HIGH-DIMENSIONAL ECONOMETRICS AND IDENTIFICATION

HIGH-DIMENSIONAL ECONOMETRICS AND IDENTIFICATION

Chihwa Kao
University of Connecticut, USA

Long Liu
The University of Texas at San Antonio, USA

NEW JERSEY · LONDON · SINGAPORE · BEIJING · SHANGHAI · HONG KONG · TAIPEI · CHENNAI · TOKYO

Published by

World Scientific Publishing Co. Pte. Ltd.

5 Toh Tuck Link, Singapore 596224

USA office: 27 Warren Street, Suite 401-402, Hackensack, NJ 07601

UK office: 57 Shelton Street, Covent Garden, London WC2H 9HE

Library of Congress Cataloging-in-Publication Data

Names: Kao, Chihwa, author. | Liu, Long, author.

Title: High-dimensional econometrics and identification /
    Chihwa Kao (University of Connecticut, USA) and
    Long Liu (The University of Texas at San Antonio, USA).

Description: New Jersey : World Scientific, [2019] |
    Includes bibliographical references and index.

Identifiers: LCCN 2019003556 | ISBN 9789811200151 (hbk : alk. paper)

Subjects: LCSH: Econometrics. | Identification.

Classification: LCC HB139 .K34 2019 | DDC 330.01/5195--dc23

LC record available at https://lccn.loc.gov/2019003556

British Library Cataloguing-in-Publication Data

A catalogue record for this book is available from the British Library.

For any available supplementary material, please visit
http://www.worldscientific.com/worldscibooks/10.1142/11273#t=suppl

Desk Editors: V. Vishnu Mohan/Karimah Samsudin

Typeset by Stallion Press
Email: enquiries@stallionpress.com

Printed in Singapore

Preface

In many applications of econometrics and economics, a large proportion of the questions of interest are identification. An economist may be interested in uncovering the true signal when the data could very noisy such as time-series spurious regression and weak instruments problems, to name a few. In this book, we illustrate the true signal and hence identification can be recovered even with noisy data in high-dimensional data, e.g., large panels. High-dimensional data in econometrics is the rule rather than the exception. One of the tools to analyze large, high-dimensional data is the panel data model. This book grew out of research work on the identification and high-dimensional econometrics that we have collaborated over the years. Some of materials are also taken from courses that we gave at various places, including graduate courses in the Economics Department of University of Connecticut, Syracuse University and the University of Texas at San Antonio.

There are three common types of data sets in econometrics: (1) cross-sectional data, e.g., observations of 100 firms (in a single year); (2) time-series data, e.g., observations of 50 years (for a single firm); and (3) panel data, which is a combination of the first two, e.g., observations of 100 firms over 50 years. This book focuses on panel data models with both large cross-sectional dimension, n, and time-series dimension, T. As a consequence, this book is complementary to Baltagi (2013), Hsiao (2014) and Pesaran (2015). It is known that, in many cases, identification could be a problem in the time-series, a cross-sectional or even a panel data with a fixed dimension n or T. We show in this book that identification can be restored in a panel data with large dimensions n and T.

In this book, we illustrate the identification and high-dimensional econometrics in five chapters. Chapter 1 discusses the panel spurious regressions.

Chapter 2 covers the estimation of autocorrelation parameter in a detrended large panel. Chapter 3 illustrates the change point estimation and testing in large panels. Chapters 1–3 drew heavily from published work with Jamie Emerson, Sanggon Na, and Badi H. Baltagi. Chapter 4 on the weak instrument problem in large panels drew our work with Badi Baltagi. Chapter 5 focuses on the incidental parameters problem in dynamic linear panels. Exercises conclude each chapter. Some of these extend the theory and others are drawn from the literature.

The main objective of this book is to provide an up-to-date presentation of the issues of identification and high-dimensional econometrics, as well as insights into the use of these results in empirical studies. This book is designed for high-level graduate courses in econometrics and statistics. We expect that this book could be part of either a third or fourth-semester econometric course, which is more theory-driven. It can be used as a reference for researchers.

This book emerged from a good collaboration between the authors. We acknowledge many people who have contributed in various ways to its completion. Bangtian Chen, Suzanne McCoskey, Jamie Emerson, Qu Feng, Sanggon Na, and Fa Wang have contributed with many original ideas as collaborators of joint research projects. We would also like to thank Badi H. Baltagi for his collaborative work that stimulated our interest in writing this book. We would like to thank Min Seong Kim for reading the drafts and providing comments. We also wish to thank World Scientific Publishing for giving us the opportunity to undertake this work.

As a personal note, the authors would like to thank their family members. Chihwa thanks his wife Ivy Liu who convinced him of the need for writing this book. Long wishes to thank his loving wife, Yue Hu, amazing daughter, Amy, and adorable son, Andrew, along with his sister and parents. The completion of this book would not have been possible without their support.

The notation used is generally standard. We use $(n, T) \to \infty$ to denote the sequential limit or the joint limit wherever it applies. We write the integral $\int_0^1 W(s)ds$ as $\int W$ and $\tilde{W}$ as $W - \int W$ when there is no ambiguity over limits. $\xrightarrow{d}$ denotes the convergence in distribution, $\equiv$ denotes equivalence in distribution, $\xrightarrow{p}$ denotes the convergence in probability, $[x]$ denotes the largest integer $\leq x$, and $I(0)$ and $I(1)$ to signify a time-series that is integrated of order zero and one, respectively. Some abbreviations frequently used in the book are: ordinary least squares (OLS), fixed effects

(FE), first difference (FD), generalized least squares (GLS), autoregressive (AR), instrumental variable (IV), two-stage least squares (2SLS), maximum likelihood estimation (MLE), independent and identically distributed (i.i.d.), the law of large numbers (LLN), central limit theorem (CLT) and continuous mapping theorem (CMT).

Chihwa Kao and *Long Liu*

About the Authors

Chihwa Kao is Professor of Economics and Department Head at UConn. He received his Ph.D. from SUNY-Stony Brook in 1983. He has held a faculty position at Syracuse University from 1985 to 2016. Chihwa's research focuses primarily on the large-dimensional econometrics such as testing and estimation arising in the cross-sectional dependence, panel change points, large factor models, and asset pricing. His work has been published in top economics and statistics journals, including *Econometrica, Journal of the American Statistical Association, Journal of Econometrics, Journal of Business and Economic Statistics, Review of Economics and Statistics, Journal of Business, Econometrics Journal,* and *Econometric Reviews.*

Long Liu is Associate Professor of Economics at the University of Texas at San Antonio. He received his Ph.D. from Syracuse University in 2008. His research interests focus on panel data problems and spatial regressions. Liu's publication have appeared in *Advances in Econometrics, Applied Economics, Econometric Journal, Econometric Reviews, Economics Letters, International Journal of Forecasting, Journal of Applied Econometrics, Journal of Forecasting, Spatial Economic Analysis, Statistical Papers* and *Statistics and Probability Letters.*

Contents

Chapter 1

Panel Data Model with Stationary and Nonstationary Regressors and Error Terms

In this book, we say a model or parameter is identifiable if it can be estimated consistently. If the parameter is not identifiable, then consistent estimators cannot exist. Before we discuss estimation, it is important to establish that they are identifiable. Here we follow Canay and Shaikh (2017)'s general notion of identifiability of a parameter in a semi-parametric setting. Let P denote the true distribution of the observed data X. Let $\mathbf{P} = \{P_\theta : \theta \in \Theta\}$ denote a model for the distribution of the observed data X. We assume that the model is correctly specified, i.e., $P \in \mathbf{P}$, where there is some $\theta \in \Theta$ such that $P_\theta = P$. We are interested in θ or some functions of f of θ. Suppose it is known that the distribution of the observed data is $P \in \mathbf{P}$. Since the model is correctly specified by assumption, it is known *a priori* that there exists some $\theta \in \Theta$ such that $P_\theta = P$. But we cannot distinguish any $\theta \in \Theta$ from any other $\theta^* \in \Theta$ such that $P_{\theta^*} = P$. Thus, from knowledge of P alone, all we can say is that $\theta \in \Theta_0(P)$, where

$$\Theta_0(P) = \{\theta \in \Theta : P_\theta = P\}.$$

We will refer to $\Theta_0(P)$ as the identified set. We say that θ is identified if $\Theta_0(P)$ is a singleton for all $P \in \mathbf{P}$. If $\Theta_0(P) = \Theta$ for all $P \in \mathbf{P}$, the parameter θ is said to be unidentified; otherwise, θ is said to be partially identified.

For example, consider the following linear regression model:

$$Y = X'\beta + \varepsilon.$$

Here, the distribution of the observed data P is the distribution of (Y, X). The model for the distribution of the observed data $\mathbf{P}$ consists of distributions P_θ for (Y, X) specified by $\theta = (P_X, \beta, P_{\varepsilon|X}) \in \Theta$, where $P_{X,\varepsilon}$ is the possible distribution for (X, ε). Suppose that $E_{P_\theta}(\varepsilon X) = 0$ and $E_{P_\theta}(XX')$ is nonsingular for each $\theta \in \Theta$, then θ is identified. In particular, $\beta = \beta(\theta)$ is identified because it may be expressed as

$$\beta(\theta) = [E_{P_\theta}(XX')]^{-1}E_{P_\theta}(XY),$$

which does not vary over the set $\Theta_0(P)$.

Suppose x_t is a nonstationary $I(1)$ process, i.e.,

$$x_t = x_{t-1} + \varepsilon_t,$$

where ε_t is white noise with variance σ_ε^2. Clearly a functional CLT (FCLT) holds,

$$W_T(r) = \frac{1}{\sqrt{T}} \sum_{t=1}^{[Tr]} \varepsilon_t \xrightarrow{d} \sigma_\varepsilon W(r)$$

for $0 \le r \le 1$ as $T \to \infty$, where $W(r)$ is a Brownian motion. Further

$$W_T(1) \xrightarrow{d} N(0, \sigma_\varepsilon^2).$$

The notion of the partial sum process $W_T(r)$ converging to $W(r)$ (up to a scale σ_ε) is defined in terms of weak convergence of their probability distributions. Weak convergence is the extension to general metric spaces of the usual notion of convergence in distribution over finite-dimensional Euclidean space, e.g., Hall and Heyde (1980). Then using a CMT, we have

$$\frac{1}{T^{3/2}} \sum_{t=1}^{T} x_t \xrightarrow{d} \sigma_\varepsilon \int_0^1 W(r)dr.$$

The above result implies that the sample mean $\bar{x} = \frac{1}{T}\sum_{t=1}^{T} x_t$ diverges as $T \to \infty$, i.e., $\bar{x} = O_p(\sqrt{T})$. This is different from when x_t is stationary. Therefore, when a regression has a nonstationary error term and/or regressors, asymptotic properties of an OLS estimator, for example, could be different from the standard textbook results such as $\sqrt{T}$-consistent and asymptotically normal. We will show in Sec. 1.1 that the OLS estimator in a spurious regression is not consistent. That is, the spurious regression is not identifiable in time-series. In Sec. 1.1, we explain the main finding of

Kao (1999) in a panel spurious regression. As far as we know, Kao (1999) is the first work to show the identification and consistency can be obtained using high-dimensional data in econometrics. Kao (1999) shows that the large panel spurious regression is identifiable where the spurious regression in time-series is not. In Sec. 1.2, we consider different cases in a large panel data regression where the regressor and the error term are either stationary, nonstationary or both. We discuss the asymptotic properties of OLS, FE, FD, and GLS estimators. As shown in Baltagi, Kao, and Liu (2008), GLS is the preferred estimator in all cases. Test of hypotheses using these standard panel data estimators is discussed in Sec. 1.3. As shown in Baltagi, Kao, and Na (2011), the simple t-ratio based on the feasible GLS (FGLS) estimator of Baltagi and Li (1991) will always converge to the standard normal random variable regardless of whether the errors and/or the regressor are stationary or not. Section 1.4 concludes.

1.1. Spurious Regression

1.1.1. *Time-series spurious regression*

We assume that x_t and y_t are both nonstationary $I(1)$ processes, i.e.,

$$x_t = x_{t-1} + \varepsilon_t$$

and

$$y_t = y_{t-1} + e_t.$$

For simplicity, we assume that for all i and t, ε_t and e_t are independent white noise with variances σ_ε^2 and σ_e^2, respectively. In this book, we purposely make the models as simple as possible so that our messages and key ideas can be delivered without sophisticated technical details. Suppose a researcher uses the following spurious regression to estimate the slope parameter β with

$$y_t = \alpha + x_t \beta + u_t$$

$t = 1, \ldots, T$. The OLS estimator of β is

$$\widehat{\beta}_{\mathrm{OLS}} = \frac{\sum_{t=1}^{T}(x_t - \bar{x})(y_t - \bar{y})}{\sum_{t=1}^{T}(x_t - \bar{x})^2}$$

and the goodness of fit R_{OLS}^2 is

$$R_{\mathrm{OLS}}^2 = \frac{\left[\sum_{t=1}^{T}(x_t - \bar{x})(y_t - \bar{y})\right]^2}{\sum_{t=1}^{T}(x_t - \bar{x})^2 \sum_{t=1}^{T}(y_t - \bar{y})^2},$$

where $\bar{x} = \frac{1}{T}\sum_{t=1}^T x_t$ and $\bar{y} = \frac{1}{T}\sum_{t=1}^T y_t$. Note

$$\frac{1}{\sqrt{T}}\sum_{t=1}^{[Tr]}\varepsilon_t \xrightarrow{d} \sigma_\varepsilon W(r)$$

and

$$\frac{1}{\sqrt{T}}\sum_{t=1}^{[Tr]}e_t \xrightarrow{d} \sigma_e^2 V(r)$$

as $T \to \infty$, where $W(r)$ and $V(r)$ are independent Brownian motions. From the time-series literature, e.g., Phillips (1986), we have the following result.

Theorem 1.1.

$$\widehat{\beta}_{\text{OLS}} \xrightarrow{d} \frac{\sigma_e \int \widetilde{W}\widetilde{V}}{\sigma_\varepsilon \int \widetilde{W}^2}$$

and

$$R_{\text{OLS}}^2 \xrightarrow{d} \frac{\left(\int \widetilde{W}\widetilde{V}\right)^2}{\int \widetilde{W}^2 \int \widetilde{V}^2}$$

as $T \to \infty$, where $\widetilde{W} = W - \int W$ and $\widetilde{V} = V - \int V$.

Proof. First, we have

$$\frac{1}{T^2}\sum_{t=1}^T (x_t - \bar{x})^2 \xrightarrow{d} \sigma_\varepsilon^2 \int \widetilde{W}^2$$

as $T \to \infty$. Similarly,

$$\frac{1}{T^2}\sum_{t=1}^T (x_t - \bar{x})(y_t - \bar{y}) \xrightarrow{d} \sigma_\varepsilon\sigma_e \int \widetilde{W}\widetilde{V}$$

as $T \to \infty$. Hence

$$\widehat{\beta}_{\text{OLS}} = \frac{\frac{1}{T^2}\sum_{t=1}^T (x_t - \bar{x})(y_t - \bar{y})}{\frac{1}{T^2}\sum_{t=1}^T (x_t - \bar{x})^2} \xrightarrow{d} \frac{\sigma_e \int \widetilde{W}\widetilde{V}}{\sigma_\varepsilon \int \widetilde{W}^2},$$

which is a random variable. Hence $\widehat{\beta}_{\text{OLS}}$ is inconsistent. Similarly,

$$\frac{1}{T^2}\sum_{t=1}^T (y_t - \bar{y})^2 \xrightarrow{d} \sigma_e^2 \int \widetilde{V}^2$$

as $T \to \infty$, we have

$$R_{\text{OLS}}^2 = \frac{\left[\frac{1}{T^2}\sum_{t=1}^T (x_t - \bar{x})(y_t - \bar{y})\right]^2}{\left[\frac{1}{T^2}\sum_{t=1}^T (x_t - \bar{x})^2\right]\left[\frac{1}{T^2}\sum_{t=1}^T (y_t - \bar{y})^2\right]} \xrightarrow{d} \frac{\left(\int \widetilde{W}\widetilde{V}\right)^2}{\int \widetilde{W}^2 \int \widetilde{V}^2}. \quad \square$$

Let us illustrate spurious regression in time-series data using the following example in R.

Example 1.1.

```
> # illustration of spurious regression in time series data
> set.seed(1234)
> T.obs <- 50
> x.t <- cumsum(rnorm(T.obs))
> y.t <- cumsum(rnorm(T.obs))
> par(mfrow=c(2,1))
> plot(x.t, type="l")
> plot(y.t, type="l")
> par(mfrow=c(1,1))
```

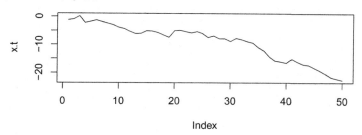

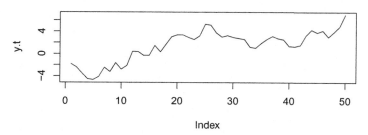

```
> reg.t <- lm(y.t~x.t)
> summary(reg.t)

Call:
lm(formula = y.t ~ x.t)

Residuals:
    Min     1Q Median     3Q    Max
-3.923 -1.370 -0.265  1.545  4.749
```

```
Coefficients:
            Estimate Std. Error t value Pr(>|t|)
(Intercept) -1.27868    0.51360  -2.490   0.0163 *
x.t         -0.29951    0.04661  -6.426 5.59e-08 ***
---
Signif. codes:  0 '***' 0.001 '**' 0.01 '*' 0.05 '.' 0.1 ' ' 1

Residual standard error: 2.074 on 48 degrees of freedom
Multiple R-squared:  0.4624,    Adjusted R-squared:  0.4512
F-statistic: 41.29 on 1 and 48 DF,  p-value: 5.586e-08
```

```
> plot(y.t~x.t)
> abline(reg.t)
```

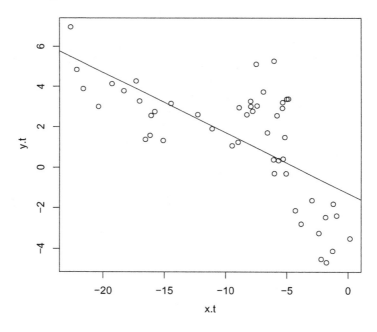

In the example above, two random walks y.t and x.t are simulated by taking the cumulative sum of two sets of random numbers using command cumsum. As we can see from the time-serious regression results above, the estimated coefficient of the slope is -0.2995 with p-value $5.59e-08$, which is smaller than 0.05. The regression goodness of fit is 0.4624, which is kind of large. Although y.t is independent of x.t, all of these regression results suggest a significant relationship between the two variables.

1.1.2. *Panel spurious regression*

We assume

$$x_{it} = x_{i,t-1} + \varepsilon_{it}$$

and

$$y_{it} = y_{i,t-1} + e_{it}$$

$i = 1, \ldots, n, t = 1, \ldots, T$, where ε_{it} and e_{it} are independent white noise for all i and t with variances σ_ε^2 and σ_e^2, respectively. Consider the following panel spurious regression:

$$y_{it} = \alpha + x_{it}\beta + u_{it}, \tag{1.1}$$

where

$$u_{it} = \mu_i + \nu_{it}.$$

The FE estimator is

$$\widehat{\beta}_{\mathrm{FE}} = \frac{\sum_{i=1}^{n} \sum_{t=1}^{T} (x_{it} - \overline{x}_i)(y_{it} - \overline{y}_i)}{\sum_{i=1}^{n} \sum_{t=1}^{T} (x_{it} - \overline{x}_i)^2}$$

with the goodness of fit

$$R_{\mathrm{FE}}^2 = \frac{\left[\sum_{i=1}^{n} \sum_{t=1}^{T} (x_{it} - \overline{x}_i)(y_{it} - \overline{y}_i)\right]^2}{\left[\sum_{i=1}^{n} \sum_{t=1}^{T} (x_{it} - \overline{x}_i)^2\right]\left[\sum_{i=1}^{n} \sum_{t=1}^{T} (y_{it} - \overline{y}_i)^2\right]},$$

where $\overline{x}_i = \frac{1}{T} \sum_{t=1}^{T} x_{it}$ and $\overline{y}_i = \frac{1}{T} \sum_{t=1}^{T} y_{it}$. Clearly,

$$\frac{1}{\sqrt{T}} \sum_{t=1}^{[Tr]} \varepsilon_{it} \overset{d}{\to} \sigma_\varepsilon W_i(r)$$

and

$$\frac{1}{\sqrt{T}} \sum_{t=1}^{[Tr]} e_{it} \overset{d}{\to} \sigma_e V_i(r)$$

as $T \to \infty$ for all i. We have the following results as in, e.g., Kao (1999).

Theorem 1.2.

$$\sqrt{n}\widehat{\beta}_{\mathrm{FE}} \overset{d}{\to} N\left(0, \frac{2\sigma_e^2}{5\sigma_\varepsilon^2}\right)$$

and

$$R_{\mathrm{FE}}^2 \xrightarrow{p} 0$$

as $(n, T) \to \infty$.

Proof. For a fixed n, we have

$$\frac{1}{nT^2} \sum_{i=1}^{n} \sum_{t=1}^{T} (x_{it} - \overline{x}_i)^2 \xrightarrow{d} \frac{1}{n} \sum_{i=1}^{n} \left(\sigma_\varepsilon^2 \int \widetilde{W}_i^2 \right)$$

as $T \to \infty$. Note that $E(\int \widetilde{W}_i^2) = \frac{1}{6}$. Therefore, by an LLN, we have

$$\frac{1}{nT^2} \sum_{i=1}^{n} \sum_{t=1}^{T} (x_{it} - \overline{x}_i)^2 \xrightarrow{p} \frac{\sigma_\varepsilon^2}{6}$$

as $(n, T) \to \infty$. Similarly, for a fixed n,

$$\frac{1}{\sqrt{n}T^2} \sum_{i=1}^{n} \sum_{t=1}^{T} (x_{it} - \overline{x}_i)(y_{it} - \overline{y}_i) \xrightarrow{d} \frac{1}{\sqrt{n}} \sum_{i=1}^{n} \left(\sigma_\varepsilon \sigma_e \int \widetilde{W}_i \widetilde{V}_i \right).$$

It can be shown that

$$E \left(\int \widetilde{W}_i \widetilde{V}_i \right) = 0$$

and

$$\mathrm{Var} \left(\int \widetilde{W}_i \widetilde{V}_i \right) = \frac{1}{90}.$$

Therefore, we have

$$\frac{1}{\sqrt{n}T^2} \sum_{i=1}^{n} \sum_{t=1}^{T} (x_{it} - \overline{x}_i)(y_{it} - \overline{y}_i) \xrightarrow{d} N \left(0, \frac{\sigma_\varepsilon^2 \sigma_e^2}{90} \right)$$

by a CLT as $(n, T) \to \infty$. Hence we have

$$\sqrt{n}\widehat{\beta}_{\mathrm{FE}} = \frac{\frac{1}{\sqrt{n}T^2} \sum_{i=1}^{n} \sum_{t=1}^{T} (x_{it} - \overline{x}_i)(y_{it} - \overline{y}_i)}{\frac{1}{nT^2} \sum_{i=1}^{n} \sum_{t=1}^{T} (x_{it} - \overline{x}_i)^2} \xrightarrow{d} N \left(0, \frac{2\sigma_e^2}{5\sigma_\varepsilon^2} \right).$$

Similarly, we have

$$\frac{1}{nT^2} \sum_{i=1}^{n} \sum_{t=1}^{T} (y_{it} - \bar{y}_i)^2 \xrightarrow{p} \frac{\sigma_e^2}{6}$$

and

$$\frac{1}{nT^2} \sum_{i=1}^{n} \sum_{t=1}^{T} (x_{it} - \overline{x}_i)(y_{it} - \overline{y}_i) \xrightarrow{p} 0$$

as $(n, T) \to \infty$. Hence, we obtain

$$R_{\text{FE}}^2 = \frac{\left[\frac{1}{nT^2} \sum_{i=1}^{n} \sum_{t=1}^{T} (x_{it} - \bar{x}_i)(y_{it} - \bar{y}_i) \right]}{\left[\frac{1}{nT^2} \sum_{i=1}^{n} \sum_{t=1}^{T} (x_{it} - \bar{x}_i)^2 \right] \left[\frac{1}{nT^2} \sum_{i=1}^{n} \sum_{t=1}^{T} (y_{it} - \bar{y}_i)^2 \right]} \xrightarrow{p} 0.$$

$\square$

Theorem 1.2 implies that $\widehat{\beta}_{\text{FE}}$ is $\sqrt{n}$-consistent in a large panel spurious regression. This is significantly different from the time-series spurious regression where the OLS is inconsistent. This indicates that the identification can be restored in high-dimension such large panels. In the panel spurious regression with the large cross-sectional dimension, the strong noise of u_{it} is attenuated by pooling the data and a consistent estimate of the signal can be extracted. Let us illustrate spurious regression in the panel data using the following example in R.

Example 1.2.

```
> # illustration of spurious regression in panel data
> library(plm)
> set.seed(1234)
> T.obs <- 50
> n.obs <- 50
> nT.obs <- n.obs * T.obs
> y.p <- c(apply(matrix(rnorm(nT.obs), T.obs, n.obs),2,cumsum))
> x.p <- c(apply(matrix(rnorm(nT.obs), T.obs, n.obs),2,cumsum))
> data.p <- data.frame(y.p,x.p)
> reg.p <- plm(y.p~x.p, plm.data(data.p, n.obs))
> summary(reg.p)

Oneway (individual) effect Within Model

Call:
plm(formula = y.p ~ x.p, data = plm.data(data.p, n.obs))

Balanced Panel: n=50, T=50, N=2500

Residuals :
      Min.    1st Qu.     Median    3rd Qu.        Max.
-13.609525  -1.591420   0.030514   1.647606    9.213355
```

```
Coefficients :
     Estimate Std. Error t-value Pr(>|t|)
x.p -0.0016941  0.0200032 -0.0847   0.9325

Total Sum of Squares:    17279
Residual Sum of Squares: 17279
R-Squared:        2.9287e-06
Adj. R-Squared: -0.020414
F-statistic: 0.00717246 on 1 and 2449 DF, p-value: 0.93251
```

```
> plot(y.p~x.p)
> abline(reg.p)
```

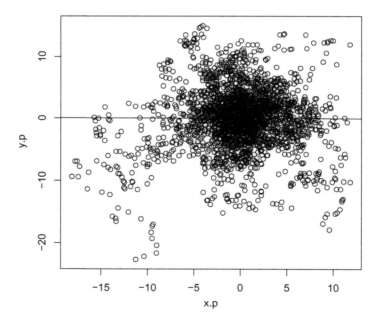

As we can see from the panel data regression results above, the estimated coefficient of the slope is -0.0017, which is very close to zero. Its p-value is 0.9325, which is larger than 0.05. The regression goodness of fit is $2.9287e-06$, which is very close to zero. With the large panel data, all the "spurious" significant regression results disappear. We recover the true relationship between the two variables.

1.2. Model with Stationary and Nonstationary Regressors and Error Terms

Consider the following panel regression:

$$y_{it} = \alpha + x_{it}\beta + u_{it}, \tag{1.2}$$

where $u_{it} = \mu_i + \nu_{it}$. For simplicity, we only consider the case of one regressor, but results will continue to hold with multiple regressors case. We assume that the individual effects μ_i are random with

Assumption 1.1. $\mu_i \overset{i.i.d.}{\sim} (0, \sigma_\mu^2)$ and ν_{it} is an AR(1) process

$$\nu_{it} = \rho \nu_{it-1} + e_{it}$$

with $|\rho| \le 1$, where e_{it} is white noise with variance σ_e^2. The μ_i's are independent of the ν_{it}'s for all i and t.

Let x_{it} be also an AR(1) process such that

$$x_{it} = \lambda x_{it-1} + \varepsilon_{it}$$

with $|\lambda| \le 1$, where ε_{it} is white noise with variance σ_ε^2. We assume that

Assumption 1.2. $E(\mu_i | x_{it}) = 0$ for all i and t.

We further assume $y_{i1} = x_{i1} = O_p(1)$ for all i. Our parameter of interest is the common slope β. This section shows that the asymptotic properties of OLS, FE, FD, and GLS estimators depend crucially on the serial correlation properties of x_{it} and ν_{it}. When y_{it} and x_{it} are both $I(1)$ but ν_{it} is $I(0)$, Eq. (1.2) is a panel cointegrated model. On the other hand, when ν_{it} is $I(1)$ and y_{it} and x_{it} are both $I(1)$, Eq. (1.2) is a panel spurious model. FE estimators for panel cointegrated and panel spurious models have been discussed in Kao and Chiang (2000) and Kao (1999). The panel time trend model, $x_{it} = t$, has been studied by Baltagi and Krämer (1997) and Kao and Emerson (2004, 2005). A survey on nonstationary panel data models is available in Baltagi and Kao (2000).

For simplicity, we assume

$$\begin{bmatrix} e_{it} \\ \varepsilon_{it} \end{bmatrix} \overset{i.i.d.}{\sim} \left(\begin{bmatrix} 0 \\ 0 \end{bmatrix}, \begin{bmatrix} \sigma_e^2 & 0 \\ 0 & \sigma_\varepsilon^2 \end{bmatrix} \right)$$

for all i and t.

1.2.1. *OLS estimator*

The OLS estimator is

$$\widehat{\beta}_{\text{OLS}} = \frac{\sum_{i=1}^{n}\sum_{t=1}^{T}(x_{it} - \overline{\overline{x}})(y_{it} - \overline{\overline{y}})}{\sum_{i=1}^{n}\sum_{t=1}^{T}(x_{it} - \overline{\overline{x}})^2} \qquad (1.3)$$

where

$$\overline{\overline{x}} = \frac{1}{nT}\sum_{i=1}^{n}\sum_{t=1}^{T}x_{it}$$

and

$$\overline{\overline{y}} = \frac{1}{nT}\sum_{i=1}^{n}\sum_{t=1}^{T}y_{it}.$$

Theorem 1.3. *As $(n, T) \to \infty$, we have the following conditions*:

(1) *If $|\rho| < 1$ and $|\lambda| < 1$, then*

$$\sqrt{nT}(\widehat{\beta}_{\text{OLS}} - \beta) \xrightarrow{d} N\left(0, \frac{\sigma_{\mu}^2}{\sigma_{\varepsilon}^2} + \frac{(1 + \rho\lambda)(1 - \lambda^2)\sigma_e^2}{(1 - \rho\lambda)(1 - \rho^2)\sigma_{\varepsilon}^2}\right).$$

(2) *If $\rho = 1$ and $|\lambda| < 1$, then*

$$\sqrt{n}(\widehat{\beta}_{\text{OLS}} - \beta) \xrightarrow{d} N\left(0, \frac{(1 - \lambda)^2\sigma_e^2}{2\sigma_{\varepsilon}^2}\right).$$

(3) *If $|\rho| < 1$ and $\lambda = 1$, then*

$$\sqrt{nT}(\widehat{\beta}_{\text{OLS}} - \beta) \xrightarrow{d} N\left(0, \frac{4\sigma_{\mu}^2}{3\sigma_{\varepsilon}^2}\right).$$

(4) *If $\rho = 1$ and $\lambda = 1$, then*

$$\sqrt{n}(\widehat{\beta}_{\text{OLS}} - \beta) \xrightarrow{d} N\left(0, \frac{2\sigma_e^2}{3\sigma_{\varepsilon}^2}\right).$$

The OLS estimator ignores the individual effects in the error term. Thus, the variance of μ_i, i.e., σ_{μ}^2, might appear in the asymptotic variance depending on the case considered. In Case 1, both μ_i and ν_{it} affect the asymptotic variance of $\widehat{\beta}_{\text{OLS}}$. In Cases 2 and 4, ν_{it} dominates μ_i. In Case 3, μ_i dominates ν_{it} and hence the convergence speed is $\sqrt{nT}$, which differs from the $\sqrt{nT}$-asymptotics in the panel cointegration. Also, the asymptotic normality of the OLS estimator comes naturally in all cases. When summing across i, the nonstandard asymptotic distribution due to unit root in the time-series dimension, such as for Cases 2–4, has been smoothed out.

1.2.2. FE estimator

The FE estimator of β is given by

$$\widehat{\beta}_{\text{FE}} = \frac{\sum_{i=1}^{n} \sum_{t=1}^{T} (x_{it} - \overline{x}_i)(y_{it} - \overline{y}_i)}{\sum_{i=1}^{n} \sum_{t=1}^{T} (x_{it} - \overline{x}_i)^2}. \tag{1.4}$$

Theorem 1.4. *As $(n, T) \to \infty$, we have the following conditions:*

(1) *If $|\rho| < 1$ and $|\lambda| < 1$, then*

$$\sqrt{nT}(\widehat{\beta}_{\text{FE}} - \beta) \xrightarrow{d} N\left(0, \frac{(1 + \rho\lambda)(1 - \lambda^2)\sigma_e^2}{(1 - \rho\lambda)(1 - \rho^2)\sigma_\varepsilon^2}\right).$$

(2) *If $\rho = 1$ and $|\lambda| < 1$, then*

$$\sqrt{n}(\widehat{\beta}_{\text{FE}} - \beta) \xrightarrow{d} N\left(0, \frac{(1 - \lambda)^2\sigma_e^2}{6\sigma_\varepsilon^2}\right).$$

(3) *If $|\rho| < 1$ and $\lambda = 1$, then*

$$\sqrt{nT}(\widehat{\beta}_{\text{FE}} - \beta) \xrightarrow{d} N\left(0, \frac{6\sigma_e^2}{(1 - \rho)^2\sigma_\varepsilon^2}\right).$$

(4) *If $\rho = 1$ and $\lambda = 1$, then*

$$\sqrt{n}(\widehat{\beta}_{\text{FE}} - \beta) \xrightarrow{d} N\left(0, \frac{2\sigma_e^2}{5\sigma_\varepsilon^2}\right).$$

Because $u_{it} - \overline{u}_i = \nu_{it} - \overline{\nu}_i$, the individual effect μ_i is eliminated. Note that Case 1 is the standard time-series textbook result under the stationarity of the regressor and the error term. Case 2 is in Baltagi *et al.* (2008). Case 3 is discussed in Kao and Chiang (2000). Case 4 is shown in Kao (1999).

1.2.3. FD estimator

The FD estimator of β is given by

$$\widehat{\beta}_{\text{FD}} = \frac{\sum_{i=1}^{n} \sum_{t=2}^{T} (x_{it} - x_{it-1})(y_{it} - y_{it-1})}{\sum_{i=1}^{n} \sum_{t=2}^{T} (x_{it} - x_{it-1})^2}. \tag{1.5}$$

Theorem 1.5. *As $(n, T) \to \infty$, we have the following conditions*

(1) *If $|\rho| < 1$ and $|\lambda| < 1$, then*

$$\sqrt{nT}(\widehat{\beta}_{\text{FD}} - \beta) \xrightarrow{d} N\left(0, \frac{(1 + \lambda)^2\left[(2 - \rho - \lambda)^2 + \frac{(1-\rho)^3}{1+\rho} + \frac{(1-\lambda)^3}{1+\lambda}\right]\sigma_e^2}{4(1 - \rho\lambda)^2\sigma_\varepsilon^2}\right).$$

(2) *If $\rho = 1$ and $|\lambda| < 1$, then*

$$\sqrt{nT}(\widehat{\beta}_{\text{FD}} - \beta) \xrightarrow{d} N\left(0, \frac{(1+\lambda)\sigma_e^2}{2\sigma_\varepsilon^2}\right).$$

(3) *If $|\rho| < 1$ and $\lambda = 1$, then*

$$\sqrt{nT}(\widehat{\beta}_{\text{FD}} - \beta) \xrightarrow{d} N\left(0, \frac{2\sigma_e^2}{(1+\rho)\sigma_\varepsilon^2}\right).$$

(4) *If $\rho = 1$ and $\lambda = 1$, then*

$$\sqrt{nT}(\widehat{\beta}_{\text{FD}} - \beta) \xrightarrow{d} N\left(0, \frac{\sigma_e^2}{\sigma_\varepsilon^2}\right).$$

Similar to the FE estimator, the individual effect μ_i is also eliminated by the FD transformation. In Cases 2 and 4, $\rho = 1$, and the FD estimator is asymptotically equivalent to the GLS estimator because both methods transform the disturbance from $I(1)$ into $I(0)$. Actually, the FD estimator is the same as the GLS estimator except for the omission of the first observation for each individual.

1.2.4.　GLS estimator

Let us rewrite Eq. (1.2) in vector form as

$$\mathbf{y} = \alpha \iota_{nT} + \beta \mathbf{x} + u \tag{1.6}$$

with $u = Z_\mu \mu + \nu$, where $u' = (u_{11}, \ldots, u_{1T}, u_{21}, \ldots, u_{2T}, \ldots, u_{n1}, \ldots, u_{nT})$ with the observations stacked such that the slower index is over individuals and the faster index is over time. μ is an $n \times 1$ vector with typical element μ_i, ν is an $nT \times 1$ vector with typical element ν_{it}, and $Z_\mu = I_n \otimes \iota_T$, where I_n is an identity matrix of dimension n, ι_T is a vector of ones of dimension T, and $\otimes$ denotes the Kronecker product. $\mathbf{y}$ is an $nT \times 1$ vector with typical element y_{it}, $\mathbf{x} = \iota_n \otimes x_i$, where ι_n is a vector of ones of dimension n and x_i is a $T \times 1$ vector. ι_{nT} is a vector of ones of dimension nT. As shown in Baltagi and Li (1991), one can write the variance–covariance matrix as

$$\Phi = E(uu') = \sigma_\mu^2(I_n \otimes \iota_T \iota_T') + \sigma_e^2(I_n \otimes \mathbf{A}), \tag{1.7}$$

where

$$\mathbf{A} = \frac{1}{1-\rho^2}\begin{bmatrix} 1 & \rho & \rho^2 & \cdots & \rho^{T-1} \\ \rho & 1 & \rho & \cdots & \rho^{T-2} \\ \rho^2 & \rho & 1 & \cdots & \rho^{T-3} \\ \vdots & \vdots & \vdots & \ddots & \vdots \\ \rho^{T-1} & \rho^{T-2} & \rho^{T-3} & \cdots & 1 \end{bmatrix} \tag{1.8}$$

when $|\rho| < 1$ and

$$
\mathbf{A} = \begin{bmatrix}
1 & 1 & 1 & \cdots & 1 \\
1 & 2 & 2 & \cdots & 2 \\
1 & 2 & 3 & \cdots & 3 \\
\vdots & \vdots & \vdots & \ddots & \vdots \\
1 & 2 & 3 & \cdots & T
\end{bmatrix}
\tag{1.9}
$$

when $\rho = 1$. When $|\rho| < 1$, one can easily verify that $\mathbf{A}^{-1} = \mathbf{C}'\mathbf{C}$, where

$$
\mathbf{C} = \begin{bmatrix}
\sqrt{1-\rho^2} & 0 & 0 & \cdots & 0 & 0 \\
-\rho & 1 & 0 & \cdots & 0 & 0 \\
0 & -\rho & 1 & \cdots & 0 & 0 \\
\vdots & \vdots & \vdots & \ddots & \vdots & \vdots \\
0 & 0 & 0 & -\rho & 1 & 0 \\
0 & 0 & 0 & 0 & -\rho & 1
\end{bmatrix}
\tag{1.10}
$$

is the Prais–Winsten (PW) transformation matrix as in Baltagi and Li (1991). As suggested in Baltagi and Li (1991), one can apply PW transformation matrix $\mathbf{C}$ to transform the remainder AR(1) errors into serially uncorrelated classical errors:

$$
y^* = \delta \iota_{nT}^* + \beta \mathbf{x}^* + u^*,
\tag{1.11}
$$

where

$$
y^* = (I_n \otimes C)\mathbf{y},
$$
$$
\mathbf{x}^* = (I_n \otimes C)\mathbf{x} = \iota_n \otimes x_i^*
$$

with $x_i^* = Cx_i$ and

$$
\iota_{nT}^* = (I_n \otimes C)\iota_{nT} = (1-\rho)(\iota_n \otimes \iota_T^\alpha)
$$

using

$$
C\iota_T = (1-\rho)\iota_T^\alpha
$$

where $\iota_T^{\alpha\prime} = (\alpha, \iota_{T-1}')$ and

$$
\alpha = \sqrt{(1+\rho)/(1-\rho)}.
$$

The transformed regression errors are in vector form

$$
u^* = (I_n \otimes C)u = (I_n \otimes C\iota_T)\mu + (I_n \otimes C)v = (1-\rho)(I_n \otimes \iota_T^\alpha)\mu + v^*,
$$

where $v^* = (I_n \otimes C)v$. As shown in Baltagi and Li (1991), the variance–covariance matrix of the transformed error is

$$\Phi^* = E(u^* u^{*\prime}) = \sigma_\mu^2 (1 - \rho)^2 (I_n \otimes \iota_T^\alpha \iota_T^{\alpha\prime}) + \sigma_\varepsilon^2 (I_n \otimes I_T) \qquad (1.12)$$

and

$$\sigma_\varepsilon \Phi^{*-1/2} = \frac{\sigma_\varepsilon}{\sigma_\alpha}(I_n \otimes \bar{J}_T^\alpha) + (I_n \otimes E_T^\alpha) \qquad (1.13)$$

where

$$E_T^\alpha = I_T - \bar{J}_T^\alpha,$$

$$\bar{J}_T^\alpha = \iota_T^\alpha \iota_T^{\alpha\prime}/d^2,$$

$$d^2 = \iota_T^{\alpha\prime} \iota_T^\alpha = \alpha^2 + T - 1,$$

$$\sigma_\alpha^2 = \sigma_e^2 + \theta\sigma_\mu^2,$$

and

$$\theta = d^2(1 - \rho)^2.$$

Premultiplying the PW transformed observations in Eq. (1.11) by $\sigma_\varepsilon \Phi^{*-1/2}$, one gets

$$\sigma_\varepsilon \Phi^{*-1/2} \mathbf{y}^* = \sigma_\varepsilon \Phi^{*-1/2} \delta \iota_{nT}^* + \sigma_\varepsilon \Phi^{*-1/2} \beta \mathbf{x}^* + \sigma_\varepsilon \Phi^{*-1/2} u^*. \qquad (1.14)$$

The OLS estimator of the transformed equation yields the GLS estimator $\hat{\beta}_{\text{GLS}}$

$$\hat{\beta}_{\text{GLS}} = [\mathbf{x}'\Phi^{-1}\mathbf{x} - \mathbf{x}'\Phi^{-1}\iota_{nT}(\iota_{nT}'\Phi^{-1}\iota_{nT})^{-1}\iota_{nT}'\Phi^{-1}\mathbf{x}]^{-1}$$
$$\times [\mathbf{x}'\Phi^{-1}\mathbf{y} - \mathbf{x}'\Phi^{-1}\iota_{nT}(\iota_{nT}'\Phi^{-1}\iota_{nT})^{-1}\iota_{nT}'\Phi^{-1}\mathbf{y}], \qquad (1.15)$$

where

$$\Phi^{-1} = I_n \otimes \left[\frac{1}{\sigma_e^2}\left(\mathbf{A}^{-1} - \frac{\sigma_\mu^2}{\sigma_e^2 + \theta\sigma_\mu^2} \mathbf{A}^{-1} \iota_T \iota_T' \mathbf{A}^{-1} \right) \right] \qquad (1.16)$$

with $\theta = \iota_T' \mathbf{A}^{-1} \iota_T$. Hence

$$\hat{\beta}_{\text{GLS}} - \beta = G_1^{-1} G_2 \qquad (1.17)$$

where

$$G_1 = \mathbf{x}'\Phi^{-1}\mathbf{x} - \mathbf{x}'\Phi^{-1}\iota_{nT}(\iota_{nT}'\Phi^{-1}\iota_{nT})^{-1}\iota_{nT}'\Phi^{-1}\mathbf{x}$$

and

$$G_2 = \mathbf{x}'\Phi^{-1}\mathbf{u} - \mathbf{x}'\Phi^{-1}\iota_{nT}(\iota_{nT}'\Phi^{-1}\iota_{nT})^{-1}\iota_{nT}'\Phi^{-1}\mathbf{u}.$$

Thus, we have the following theorem.

Theorem 1.6. *As $(n, T) \to \infty$, we have the following conditions:*

(1) *If $|\rho| < 1$ and $|\lambda| < 1$, then*

$$\sqrt{nT}(\widehat{\beta}_{\mathrm{GLS}} - \beta) \xrightarrow{d} N\left(0, \frac{(1 - \lambda^2)\sigma_e^2}{(1 - 2\rho\lambda + \rho^2)\sigma_\varepsilon^2}\right).$$

(2) *If $\rho = 1$ and $|\lambda| < 1$, then*

$$\sqrt{nT}(\widehat{\beta}_{\mathrm{GLS}} - \beta) \xrightarrow{d} N\left(0, \frac{(1 + \lambda)\sigma_e^2}{2\sigma_\varepsilon^2}\right).$$

(3) *If $|\rho| < 1$ and $\lambda = 1$, then*

$$\sqrt{n}T(\widehat{\beta}_{\mathrm{GLS}} - \beta) \xrightarrow{d} N\left(0, \frac{6\sigma_e^2}{(1 - \rho)^2\sigma_\varepsilon^2}\right).$$

(4) *If $\rho = 1$ and $\lambda = 1$, then*

$$\sqrt{nT}(\widehat{\beta}_{\mathrm{GLS}} - \beta) \xrightarrow{d} N\left(0, \frac{\sigma_e^2}{\sigma_\varepsilon^2}\right).$$

Case 1 is standard. Case 3 is discussed in Choi (1999). Cases 2 and 4 are in Baltagi *et al.* (2008). It is worth pointing out that when $\rho = 1$, the GLS transformation given by Baltagi and Li (1991) is identical to the FD transformation. In fact, it omits the first observation for each individual and the Cochrane–Orcutt transformation from period 2 up to T becomes the FD transformation. Hence, the GLS estimator will be the same as the FD estimator and the conditional expectation of μ_i given x_{it} need not be zero when $\rho = 1$. When $\rho < 1$, $E(\mu_i|x_{it}) = 0$ is required, otherwise $\widehat{\beta}_{\mathrm{GLS}}$ would be biased and inconsistent. This is the case for the Mundlak (1978) model where the μ_i's are explicitly formulated as a function of the means of all the regressors, in this case ($\overline{x}_i$). The result is that under this Mundlak model, OLS and GLS suffer from omitted variable bias, i.e., the omission of $\overline{x}_i$, while FD and FE wipe out this source of endogeneity and remain consistent. In this case, one may use the within or FD transformation to wipe out μ_i and then run GLS estimation in case of serial correlation in the remainder error.

1.2.5. *Feasible GLS estimator*

It is clear that the GLS estimator in Sec. 1.2.4 is not feasible. In this section, we discuss the FGLS estimation. An FGLS estimator can be calculated by estimating the autocorrelation coefficient ρ and the variance components σ_μ^2 and σ_e^2. To estimate these parameters, we first retrieve the residual estimator $\widehat{\nu}_{it}$ from the FE regression in (1.2). As suggested by Baltagi and Li (1991), one can estimate ρ by

$$\widehat{\rho} = \frac{\sum_{i=1}^{n}\sum_{t=2}^{T}\widehat{\nu}_{it}\widehat{\nu}_{i,t-1}}{\sum_{i=1}^{n}\sum_{t=2}^{T}\widehat{\nu}_{i,t-1}^{2}} \tag{1.18}$$

and

$$\widehat{\sigma}_{e}^{2} = \frac{1}{nT}\sum_{i=1}^{n}\sum_{t=2}^{T}(\widehat{\nu}_{it} - \widehat{\rho}\widetilde{\nu}_{it-1})^{2}.$$

The following theorem is taken from Baltagi *et al.* (2011).

Theorem 1.7. *As $(n, T) \to \infty$, we have the following conditions*:

(1) *If $|\rho| < 1$ with $\frac{n}{T} \to 0$, then $\sqrt{nT}(\widehat{\rho} - \rho) \xrightarrow{d} N(0, 1 - \rho^2)$ and $\widehat{\sigma}_{e}^{2} \xrightarrow{p} \sigma_{e}^{2}$.*
(2) *If $\rho = 1$, then $T(\widehat{\rho} - 1) \xrightarrow{p} -3$ and $\widehat{\sigma}_{e}^{2} \xrightarrow{p} \sigma_{e}^{2}$.*

1.2.6.   *Efficiency comparisons*

This section summarizes the relative efficiency of OLS, FE, GLS and FD estimators. First, the speeds of convergence for the different cases considered are summarized as follows:

	OLS	FE	FD	GLS
Case 1: $|\rho| < 1$ and $|\lambda| < 1$	$\sqrt{nT}$	$\sqrt{nT}$	$\sqrt{nT}$	$\sqrt{nT}$
Case 2: $\rho = 1$ and $|\lambda| < 1$	$\sqrt{n}$	$\sqrt{n}$	$\sqrt{nT}$	$\sqrt{nT}$
Case 3: $|\rho| < 1$ and $\lambda = 1$	$\sqrt{nT}$	$\sqrt{nT}$	$\sqrt{nT}$	$\sqrt{nT}$
Case 4: $\rho = 1$ and $\lambda = 1$	$\sqrt{n}$	$\sqrt{n}$	$\sqrt{nT}$	$\sqrt{nT}$

In Case 1, the four estimators have the same convergence speed $\sqrt{nT}$. The efficiency of the OLS estimator is hard to compare with the remaining estimators because OLS does not difference out μ_i, and as a result, its variance still contains σ_{μ}^{2}. That GLS is more efficient than FE and FD which is evident from the Gauss–Markov theorem. Since these estimators all converge at the same rate $\sqrt{nT}$, we further compare their asymptotic variances. The relative efficiency of the FE estimator with respect to true GLS is given by

$$\text{var}(\widehat{\beta}_{\text{FE}})/\text{var}(\widehat{\beta}_{\text{GLS}}) = \frac{(1+\rho\lambda)(1-\lambda^2)\sigma_{e}^{2}}{(1-\rho\lambda)(1-\rho^2)\sigma_{\varepsilon}^{2}} \bigg/ \frac{(1-\lambda^2)\sigma_{e}^{2}}{(1-2\rho\lambda+\rho^2)\sigma_{\varepsilon}^{2}}$$

$$= \frac{(1+\rho\lambda)(1-2\rho\lambda+\rho^2)}{(1-\rho\lambda)(1-\rho^2)}.$$

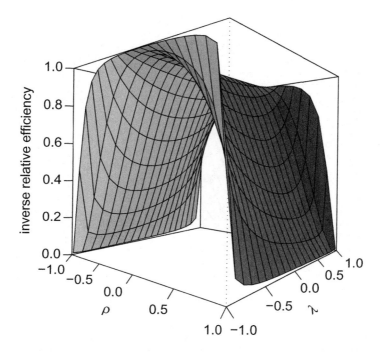

Fig. 1.1.   Inverse relative efficiency of FE to GLS estimator.

The relative efficiency of the FD estimator with respect to true GLS is given by

$$\mathrm{var}(\widehat{\beta}_{\mathrm{FD}})/\mathrm{var}(\widehat{\beta}_{\mathrm{GLS}})$$

$$= \frac{(1+\lambda)^2 \left[(2-\rho-\lambda)^2 + \frac{(1-\rho)^3}{1+\rho} + \frac{(1-\lambda)^3}{1+\lambda}\right]\sigma_e^2}{4(1-\rho\lambda)^2\sigma_\varepsilon^2} \Bigg/ \frac{(1-\lambda^2)\sigma_e^2}{(1-2\rho\lambda+\rho^2)\sigma_\varepsilon^2}$$

$$= \frac{(1+\lambda)(1-2\rho\lambda+\rho^2)\left[(2-\rho-\lambda)^2 + \frac{(1-\rho)^3}{1+\rho} + \frac{(1-\lambda)^3}{1+\lambda}\right]}{4(1-\lambda)(1-\rho\lambda)^2}.$$

One can easily verify that both relative efficiencies are larger or equal to 1. We plot the inverse relative efficiency of the FE and FD estimators with respect to true GLS in Figs. 1.1 and 1.2. Comparing the GLS estimator with the FE and FD estimators, the relative efficiency depends on the values of ρ and λ. As shown in Figs. 1.1 and 1.2, when ρ is small, the FE estimator performs well in terms of relative efficiency with respect to true GLS. When

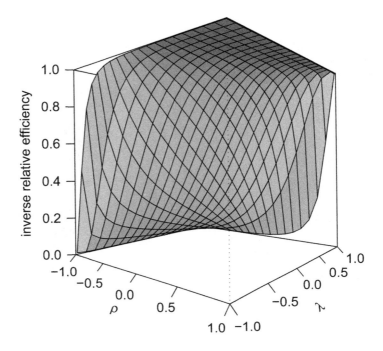

Fig. 1.2.   Inverse relative efficiency of FD to GLS estimator.

ρ is large, the FD estimator performs well in terms of relative efficiency with respect to true GLS.

In Case 2, the error is $I(1)$ but the regressor is $I(0)$. The noise is strong so that it dominates the signal. In the time-series case, the OLS estimator is not consistent. After double smoothing using panel data, the asymptotic distribution becomes normal and the convergence speed is $\sqrt{n}$. GLS estimation, however, transforms the disturbance into $I(0)$. Therefore, the convergence speed is $\sqrt{nT}$. When the error is $I(1)$, FD estimation will be the same as GLS except for the first observation. Hence it is also $\sqrt{nT}$-consistent.

In Case 3, the error is $I(0)$ but the regressor is $I(1)$. This is the cointegration case. The cointegration literature shows that the GLS estimator is T consistent in time-series models. In the panel data model, both GLS and FE are $\sqrt{nT}$-consistent.

In Case 4, both the error and the regressor are $I(1)$. This is the spurious regression case. As shown in Kao (1999), the FE estimator is $\sqrt{n}$-consistent.

For the same reason given in Case 2, FD transforms the error term from $I(1)$ to $I(0)$. Therefore, the convergence speed of both the GLS and the FD estimators is $\sqrt{nT}$.

To compare the FD estimator with the FE estimator, in Case 3, the FE estimator is more efficient when v_{it} is stationary, including the special case when v_{it} is serially uncorrelated. In Cases 2 and 4, the FD estimator is more efficient when v_{it} follows a random walk. These results verify the conclusion in Wooldridge (2002). However, in Case 1, when ρ is large, even though v_{it} does not follow a random walk, the FD estimator is still more efficient than the FE estimator.

1.3.   Test of Hypotheses

In this section, we focus on testing the common slope β in Eq. (1.2),

$$H_0 : \beta = \beta_0.$$

We start by investigating the asymptotic distributions of the t-statistics for H_0 based on the FE and FD estimators. Let us denote these by t_{FE} and t_{FD}, respectively. We derive these asymptotic distributions under four scenarios where the errors and the regressor are allowed to be $I(0)$ or $I(1)$ or both.

1.3.1.   *FE estimator*

If v_{it} is $I(0)$, the corresponding t-test for H_0 using the FE estimator $\widehat{\beta}_{\text{FE}}$, is given by

$$t_{\text{FE}} = \frac{\widehat{\beta}_{\text{FE}} - \beta_0}{s_{\text{FE}}}, \tag{1.19}$$

where

$$s_{\text{FE}} = \sqrt{\frac{\widehat{\sigma}_\nu^2}{\sum_{i=1}^{n}\sum_{t=1}^{T}(x_{it} - \bar{x}_i)^2}}$$

with $\widehat{\sigma}_\nu^2 = \frac{\widehat{\sigma}_e^2}{1-\widehat{\rho}^2}$ and

$$\widehat{\sigma}_e^2 = \frac{1}{nT}\sum_{i=1}^{n}\sum_{t=2}^{T}(\widehat{\nu}_{it} - \widehat{\rho}\widehat{\nu}_{it-1})^2.$$

Here

$$\widehat{\nu}_{it} = (y_{it} - \bar{y}_i) - \widehat{\beta}_{\text{FE}}(x_{it} - \bar{x}_i)$$

denotes the FE residuals from Eq. (1.2), and

$$\widehat{\rho} = \frac{\sum_{i=1}^{n} \sum_{t=2}^{T} \widehat{\nu}_{it} \widehat{\nu}_{it-1}}{\sum_{i=1}^{n} \sum_{t=2}^{T} \widehat{\nu}_{it-1}^2}$$

is the estimator of ρ suggested by Baltagi and Li (1991). Theorem 1.8 derives the corresponding asymptotic distribution of the t-statistic based on the FE estimator, t_{FE}, under various scenarios involving the stationarity or nonstationarity of the regressor and the error term.

Theorem 1.8. *Assume* $(n, T) \to \infty$ *with* $\frac{n}{T} \to 0$.

(1) *If* $|\rho| < 1$, $|\lambda| < 1$, *then*

$$t_{\mathrm{FE}} \xrightarrow{d} N\left(0, \frac{1 + \rho\lambda}{1 - \rho\lambda}\right).$$

(2) *If* $\rho = 1$, $|\lambda| < 1$, *then*

$$t_{\mathrm{FE}} \xrightarrow{d} N\left(0, \frac{1 - \lambda}{1 + \lambda}\right).$$

(3) *If* $|\rho| < 1$, $\lambda = 1$, *then*

$$t_{\mathrm{FE}} \xrightarrow{d} N\left(0, \frac{1 + \rho}{1 - \rho}\right).$$

(4) *If* $\rho = 1$, $\lambda = 1$, *then*

$$\frac{t_{\mathrm{FE}}}{\sqrt{T}} \xrightarrow{d} N\left(0, \frac{2}{5}\right).$$

Theorem 1.8 shows that, under the null, t_{FE} follows a normal distribution asymptotically in Cases 1–3. However, $t_{\mathrm{FE}} = O_p(\sqrt{T})$ in Case 4. This has also been pointed out by Kao (1999).

1.3.2.   FD estimator

Next, we turn to the FD estimator, $\widehat{\beta}_{\mathrm{FD}}$. The corresponding t-test for H_0 using the FD estimator $\widehat{\beta}_{\mathrm{FD}}$ is given by

$$t_{\mathrm{FD}} = \frac{\widehat{\beta}_{\mathrm{FD}} - \beta_0}{s_{\mathrm{FD}}}, \tag{1.20}$$

where

$$s_{\mathrm{FD}} = \sqrt{\frac{\widehat{\sigma}_{\triangle\nu}^2}{\sum_{i=1}^{n} \sum_{t=2}^{T} (x_{it} - x_{it-1})^2}}$$

with

$$\widehat{\sigma}^2_{\triangle\nu} = \frac{1}{nT} \sum_{i=1}^{n} \sum_{t=2}^{T} (\triangle y_{it} - \widehat{\beta}_{\text{FD}} \triangle x_{it})^2.$$

Theorem 1.9. *Assume* $(n, T) \to \infty$ *and* $\frac{n}{T} \to 0$.

(1) *If* $|\rho| < 1$, $|\lambda| < 1$, *then*

$$t_{\text{FD}} \xrightarrow{d} N\left(0, \frac{(1+\rho)(1+\lambda)\left[(2-\rho-\lambda)^2 + \frac{(1-\rho)^3}{1+\rho} + \frac{(1-\lambda)^3}{1+\lambda}\right]}{4(1-\rho\lambda)^2}\right).$$

(2) *If* $\rho = 1$, $|\lambda| < 1$, *then*

$$t_{\text{FD}} \xrightarrow{d} N(0, 1).$$

(3) *If* $|\rho| < 1$, $\lambda = 1$, *then*

$$t_{\text{FD}} \xrightarrow{d} N(0, 1).$$

(4) *If* $\rho = 1$, $\lambda = 1$, *then*

$$t_{\text{FD}} \xrightarrow{d} N(0, 1).$$

Theorem 1.9 shows that, under the null, t_{FD} follows asymptotically a standard normal distribution in Cases 2–4, while not in Case 1.

1.3.3.   *GLS estimator*

In order to obtain the FGLS estimator $\widehat{\beta}_{\text{FGLS}}$, we use an estimate of ρ suggested by Baltagi and Li (1991). The asymptotic distribution of $\widehat{\rho}$ was derived in Theorem 1.7. Define

$$\hat{\alpha} = \sqrt{(1 + \widehat{\rho})/(1 - \widehat{\rho})}$$

and $\widehat{\iota}_T^{\alpha\prime} = (\hat{\alpha}, \iota'_{T-1})$, where ι_{T-1} is a vector of ones of dimension $T - 1$. Using a trick by Wansbeek and Kapteyn (1983), we define $\widehat{J}_T^{\alpha} = \widehat{\iota}_T^{\alpha}\widehat{\iota}_T^{\alpha\prime}/\hat{d}^2$,

where

$$\hat{d}^2 = \hat{\iota}_T^{\alpha\prime}\hat{\iota}_T^{\alpha} = \frac{2\widehat{\rho}}{1-\widehat{\rho}} + T.$$

Then,

$$\hat{E}_T^{\alpha} = I_T - \widehat{\bar{J}}_T^{\alpha}.$$

Also, let

$$\sigma_\alpha^2 = \theta\sigma_\mu^2 + \sigma_e^2,$$

where

$$\theta = (1-\rho)^2 d^2.$$

Estimates for σ_e^2 and σ_μ^2 can be obtained from

$$\hat{\sigma}_e^2 = \frac{1}{n(T-1)}\hat{\mathbf{u}}^{*\prime}(I_n \otimes \hat{E}_T^{\alpha})\hat{\mathbf{u}}^*$$

and

$$\hat{\sigma}_\alpha^2 = \frac{1}{n}\hat{\mathbf{u}}^{*\prime}(I_n \otimes \widehat{\bar{J}}_T^{\alpha})\hat{\mathbf{u}}^*$$

where $\hat{\mathbf{u}}^*$ are the PW transformed residuals, see Baltagi and Li (1991) for more details. Hence, $\hat{\sigma}_\mu^2$ can be estimated as

$$\hat{\sigma}_\mu^2 = \frac{1}{\hat{\theta}}(\hat{\sigma}_\alpha^2 - \hat{\sigma}_e^2).$$

Substituting $\hat{\sigma}_e^2$, $\hat{\sigma}_\mu^2$, and $\widehat{\rho}$ into Eq. (1.16), one obtains $\widehat{\beta}_{\text{FGLS}}$. The corresponding t-test for H_0 using the FGLS estimator $\widehat{\beta}_{\text{FGLS}}$ is

$$t_{\text{FGLS}} = \frac{\hat{\beta}_{\text{FGLS}} - \beta}{\sqrt{\widehat{\text{Var}}(\hat{\beta}_{\text{FGLS}})}} = \frac{\widehat{G}_1^{-1}\widehat{G}_2}{\sqrt{\widehat{G}_1^{-1}}} = \widehat{G}_1^{-1/2}\widehat{G}_2, \tag{1.21}$$

where $\widehat{G}_1$ and $\widehat{G}_2$ are given as Eq. (1.17) with the replacement of Φ by $\hat{\Phi}$. This section derives the asymptotic distribution of t_{FGLS} given in (1.21).

Theorem 1.10. *Assume $(n,T) \to \infty$ and $\frac{n}{T} \to 0$.*

(1) *If $|\rho| < 1$ and $|\lambda| < 1$, we have $\hat{\sigma}_e^2 \xrightarrow{p} \sigma_e^2$, $\hat{\sigma}_\mu^2 \xrightarrow{p} \sigma_\mu^2$ and*

$$t_{\text{FGLS}} \xrightarrow{d} N(0,1).$$

(2) *If $\rho = 1$ and $|\lambda| < 1$, we have $\hat{\sigma}_e^2 \xrightarrow{p} \sigma_e^2$, $(1-\hat{\rho})\hat{\sigma}_\mu^2 \xrightarrow{p} \frac{16}{25}\sigma_e^2$ and*

$$t_{\text{FGLS}} \xrightarrow{d} N(0,1).$$

(3) *If $|\rho| < 1$ and $\lambda = 1$, we have $\hat{\sigma}_e^2 \xrightarrow{p} \sigma_e^2$, $\hat{\sigma}_\mu^2 \xrightarrow{p} \sigma_\mu^2$ and*

$$t_{\text{FGLS}} \xrightarrow{d} N(0,1).$$

(4) *If $\rho = 1$ and $\lambda = 1$, we have $\hat{\sigma}_e^2 \xrightarrow{p} \sigma_e^2$, $(1-\hat{\rho})\hat{\sigma}_\mu^2 \xrightarrow{p} \frac{16}{25}\sigma_e^2$ and*

$$t_{\text{FGLS}} \xrightarrow{d} N(0,1).$$

Theorem 1.10 implies that the t-ratio based on $\hat{\rho}$ by Baltagi and Li (1991) asymptotically leads to the standard normal distribution regardless of the stationarity or nonstationarity of the regressor and/or the error term. This is an interesting finding because despite the fact that we do not have a consistent estimate of σ_μ^2 when $\rho = 1$, we can still obtain t_{FGLS} converging in distribution to $N(0,1)$.

1.4. Conclusion

This chapter has provided insights into some of the results that have developed for panel spurious regression models. We first show that large panel spurious regression is identifiable. That is, the large cross-sectional dimension helps to recover the identification. Next, we provide a comprehensive treatment of four panel estimators, OLS, FE, FD and GLS when the regression error and/or the regressor are either stationary or nonstationary. We show the GLS is the preferred estimator since GLS converges at as good or better rate in all cases and FD estimator is also a good choice for applied users due to its robustness. We also show the t-statistic of the FGLS always follows asymptotically a standard normal distribution.

1.5. Technical Proofs

Proof of Theorems 1.3–1.6 can be found in Baltagi *et al.* (2008). Proof of Theorems 1.7–1.10 can be found in Baltagi *et al.* (2011).

1.6. Exercises

(1) Prove Theorem 1.2 using the joint limit.
(2) Show $E(\int \widetilde{W}_i \widetilde{V}_i) = 0$ and $\text{Var}(\int \widetilde{W}_i \widetilde{V}_i) = \frac{1}{90}$ in Theorem 1.2.
(3) Revisit Theorem 1.2 if x_{it} and y_{it} have nonzero drifts as

$$x_{it} = \mu_i + x_{i,t-1} + \varepsilon_{it}$$

and

$$y_{it} = v_i + y_{i,t-1} + e_{it}$$

with $\mu_i \neq 0$ and $\nu_i \neq 0$.

(4) In the panel spurious regression model in Eq. (1.1), show that the t-statistic t_β has the following asymptotic distribution:

$$\frac{1}{\sqrt{T}} t_\beta \xrightarrow{d} N\left(0, \frac{2}{5}\right)$$

as $(n, T) \to \infty$.

(5) In the panel spurious regression model in Eq. (1.1), the Durbin–Watson Statistic is given by

$$DW = \frac{\sum_{i=1}^{n} \sum_{t=2}^{T} (\hat{\nu}_{it} - \hat{\nu}_{i,t-1})^2}{\sum_{i=1}^{n} \sum_{t=1}^{T} \hat{\nu}_{it}^2},$$

where $\hat{\nu}_{it}$ are within residuals. Show that $T \times DW \xrightarrow{p} 6$ as $(n, T) \to \infty$.

(6) Theorems 1.2 and 1.4 assume strong exogeneity in the absence of serial correlation as follows.

Assumption 1.3. Assume $E(e_{it}\varepsilon_{i,t+k}) = 0$ for all i and k. Both ε_{it} and e_{it} are independent.

This strong assumption is used to simplify proofs and can be relaxed. Let $\mathbf{w}_{it} = (e_{it}, \varepsilon_{it})'$. To be general, we can assume that $\mathbf{w}_{it}$ is a linear process that satisfies the following assumptions.

Assumption 1.4. For each i, we assume:

(a) $\mathbf{w}_{it} = \Pi(L)\eta_{it} = \sum_{j=0}^{\infty} \Pi_j \eta_{it-j}$, $\sum_{j=0}^{\infty} j^a \|\Pi_j\| < \infty$, $|\Pi(1)| \neq 0$ for some $a > 1$;

(b) for a given i, η_{it} is i.i.d. with zero mean, variance–covariance matrix Ξ, and finite fourth-order cumulants.

Assumption 1.5. We assume η_{it} and η_{jt} are independent for $i \neq j$. That is, we assume cross-sectional independence for our model.

Assumption 1.4 implies that the partial sum process $\frac{1}{\sqrt{T}}\sum_{t=1}^{[Tr]}\mathbf{w}_{it}$ satisfies the following multivariate FCLT:

$$\frac{1}{\sqrt{T}}\sum_{t=1}^{[Tr]}\mathbf{w}_{it} \xrightarrow{d} \mathbf{B}_i(r) = \mathbf{BM}_i(\Omega) \text{ as } T \to \infty \text{ for all } i,$$

where $\mathbf{B}_i = \begin{bmatrix} B_{ei} \\ B_{\varepsilon i} \end{bmatrix}$. The long-run 2×2 covariance matrix of $\{\mathbf{w}_{it}\}$ is given by

$$\Omega = \sum_{j=-\infty}^{\infty} E(\mathbf{w}_{ij}\mathbf{w}_{i0}') = \begin{bmatrix} \varpi_e^2 & \varpi_{e\varepsilon} \\ \varpi_{e\varepsilon} & \varpi_\varepsilon^2 \end{bmatrix} \tag{1.22}$$

which can be decomposed into $\Omega = \Sigma + 2\Gamma$, where

$$\Gamma = \sum_{j=1}^{\infty} E(\mathbf{w}_{ij}\mathbf{w}_{i0}') = \begin{bmatrix} \gamma_e^2 & \gamma_{e\varepsilon} \\ \gamma_{e\varepsilon} & \gamma_\varepsilon^2 \end{bmatrix}$$

and

$$\Sigma = E(\mathbf{w}_{i0}\mathbf{w}_{i0}') = \begin{bmatrix} \sigma_e^2 & \sigma_{e\varepsilon} \\ \sigma_{e\varepsilon} & \sigma_\varepsilon^2 \end{bmatrix}.$$

The one-sided long-run covariance can be further defined as

$$\Delta = \Sigma + \Gamma = \sum_{j=0}^{\infty} E(\mathbf{w}_{ij}\mathbf{w}_{i0}') = \begin{bmatrix} \delta_e^2 & \delta_{e\varepsilon} \\ \delta_{e\varepsilon} & \delta_\varepsilon^2 \end{bmatrix}.$$

Assuming ϖ_ε^2 is nonzero, we define $\varpi_{e.\varepsilon}^2 = \varpi_e^2 - \frac{\varpi_{e\varepsilon}^2}{\varpi_\varepsilon^2}$. It is worth pointing out that Assumption 1.3 implies $\Gamma = 0$ and $\Omega = \Sigma = \begin{bmatrix} \sigma_e^2 & 0 \\ 0 & \sigma_\varepsilon^2 \end{bmatrix}$. Therefore, $\varpi_{e.\varepsilon} = \sigma_e$, $\varpi_\varepsilon = \sigma_\varepsilon$ and $\varpi_{e\varepsilon} = 0$. Hence $\mathbf{B}_i$ can be rewritten as $\mathbf{B}_i = \begin{bmatrix} B_{ei} \\ B_{ei} \end{bmatrix} = \begin{bmatrix} \sigma_e & 0 \\ 0 & \sigma_\varepsilon \end{bmatrix}\begin{bmatrix} V_i \\ W_i \end{bmatrix}$, where $\begin{bmatrix} V_i \\ W_i \end{bmatrix}$ is a standard Brownian motion. Show that without Assumption 1.3, i.e., under Assumptions (1.1)–(1.5), the case of spurious regression in Theorems 1.2 and 1.4 can be extended to the following: If $\rho = 1$ and $\lambda = 1$,

(a) $\widehat{\beta}_{\text{FE}} - \beta \xrightarrow{p} \frac{\varpi_{e\varepsilon} + 6\delta_{e\varepsilon}}{\varpi_\varepsilon^2}$,

(b) $\sqrt{n}(\widehat{\beta}_{\text{FE}} - \beta - \tau_{4nT}^{\text{FE}}) \xrightarrow{d} N(0, \kappa_4^{\text{FE}})$, where

$$\tau_{4nT}^{\text{FE}} = \frac{\left(\frac{1}{n}\sum_{i=1}^{n}\frac{1}{T^2}\sum_{t=1}^{T}(x_{it} - \overline{x}_i)^2\right)\frac{\varpi_{e\varepsilon}}{\varpi_\varepsilon^2} + \delta_{e\varepsilon}}{\frac{1}{n}\sum_{i=1}^{n}\frac{1}{T^2}\sum_{t=1}^{T}(x_{it} - \overline{x}_i)^2} \text{ and } \kappa_4^{\text{FE}} = \frac{2\varpi_{e.\varepsilon}}{5\varpi_\varepsilon^2}.$$

Note that the bias term is $\frac{\varpi_{\varepsilon e} + 6\delta_{\varepsilon e}}{\varpi_\varepsilon^2}$, which depends on $\varpi_{\varepsilon e}$ and $\delta_{\varepsilon e}$. Of them, $\varpi_{\varepsilon e}$ is due to the endogeneity of the regressor x_{it}, and $\delta_{\varepsilon e}$ is due to serial correlation. Of course, when $\varpi_{\varepsilon e} = 0$ and $\delta_{\varepsilon e} = 0$, the bias reduces to 0.

(7) Show that without Assumption 1.3, i.e., under Assumptions (1.1)–(1.5), the case of spurious regression in Theorem 1.4 can be extended to the following:

If $|\rho| < 1$ and $\lambda = 1$,

(a) $T(\widehat{\beta}_{\text{FE}} - \beta) \xrightarrow{p} \frac{-3\varpi_{\varepsilon e} + 6\delta_{\varepsilon e}}{(1-\rho)\varpi_\varepsilon^2}$,

(b) $\sqrt{n}T(\widehat{\beta}_{\text{FE}} - \beta) - \sqrt{n}\tau_{3nT}^{\text{FE}} \xrightarrow{d} N(0, \kappa_3^{\text{FE}})$, where

$$\tau_{3nT}^{\text{FE}} = \frac{\left(\frac{1}{n}\sum_{i=1}^{n}\frac{1}{T}\sum_{t=1}^{T}(x_{it} - \overline{x}_i)\varepsilon_{it}\right)\frac{\varpi_{\varepsilon e}}{\varpi_\varepsilon^2} + \delta_{\varepsilon e}}{(1-\rho)\frac{1}{n}\sum_{i=1}^{n}\frac{1}{T^2}\sum_{t=1}^{T}(x_{it} - \overline{x}_i)^2} \quad \text{and}$$

$$\kappa_3^{\text{FE}} = \frac{6\varpi_{e.\varepsilon}}{(1-\rho)^2\varpi_\varepsilon^2}.$$

Note that if $|\rho| < 1$ and $\lambda = 1$, Eq. (1.2) is a cointegration regression, i.e., y_{it} is cointegrated with x_{it}.

(8) Kao (1999) proposes several residual-based cointegration Dickey–Fuller (DF) test and augmented DF (ADF) test. In model (1.1), we are interested in the null hypothesis $H_0 : \rho = 1$. Consider the estimator

$$\hat{\rho} = \frac{\sum_{i=1}^{n}\sum_{t=2}^{T}\hat{\nu}_{it}\hat{\nu}_{i,t-1}}{\sum_{i=1}^{n}\sum_{t=2}^{T}\hat{\nu}_{it}^2},$$

which is the OLS estimator from a regression $\hat{\nu}_{it}$ on $\hat{\nu}_{i,t-1}$. The null hypothesis that $\rho = 1$ can be tested by

$$\sqrt{n}T(\hat{\rho} - 1) = \sqrt{n}\frac{\frac{1}{nT}\sum_{i=1}^{n}\sum_{t=2}^{T}\Delta\hat{\nu}_{it}\hat{\nu}_{i,t-1}}{\frac{1}{nT^2}\sum_{i=1}^{n}\sum_{t=2}^{T}\hat{\nu}_{it}^2} = \sqrt{n}\frac{\xi_{3nT}}{\xi_{4nT}}.$$

Theorem 2 in Kao (1999) shows that

$$\sqrt{n}T(\hat{\rho} - 1) - \sqrt{n}\frac{\mu_{3T}}{\mu_{4T}} \xrightarrow{d} N\left(0, 3 + \frac{36\sigma_\nu^4}{5\sigma_{0\nu}^4}\right), \qquad (1.23)$$

where $\mu_{3T} = E(\xi_{3nT})$ and $\mu_{4T} = E(\xi_{4nT})$, which can be approximated by $-\sigma_\nu^2/2$ and $\sigma_{0\nu}^2/6$, respectively. σ_ν^2 and $\sigma_{0\nu}^2$ are short- and long-run variances, respectively. (In our notations in Eq. (1.22), they are $\varpi_{e.\varepsilon} = \varpi_e^2 - \frac{\varpi_{e\varepsilon}^2}{\varpi_\varepsilon^2}$ and $\sigma_{e.\varepsilon} = \sigma_e^2 - \frac{\sigma_{e\varepsilon}^2}{\sigma_\varepsilon^2}$, respectively.) The t-statistic to test $\rho = 1$ is defined as

$$t_\rho = \frac{(\hat{\rho} - 1)\sqrt{\sum_{i=1}^{n} \sum_{t=2}^{T} \hat{e}_{i,t-1}^{*2}}}{s_e},$$

where

$$s_e = \sqrt{\frac{1}{nT} \sum_{i=1}^{n} \sum_{t=2}^{T} (\hat{e}_{it}^* - \hat{\rho}\hat{e}_{i,t-1}^*)^2},$$

$$\hat{e}_{it}^* = y_{it}^* - \hat{\alpha}_i - \hat{\beta}^* x_{it}^*,$$

$$y_{it}^* = y_{it} - \sigma_{0u\epsilon}\sigma_{0\epsilon}^{-2} x_{it},$$

and $x_{it}^* = \sigma_{0\epsilon}^{-1} x_{it}$. Theorem 2 in Kao (1999) shows that

$$t_\rho - \frac{\sqrt{n}\mu_{3T}}{s_e\sqrt{\mu_{4T}}} \xrightarrow{d} N\left(0, \frac{\sigma_{0v}^2}{2\sigma_v^2} + \frac{3\sigma_v^2}{10\sigma_{0v}^2}\right).$$

Hence, DF tests based on ρ and t_ρ can be derived as

$$DF_\rho^* = \frac{\sqrt{n}T(\hat{\rho} - 1) + 3\sqrt{n}\frac{\hat{\sigma}_v^2}{\hat{\sigma}_{0v}^2}}{\sqrt{3 + \frac{36}{5}\frac{\hat{\sigma}_v^4}{\hat{\sigma}_{0v}^4}}} \xrightarrow{d} N(0, 1)$$

and

$$DF_t^* = \frac{t_\rho + \frac{\sqrt{6n}\hat{\sigma}_v}{2\hat{\sigma}_{0v}}}{\sqrt{\frac{\hat{\sigma}_{0v}^2}{2\hat{\sigma}_v^2} + \frac{3\hat{\sigma}_v^2}{10\hat{\sigma}_{0v}^2}}} \xrightarrow{d} N(0, 1).$$

Show Eq. (1.23).

(9) Kao (1999) also extends the residual-based cointegration DF test and ADF test to the models with deterministic trends. In model (1.1), now we consider that

$$\Delta x_{it} = \gamma_i + \varepsilon_{it},$$

which is equivalent to

$$x_{it} = \gamma_i t + \sum_{s=1}^{t} \varepsilon_{is}.$$

When $\gamma_i = 0$, x_{it} reduces to $x_{it} = \sum_{s=1}^{t} \varepsilon_{is}$, which is a random walk. When $\gamma_i \neq 0$, the stochastic part, $\sum_{s=1}^{t} \varepsilon_{is}$, is asymptotically dominated by the deterministic part, t. To test the null hypothesis $H_0 : \rho = 1$, consider the estimator

$$\hat{\rho} = \frac{\sum_{i=1}^{n} \sum_{t=2}^{T} \tilde{y}_{it}\tilde{y}_{i,t-1}}{\sum_{i=1}^{n} \sum_{t=2}^{T} \tilde{y}_{it}^2},$$

where $\tilde{y}_{it} = y_{it} - \bar{y}_i - d_i$

$$d_i = \frac{\sum_{t=1}^{T}(t - \bar{t})y_{it}}{\sum_{t=1}^{T}(t - \bar{t})^2}.$$

Under the null of no cointegration, $\rho = 1$,

$$\sqrt{n}T(\hat{\rho} - 1) = \sqrt{n}\frac{\frac{1}{nT}\sum_{i=1}^{n} \sum_{t=2}^{T} \epsilon_{it}\tilde{y}_{i,t-1}}{\frac{1}{nT}\sum_{i=1}^{n} \sum_{t=2}^{T} \tilde{y}_{it}^2}.$$

Theorem 4 in Kao (1999) shows that result in Eq. (1.23) becomes

$$\sqrt{n}\left[T(\hat{\rho} - 1) - \frac{\mu_{7T}}{\mu_{8T}}\right] \xrightarrow{d} N\left(0, \frac{15}{4} + \frac{2475}{112}\frac{\sigma_u^4}{\sigma_{0u}^4}\right), \qquad (1.24)$$

where

$$\mu_{7T} = E\left(\frac{1}{T}\sum_{t=2}^{T} \epsilon_{it}\tilde{y}_{i,t-1}\right),$$

and

$$\mu_{8T} = E\left(\frac{1}{T}\sum_{t=2}^{T} \tilde{y}_{it}^2\right),$$

σ_u^2 and σ_{0u}^2 are short- and long-run variances, respectively. (In our notations in Eq. (1.22), they are $\varpi_{e.\varepsilon} = \varpi_e^2 - \frac{\varpi_{e\varepsilon}^2}{\varpi_\varepsilon^2}$ and $\sigma_{e.\varepsilon} = \sigma_e^2 - \frac{\sigma_{e\varepsilon}^2}{\sigma_\varepsilon^2}$, respectively.) The t-statistic to test $\rho = 1$ hence can be derived as

$$t_\rho = \frac{(\hat{\rho} - 1)\sqrt{\sum_{i=1}^{n} \sum_{t=2}^{T} \tilde{y}_{i,t-1}^2}}{s_e},$$

where

$$s_e = \sqrt{\frac{1}{nT}\sum_{i=1}^{n}\sum_{t=2}^{T} \hat{\epsilon}_{it}^2}.$$

Theorem 4 in Kao (1999) shows that

$$t_\rho - \frac{\sqrt{n}\mu_{7T}}{s_e\sqrt{\mu_{8T}}} \xrightarrow{d} N\left(0, \frac{\sigma_{0u}^2}{4\sigma_u^2} + \frac{165}{448}\frac{\sigma_u^2}{\sigma_{0u}^2}\right).$$

Prove Eq. (1.24).

(10) Gengenbach, Palm, and Urbain (2006) extend the panel cointegration test in Kao (1999) by allowing an unobserved common factor structure. Define $Z_{it} = (y_{it}, x'_{it})'$ with

$$Z_{it} = \Lambda_i F_t + E_{it},$$

where F_t is a k-vector of common $I(1)$ factors given by

$$F_t = F_{t-1} + f_t$$

where $f_t = \Phi(L)\eta_t$, η_t is a sequence of $(k \times 1)$ i.i.d. random vectors, and $\Phi(L) = \sum_{j=0}^{\infty} \Phi_j L^j$. The $(1+m) \times k$ matrix of factor loadings Λ_i is assumed to be of full rank and block-diagonal, with block diagonality corresponding to the partition of Z_{it}, and diagonal blocks denote a λ'_{1i} and λ'_{2i} for the upper left and lower right block, respectively. The idiosyncratic component E_{it} could be either stationary and nonstationary. For the former case, we have

$$E_{it} = e_{it}$$

while in the latter case we have

$$E_{it} = E_{i,t-1} + e_{it}$$

where the stationary vector $e_{it} = \Gamma_i(L)\epsilon_{it}$ with ϵ_{it} being a sequence of i.i.d. $(0, \Sigma_i)$ random vectors and $\Gamma_i(L) = \sum_{j=0}^{\infty} \Gamma_{ij} L^j$. Show the following results, which are from Proposition 1 in Gengenbach, Palm and Urbain (2006):

(a) If the idiosyncratic component is stationary $E_{it} = e_{it}$, as $(n, T) \to \infty$, show that

$$\tilde{\beta} \xrightarrow{d} \left(\int \tilde{B}_{F\Lambda}^Y \tilde{B}_{F\Lambda}^{X'} \right) \left(\int \tilde{B}_{F\Lambda}^X \tilde{B}_{F\Lambda}^{X'} \right)^{-1} \equiv \tilde{\mathbf{b}}_A$$

and

$$T(\tilde{\rho} - 1) \xrightarrow{d} \frac{(1, -\tilde{\mathbf{b}}_A) \left(\int dB_{F\Lambda} \tilde{B}'_{F\Lambda} + \Theta_{F\Lambda} + \gamma_1 - \Upsilon \right) (1, -\tilde{\mathbf{b}}_A)'}{(1, -\tilde{\mathbf{b}}_A) \left(\int \tilde{B}_{F\Lambda} \tilde{B}'_{F\Lambda} \right) (1, -\tilde{\mathbf{b}}_A)'}$$

where $\gamma_1 = E(\gamma_{i1})$ and $\gamma_{i1} = E(\tilde{e}_{i,t-1} \tilde{e}'_{it})$. Furthermore, $t_{\tilde{\rho}}$ diverges at the rate $\sqrt{n}$.

(b) If the idiosyncratic component is stationary $E_{it} = E_{i,t-1} + e_{it}$, as $(n, T) \to \infty$, show that

$$\tilde{\beta} \xrightarrow{d} \left(\int \tilde{B}^Y_{F\Lambda} \tilde{B}^{X\prime}_{F\Lambda} + \frac{1}{6} \Psi^{YX} \right) \left(\int \tilde{B}^X_{F\Lambda} \tilde{B}^{X\prime}_{F\Lambda} + \frac{1}{6} \Psi^{XX} \right)^{-1} \equiv \tilde{b}_B$$

and

$$T(\tilde{\rho} - 1) \xrightarrow{d} \frac{(1, -\tilde{b}_B) \left(\int dB_{F\Lambda} \tilde{B}'_{F\Lambda} + \Theta_{F\Lambda} - \frac{1}{2}\Psi + \Delta \right) (1, -\tilde{b}_B)'}{(1, -\tilde{b}_B) \left(\int dB_{F\Lambda} \tilde{B}'_{F\Lambda} + \frac{1}{6}\Psi \right) (1, -\tilde{b}_B)'}.$$

Furthermore, $t_{\tilde{\rho}}$ diverges at the rate $\sqrt{n}$.

(11) Wu (1981) considers

$$y_i = f(x_i, \theta_0) + \varepsilon_i,$$

where θ_0 is the unknown $p \times 1$ vector parameter, $f_i(\theta) = f(x_i, \theta)$ are continuous functions in θ, and ε_i are i.i.d. with mean zero and variance σ^2.

(a) Show that there exists a consistent estimator $\widehat{\theta}$ such that $\widehat{\theta} \xrightarrow{p} \theta_0$ if and only if

$$D_n(\theta, \theta') = \sum_{i=1}^{n} [f_i(\theta) - f_i(\theta')]^2 \to \infty$$

as $n \to \infty$ for all $\theta \neq \theta'$.

(b) Show that the nonlinear least squares estimator $\widehat{\theta}$ is inconsistent for the following models:

(i) $f_t(\theta) = e^{-\theta t}$, $\theta \in (0, 2\pi)$.

(ii) $f_t(\theta) = \frac{\theta_1 \theta_2}{\theta_2 - \theta_3} (e^{-\theta_3 t} - e^{-\theta_2 t})$, $\theta = (\theta_1, \theta_2, \theta_3) > 0$.

(12) Van de Geer and Wegkamp (1996) consider the following regression model:

$$y_i = g_0(x_i) + \varepsilon_i,$$

where x_i is a random variable with values in R^k and probability distribution P, and ε_i is a real-valued random variable with distribution K. We assume that ε_i and x_i are independent, and that $E(\varepsilon_i) = 0$,

$E(\varepsilon_i^2) = \sigma^2$. We also require $\int g_0^2 dP < \infty$, that is, $g_0 \in L^2(P)$. Let $\widehat{g}_n$ be the nonparametric least squares estimator

$$\widehat{g}_n = \arg\inf_g \frac{1}{n} \sum_{i=1}^{n} (y_i - g(x_i))^2.$$

Let

$$\|g\|_n^2 = \frac{1}{n} \sum_{i=1}^{n} g^2(x_i).$$

Show that

$$\|\widehat{g}_n - g_0\|_n \xrightarrow{p} 0$$

and spell out the conditions you need.

(13) Consider a binary response model

$$Y = 1\{X'\beta - \varepsilon \geq 0\}.$$

In economics, Y indicates a utility-maximizing decision-maker's observable choice between two alternatives. Then, the latent index $X'\beta - \varepsilon$ can be interpreted as the difference between these two choices. Let $\theta = (P_X, \beta, P_{\varepsilon|X})$ and Θ be the set of all possible values of θ. Assume $P_{\varepsilon|X} = N(0, \sigma^2)$ and there exists no $A \subseteq R^k$ such that A has probability 1 under P_X and A is a proper linear subspace of R^k. Show that $(P_X, \frac{\beta}{\sigma})$ is identified.

(14) Hong and Tamer (2003) consider the binary choice model

$$y = 1[y^* \geq 0]$$

with

$$y^* = x'\beta + \varepsilon,$$

where $x \in R^k$ is a vector of regressors, ε is a random variable such that $Med[\varepsilon|z] = 0$ where $z \in R^d$ is a vector of exogenous instruments. We observe an i.i.d. sample (y_i, x_i, z_i) and are interested in the parameter $\beta \in \mathbf{B}$. Show that the parameter β is point identified if, for all $b \in \mathbf{B}$, $b \neq \beta$, we have

$$P\{z : P(x'b < 0 \leq x'\beta|z) = 1 \cup P(x'\beta < 0 \leq x'b|z) = 1\} > 0. \quad (1.25)$$

(15) Shaikh and Vyltlacil (2008) consider

$$y = 1[y^* \geq 0]$$

with

$$y^* = \beta_0 + \beta_1 x_1 + \beta_2 x_2 + \varepsilon$$

with $z = (x_1, w)$ and $Med(\varepsilon|z) = 0$. Assume $\beta_1 = 1$ and x_2 is a Bernoulli random variable. Show that if

$$P\{z : P\{x_2 = 0|z\} > 0\} = 1 \text{ or } P\{z : P\{x_2 = 1|z\} > 0\} = 1$$

then Eq. (1.25) does not hold for some $b \in B$ such that $b \neq \beta$.

(16) Honore and Tamer (2006) consider

$$P(y_{i1} = 1|\alpha_i) = P_1(\alpha_i)$$

and

$$P(y_{it} = 1|\alpha_i, y_{i1}, \ldots, y_{i,t-1}) = P_1(\alpha_i + \rho y_{i,t-1})$$

where P_1 is an unknown function taking values between 0 and 1. Show the sign of ρ is identified.

Chapter 2

Panel Time Trend Model with Stationary and Nonstationary Error Terms

This chapter discusses the panel regression models when the regressor x_t has a time trend, i.e.,

$$x_t = t$$

and

$$\bar{t} = \frac{1}{T} \sum_{t=1}^{T} t = \frac{T+1}{2}.$$

Hence $\bar{t} = O(T)$, which diverges even faster than an $I(1)$ process. In a regression including a time trend t together with an $I(1)$ random walk and/or stationary variables as regressors, the time trend dominates. For example, if the error term is stationary $I(0)$, FE and GLS estimators in a panel time trend model could be asymptotically equivalent. Even if the regression error term is a nonstationary $I(1)$ process, the slope coefficient of the time trend variable could still be identified.

In Sec. 2.1, we illustrate the estimation of the autocorrelation parameter of nonstationary $I(1)$ error term for a de-trended model. By comparing the result in Perron and Yabu (2009a) for the time-series and the result in Baltagi, Kao and Liu (2014) for panel data, we demonstrate the advantage of using the panel model with large dimensions n and T. In Sec. 2.2, we further consider different cases in a panel data regression model where the error terms are either stationary or nonstationary. We compare the asymptotic distributions of the OLS, FE, FD, and GLS estimators. As shown in Kao and Emerson (2004, 2005), GLS is the preferred estimator in all cases. Test of hypotheses using these standard panel data estimators is discussed in Sec. 2.3. In particular, as shown in Baltagi, Kao and Liu (2014), the estimator of the autocorrelation parameter in Baltagi and Li (1991) is asymptotically biased. Baltagi, Kao, and Liu (2014) therefore propose a bias-corrected estimator. The simple t-ratio based on the FGLS using bias-corrected estimator will always converge to a standard normal random variable regardless of whether the errors are stationary or nonstationary. Section 2.4 concludes.

2.1. Estimation in a Time Trend Model

2.1.1. *Estimation of autocorrelation parameter in a detrended model*

Consider the following time trend model as in Perron and Yabu (2009a):

$$y_t = \delta + \beta t + u_t$$

for $t = 1, \ldots, T$, where u_t follows an AR(1) process

$$u_t = \rho u_{t-1} + e_t$$

with $|\rho| \leq 1$, where e_t is a white noise with variance σ_e^2. Our primary interest is to test if a trend is present, i.e., $H_0 : \beta = 0$. Since the error term is autocorrelated, we use an FGLS estimator $\hat{\beta}_{\text{FGLS}}$. Its t-statistic for testing $\beta = 0$ is given by

$$t_{\text{FGLS}} = \frac{\hat{\beta}_{\text{FGLS}} - \beta}{\sqrt{\widehat{\text{Var}}(\hat{\beta}_{\text{FGLS}})}}. \tag{2.1}$$

To perform the GLS transformation, we first need to obtain an estimator of ρ,

$$\hat{\rho} = \frac{\sum_{t=2}^{T} \hat{u}_t \hat{u}_{t-1}}{\sum_{t=2}^{T} \hat{u}_{t-1}^2},$$

where $\hat{u}_t$ is the OLS residual, i.e.,

$$\hat{u}_t = (y_t - \bar{y}) - \hat{\beta}_{\text{OLS}}(t - \bar{t})$$

with $\bar{y} = \frac{1}{T} \sum_{t=1}^{T} y_t$. When $|\rho| < 1$, it is easy to show $T(\hat{\rho} - 1) \xrightarrow{p} 0$ and the t-statistics of the FGLS estimator of β using $\hat{\rho}$ asymptotically follows a standard normal distribution, i.e., $t_{\text{FGLS}} \xrightarrow{d} N(0, 1)$. However, when $\rho = 1$, based on Perron and Yabu (2009a), the asymptotic property of $\hat{\rho}$ is as follows.

Theorem 2.1. *If $\rho = 1$, we have $T(\hat{\rho} - 1) = O_p(1)$.*

Proof. Note that

$$\hat{\rho} - 1 = \frac{\sum_{t=2}^{T} \Delta \hat{u}_t \hat{u}_{t-1}}{\sum_{t=2}^{T} \hat{u}_{t-1}^2}.$$

For the denominator, we have

$$\frac{1}{T^2} \sum_{t=2}^{T} \hat{u}_{t-1}^2 = \frac{1}{T^2} \sum_{t=2}^{T} (u_{t-1} - \bar{u})^2$$

$$+ [\sqrt{T}(\hat{\beta}_{\text{OLS}} - \beta)]^2 \left[\frac{1}{T^3} \sum_{t=2}^{T} (t - 1 - \bar{t})^2 \right]$$

$$- 2[\sqrt{T}(\hat{\beta}_{\text{OLS}} - \beta)] \left[\frac{1}{T^{5/2}} \sum_{t=2}^{T} (t - 1 - \bar{t})(u_{t-1} - \bar{u}) \right]$$

$$= O_p(1).$$

Similarly, for the numerator, we have

$$\frac{1}{T} \sum_{t=2}^{T} \Delta \hat{u}_t \hat{u}_{t-1} = \frac{1}{T} \sum_{t=2}^{T} [e_t(u_{t-1} - \bar{u})]$$

$$+ [\sqrt{T}(\hat{\beta}_{\text{OLS}} - \beta)] \left[\frac{1}{T^{3/2}} \sum_{t=2}^{T} (t - 1 - \bar{t})e_t \right]$$

$$+ \frac{1}{T^{3/2}} [\sqrt{T}(\hat{\beta}_{\text{OLS}} - \beta)] \left[\frac{1}{T^{3/2}} \sum_{t=2}^{T} (u_{t-1} - \bar{u}) \right]$$

$$+ \frac{1}{T} [\sqrt{T}(\hat{\beta}_{\text{OLS}} - \beta)]^2 \left[\frac{1}{T} \sum_{t=2}^{T} (t - 1 - \bar{t}) \right]$$

$$= O_p(1)$$

in which the first two terms are $O_p(1)$ and others are of smaller terms. Therefore,

$$T(\hat{\rho} - 1) = \frac{\frac{1}{T} \sum_{t=2}^{T} \Delta \hat{u}_t \hat{u}_{t-1}}{\frac{1}{T^2} \sum_{t=2}^{T} \hat{u}_{t-1}^2} = O_p(1). \qquad \square$$

Theorem 2.1 shows that $T(\hat{\rho} - 1)$ does not converge to 0 when the error term is $I(1)$. Instead, it converges to a random variable. As a result, the *t*-statistics of the FGLS estimator of β using $\hat{\rho}$ does not follow a standard normal distribution asymptotically. In fact, as shown in Perron and Yabu (2009a), we have

$$T(\hat{\rho} - 1) \xrightarrow{d} \frac{\int_0^1 W^*(r)dW(r)}{\int_0^1 W^{*2}(r)dr} \equiv \kappa,$$

where $W^*(r)$ is the residual process from a continuous time regression of a Brownian motion $W(r)$ on $\{1, r\}$. Hence,

$$t_{\text{FGLS}} \xrightarrow{d} \frac{W(1) - \kappa \int_0^1 W(r)dr - \kappa[\int_0^1 rdW(r) - \kappa \int_0^1 rW(r)dr]}{(1 - \kappa + \kappa^2/3)^{1/2}},$$

which is not normally distributed and depends on κ. Therefore, Perron and Yabu (2009a) suggest a super-efficient estimate of ρ as a solution. Let us illustrate estimation of autocorrelation parameter in time-series data using the following example in R.

Example 2.1.

```
> # time series
> set.seed(12345)
> T.obs <- 50
> x.t <- 1:T.obs
> u.t <- cumsum(rnorm(T.obs))
> y.t <- 1 + 0.5*x.t + u.t
> beta.hat <- sum((x.t-mean(x.t))*(y.t-mean(y.t)))
              /sum((x.t-mean(x.t))^2)
> u.hat <- (y.t-mean(y.t))-beta.hat*(x.t-mean(x.t))
> rho.hat <- sum(u.hat[1:(T.obs-1)]*u.hat[2:T.obs])
             /sum(u.hat[1:(T.obs-1)]^2)
> rho.hat

[1] 0.8100922

> T.obs*(rho.hat-1)

[1] -9.49539
```

In the time-series example above, the variables are created as $T = 50$. The true value of ρ is 1. The estimated value is 0.8101, which is less than the true value of 1. After multiplying T, the bias is -9.4954, which is large.

2.1.2. *Estimation of autocorrelation parameter in a panel detrended model*

Let us illustrate the benefits of a large panel using a simple model without individual effects. The general model with individual effects will be discussed in the next section. Consider the following panel data time trend model:

$$y_{it} = \delta + \beta t + u_{it}$$

for $i = 1, \ldots, n$, $t = 1, \ldots, T$, where u_{it} follows an AR(1) process

$$u_{it} = \rho u_{i,t-1} + e_{it}$$

with $|\rho| \le 1$, where e_{it} is a white noise process with variance σ_e^2. An estimator of ρ is

$$\hat{\rho} = \frac{\sum_{i=1}^{n} \sum_{t=2}^{T} \hat{u}_{it} \hat{u}_{i,t-1}}{\sum_{i=1}^{n} \sum_{t=2}^{T} \hat{u}_{i,t-1}^2},$$

where $\hat{u}_{it}$ is the OLS residual, i.e.,

$$\hat{u}_{it} = (y_{it} - \overline{\overline{y}}) - \hat{\beta}_{\text{OLS}}(t - \overline{t}).$$

Using $\hat{\rho}$, a t-statistic for testing $\beta = 0$ using an FGLS estimator $\hat{\beta}_{\text{FGLS}}$ is still given in Eq. (2.1). Different from time-series, we present the following theorem.

Theorem 2.2. *Assuming* $(n, T) \to \infty$, *we have* $T(\hat{\rho} - 1) \overset{p}{\to} 0$ *for both* $|\rho| < 1$ *and* $\rho = 1$.

Proof. The proof for $|\rho| < 1$ is a textbook result and hence omitted here. We only discuss the case $\rho = 1$.

Note that

$$\hat{\rho} - 1 = \frac{\sum_{i=1}^{n} \sum_{t=2}^{T} \Delta \hat{u}_{it} \hat{u}_{i,t-1}}{\sum_{i=1}^{n} \sum_{t=2}^{T} \hat{u}_{i,t-1}^2}.$$

For the denominator, we have

$$\frac{1}{nT^2} \sum_{i=1}^{n} \sum_{t=2}^{T} \hat{u}_{i,t-1}^2$$

$$= \frac{1}{nT^2} \sum_{i=1}^{n} \sum_{t=2}^{T} (v_{i,t-1} - \overline{\overline{v}})^2$$

$$+ \frac{1}{n}[\sqrt{nT}(\hat{\beta}_{\text{OLS}} - \beta)]^2 \left[\frac{1}{nT^3} \sum_{i=1}^{n} \sum_{t=2}^{T} (t - 1 - \bar{t})^2 \right]$$

$$- \frac{2}{n}[\sqrt{nT}(\hat{\beta}_{\text{OLS}} - \beta)] \left[\frac{1}{\sqrt{n}T^{5/2}} \sum_{i=1}^{n} \sum_{t=2}^{T} (t - 1 - \bar{t})(v_{i,t-1} - \bar{\bar{v}}) \right]$$

$$\xrightarrow{p} \frac{\sigma_e^2}{2}$$

as $(n, T) \to \infty$ since the first term is

$$\frac{1}{nT^2} \sum_{i=1}^{n} \sum_{t=2}^{T} (v_{i,t-1} - \bar{\bar{v}})^2 \xrightarrow{p} \frac{\sigma_e^2}{2}$$

and others are of smaller terms. Similarly, for the numerator, we have

$$\frac{1}{nT} \sum_{i=1}^{n} \sum_{t=2}^{T} \Delta \hat{u}_{it} \hat{u}_{i,t-1}$$

$$= \frac{1}{nT} \sum_{i=1}^{n} \sum_{t=2}^{T} [e_{it}(v_{i,t-1} - \bar{\bar{v}})]$$

$$+ \frac{1}{n}[\sqrt{nT}(\hat{\beta}_{\text{OLS}} - \beta)] \left[\frac{1}{\sqrt{n}T^{3/2}} \sum_{i=1}^{n} \sum_{t=2}^{T} (t - 1 - \bar{t})e_{it} \right]$$

$$+ \frac{1}{\sqrt{n}T^{3/2}}[\sqrt{nT}(\hat{\beta}_{\text{OLS}} - \beta)] \left[\frac{1}{\sqrt{n}T^{3/2}} \sum_{i=1}^{n} \sum_{t=2}^{T} (v_{i,t-1} - \bar{\bar{v}}) \right]$$

$$+ \frac{1}{nT}[\sqrt{nT}(\hat{\beta}_{\text{OLS}} - \beta)]^2 \left[\frac{1}{nT} \sum_{i=1}^{n} \sum_{t=2}^{T} (t - 1 - \bar{t}) \right]$$

$$\xrightarrow{p} 0$$

as $(n, T) \to \infty$ since the first term is

$$\frac{1}{nT} \sum_{i=1}^{n} \sum_{t=2}^{T} [e_{it}(v_{i,t-1} - \bar{\bar{v}})] \xrightarrow{p} 0$$

and others are of smaller terms. Therefore,

$$T(\hat{\rho} - 1) = \frac{\frac{1}{nT} \sum_{i=1}^{n} \sum_{t=2}^{T} \Delta \hat{u}_{it} \hat{u}_{i,t-1}}{\frac{1}{nT^2} \sum_{i=1}^{n} \sum_{t=2}^{T} \hat{u}_{i,t-1}^2} \xrightarrow{p} 0$$

as $(n, T) \to \infty$. $\square$

Theorem 2.2 shows that as $(n, T) \to \infty$, $T(\hat{\rho} - 1)$ converges to 0. As a result, we have $t_{\text{FGLS}} \xrightarrow{d} N(0, 1)$ using $\hat{\rho}$ for both $|\rho| < 1$ and $\rho = 1$. This implies that inference on the slope parameter can be performed using the standard normal distribution. This is an interesting result since the t-ratio based on FGLS effectively bridges the gap between the $I(0)$ and $I(1)$ error terms. This is different from the time-series model as in Perron and Yabu (2009a) which requires a super-efficient estimate in order to achieve this goal. It is worth pointing out that the nice result above is for the special case where there are no individual effects in the model. We will discuss the general case in the next section. Besides the GLS estimator, we will also discuss OLS, FE and FD estimators. Let us illustrate estimation of autocorrelation parameter in the panel data using the following example in R.

Example 2.2.

```
> # panel data
> set.seed(12345)
> T.obs <- 50
> n.obs <- 100
> nT.obs <- n.obs * T.obs
> x <- 1:T.obs
> u <- apply(matrix(rnorm(nT.obs), T.obs, n.obs),2,cumsum)
> y <- x + u
> beta.hat <- sum((x-mean(x))*(y-mean(y)))
            /(n.obs*sum((x-mean(x))^2))
> u.hat <- (y-mean(y))-beta.hat*(x-mean(x))
> rho.hat <- sum(u.hat[1:(T.obs-1),]*u.hat[2:T.obs,])
            /sum(u.hat[1:(T.obs-1),]^2)
> rho.hat

[1] 0.9983507

> T.obs*(rho.hat-1)

[1] -0.08246515
```

In the panel data example above, we have $n = 100$ and $T = 50$. The estimated value is 0.9984, which is still slightly less than the true value of 1. After multiplying T, the bias reduces to -0.0825, which is very small.

2.2. Estimation in a Time Trend Model with Stationary and Nonstationary Error Terms

Consider the following panel time trend model:

$$y_{it} = \delta + \beta t + u_{it}, \tag{2.2}$$

where $u_{it} = \mu_i + \nu_{it}$. We assume $\mu_i \overset{i.i.d.}{\sim} (0, \sigma_\mu^2)$ and ν_{it} following an AR(1) process

$$\nu_{it} = \rho \nu_{i,t-1} + e_{it} \tag{2.3}$$

with $|\rho| \leq 1$, where e_{it} is a white noise with variance σ_e^2. The μ_i's are independent of the ν_{it}'s for all i and t. Our interest is to estimate the trend coefficient β. The estimators to be considered are the OLS, FE, FD, and GLS estimators. Indeed, the model considered in (2.2) is rather restrictive, e.g., (i) there are no regressors in the model, (ii) the time trend slope is restricted to being the same across all i, and (iii) the AR(1) parameter, ρ, and error variance are assumed to be the same for all i. However, this model should be viewed as a first step in understanding more complicated ones by analyzing restricted versions of them. For example, model (2.2) can be seen as a panel regression with a nonzero drift $I(1)$ regressor. This model has been studied by Baltagi and Krämer (1997) and Kao and Emerson (2004, 2005). In fact, Baltagi and Krämer (1997) show the equivalence of OLS, GLS and FE estimators for the panel data time trend model in Eq. (2.2), but without serial correlation. Baltagi and Krämer (1997) also investigate the relative efficiency of the FD estimator with respect to the other estimators of β as $T \to \infty$. Kao and Emerson (2004) extend Baltagi and Krämer (1997) to model (2.2) with serially correlated errors (2.3). This model could be further extended to a polynomial trend model by following similar steps as in Sec. 6 of Emerson and Kao (2001). We follow Canjels and Watson (1997) to assume the following initial conditions.

Assumption 2.1. $v_{i1} = \sum_{j=0}^{[\pi T]} \rho^j e_{i,1-j.}$, where π is a parameter that governs the variance of the initial condition.

When $\rho = 1$, v_{it} is $I(1)$. From Assumption 2.1, we have

$$\frac{1}{\sqrt{T}} v_{i1} = \frac{1}{\sqrt{T}} \sum_{j=0}^{[\pi T]} e_{i,1-j} \overset{d}{\to} N(0, \pi \sigma_e^2)$$

for all i. For simplicity, we assume $[\pi T] \to \infty$.

2.2.1. *FE estimator*

First of all, we note that the OLS and FE estimators are the same for the time trend model with an intercept in Eq. (2.2). They are

$$\widehat{\beta}_{\text{OLS}} = \widehat{\beta}_{\text{FE}} = \frac{\sum_{i=1}^{N}\sum_{t=1}^{T}(t - \bar{t})y_{it}}{\sum_{i=1}^{N}\sum_{t=1}^{T}(t - \bar{t})^2}. \tag{2.4}$$

Theorem 2.3. *Under Assumption 2.1, as* $(n, T) \to \infty$,

(1) *if* $|\rho| < 1$,

$$\sqrt{nT^3}(\widehat{\beta}_{\text{FE}} - \beta) \xrightarrow{d} N\left(0, \frac{12\sigma_e^2}{(1 - \rho)^2}\right);$$

(2) *if* $\rho = 1$,

$$\sqrt{nT}(\widehat{\beta}_{\text{FE}} - \beta) \xrightarrow{d} N\left(0, \frac{6}{5}\sigma_e^2\right).$$

Note that the inclusion of a fitted intercept in Eq. (2.2) does not alter the FE estimator $\widehat{\beta}_{\text{FE}}$. Thus, the FE estimator has the same limiting distribution whether or not an intercept is included in the regression. However, without the intercept, the OLS estimator $\widehat{\beta}_{\text{OLS}}$ becomes

$$\widehat{\beta}_{\text{OLS}} = \frac{\sum_{i=1}^{n}\sum_{t=1}^{T} ty_{it}}{\sum_{i=1}^{n}\sum_{t=1}^{T} t^2}$$

so that the limiting distribution of $\widehat{\beta}_{\text{OLS}}$ will be affected by a fitted intercept.

2.2.2. *FD estimator*

The FD estimator of β for a regressor x_{it} is given by

$$\widehat{\beta}_{\text{FD}} = \frac{\sum_{i=1}^{n}\sum_{t=2}^{T}(x_{it} - x_{it-1})(y_{it} - y_{it-1})}{\sum_{i=1}^{n}\sum_{t=2}^{T}(x_{it} - x_{it-1})^2}.$$

For the time trend regressor $x_{it} = t$, the FD estimator $\widehat{\beta}_{\text{FD}}$ is reduced to

$$\widehat{\beta}_{\text{FD}} = \frac{\sum_{i=1}^{n}(y_{iT} - y_{i1})}{n(T - 1)}.$$

Theorem 2.4. *Under Assumption 2.1, as* $(n, T) \to \infty$,

(1) *if* $|\rho| < 1$,

$$\sqrt{nT}(\widehat{\beta}_{\text{FD}} - \beta) \xrightarrow{d} N\left(0, \frac{2\sigma_e^2}{1 - \rho^2}\right);$$

(2) *if $\rho = 1$,*

$$\sqrt{nT}(\widehat{\beta}_{\text{FD}} - \beta) \xrightarrow{d} N(0, \sigma_e^2).$$

2.2.3. GLS estimator

Rewrite Eq. (2.2) in matrix form

$$\mathbf{y} = \delta\iota_{nT} + \beta\mathbf{x} + u \tag{2.5}$$

with $u = Z_\mu\mu + \nu$, which is the same defined as in Eq. (1.6) except $\mathbf{x} = \iota_n \otimes x$, and x is a $T \times 1$ vector indicating a time trend with elements $(1, 2, \ldots, T)$. The variance–covariance matrix Φ and its inverse are given in Eqs. (1.7) and (1.16), respectively. As we showed in Eq. (1.15), the GLS estimator $\widehat{\beta}_{\text{GLS}}$ is given by

$$\widehat{\beta}_{\text{GLS}} = [\mathbf{x}'\Phi^{-1}\mathbf{x} - \mathbf{x}'\Phi^{-1}\iota_{nT}(\iota'_{nT}\Phi^{-1}\iota_{nT})^{-1}\iota'_{nT}\Phi^{-1}\mathbf{x}]^{-1}$$
$$\times [\mathbf{x}'\Phi^{-1}\mathbf{y} - \mathbf{x}'\Phi^{-1}\iota_{nT}(\iota'_{nT}\Phi^{-1}\iota_{nT})^{-1}\iota'_{nT}\Phi^{-1}\mathbf{y}]. \tag{2.6}$$

Theorem 2.5. *Under Assumption 2.1, as $(n, T) \to \infty$,*

(1) *if $|\rho| < 1$,*

$$\sqrt{nT^3}(\widehat{\beta}_{\text{GLS}} - \beta) \xrightarrow{d} N\left(0, \frac{12\sigma_e^2}{(1-\rho)^2}\right);$$

(2) *if $\rho = 1$,*

$$\sqrt{nT}(\widehat{\beta}_{\text{GLS}} - \beta) \xrightarrow{d} N(0, \sigma_e^2).$$

Kao and Emerson (2004) show that the FE estimator is asymptotically equivalent to GLS when the error term is $I(0)$ but that GLS is more efficient than FE when the error term is $I(1)$. Kao and Emerson further show that the properties of FE, FD, and GLS estimators of β depend crucially upon the value of ρ. When ν_{it} is $I(0)$, i.e., $|\rho| < 1$, the FE and GLS estimators are both $\sqrt{n}T^{3/2}$-consistent and asymptotically equivalent. However, when ν_{it} is $I(1)$, i.e., $\rho = 1$, this asymptotic equivalence breaks down and the GLS estimator is more efficient than the FE estimator. This has serious implications for applied research when ν_{it} is serially correlated and it is unknown whether the remainder errors are $I(0)$ or $I(1)$. These are consistent with the findings in Chapter 1.

2.3.   Test of Hypotheses

In this section, we are interested in testing

$$H_0 : \beta = \beta_0$$

without knowing whether v_{it} is $I(0)$ or $I(1)$. However, the results in this chapter for a panel time trend model with serially correlated error component disturbances are different. Hypothesis testing on the slope of the trend has been studied in the time-series econometric literature, e.g., Canjels and Watson (1997), Vogelsang and Fomby (2002), Bunzel and Vogelsang (2005), Roy, Falk, and Fuller (2004), and Perron and Yabu (2009b). The focus of here is on the testing in large panel time trend models.

2.3.1.   *FE estimator*

The t-statistic for the null hypothesis H_0 can be constructed using the FE estimator as follows:

$$t_{\text{FE}} = \frac{\hat{\beta}_{\text{FE}} - \beta_0}{\sqrt{\widehat{\text{Var}}(\hat{\beta}_{\text{FE}})}}, \tag{2.7}$$

where

$$\widehat{\text{Var}}(\hat{\beta}_{\text{FE}}) = \frac{\hat{\sigma}_v^2}{n \sum_{t=1}^{T}(t - \bar{t})^2}$$

with

$$\hat{\sigma}_v^2 = \frac{1}{n(T-1) - 1} \sum_{i=1}^{n} \sum_{t=2}^{T} \hat{v}_{it}^2$$

and $\hat{v}_{it}$ are the within residuals from Eq. (2.2), i.e.,

$$\hat{v}_{it} = (y_{it} - \bar{y}_i) - \hat{\beta}_{\text{FE}}(t - \bar{t}).$$

The next theorem derives the limiting distribution of t_{FE}.

Theorem 2.6. *Assume* $(n, T) \to \infty$.

(1) *If* $|\rho| < 1$,

$$t_{\text{FE}} \xrightarrow{d} N(0, 1).$$

(2) *If* $\rho = 1$,

$$\frac{1}{\sqrt{T}} t_{\text{FE}} \xrightarrow{d} N\left(0, \frac{3}{5}\right).$$

From Theorem 2.6, we note that t_{FE} in Eq. (2.7) converges to a standard normal only when v_{it} is $I(0)$, and t_{FE} diverges when the error term is $I(1)$.

This is not surprising since $\hat{\sigma}_v^2 = O_p(T)$, i.e., σ_v^2 is not identified when v_{it} is $I(1)$.

2.3.2.   *FD estimator*

Next, we turn to the FD estimator, $\hat{\beta}_{\text{FD}}$. The corresponding t-statistic is given by

$$t_{\text{FD}} = \frac{\hat{\beta}_{\text{FD}} - \beta_0}{\sqrt{\widehat{\text{Var}}(\hat{\beta}_{\text{FD}})}}, \tag{2.8}$$

where

$$\widehat{\text{Var}}(\hat{\beta}_{\text{FD}}) = \frac{\hat{\sigma}_e^2}{nT}$$

with

$$\hat{\sigma}_e^2 = \frac{1}{n(T-1)-1} \sum_{i=1}^{n} \sum_{t=2}^{T} (\Delta y_{it} - \hat{\beta}_{\text{FD}})^2.$$

If v_{it} is known to be $I(1)$, then the optimal test for testing the null hypothesis H_0 is based on the t-statistic using the FD estimator, $\hat{\beta}_{\text{FD}}$. Next theorem derives the limiting distribution of t_{FD}.

Theorem 2.7. *Assume* $(n, T) \to \infty$.

(1) *If* $|\rho| < 1$,

$$\sqrt{T} t_{\text{FD}} \xrightarrow{d} N\left(0, \frac{1}{1-\rho}\right).$$

(2) *If* $\rho = 1$,

$$t_{\text{FD}} \xrightarrow{d} N(0, 1).$$

Theorem 2.7 shows that $t_{\text{FD}} \xrightarrow{d} N(0, 1)$ when v_{it} is, in fact, $I(1)$, under the null. On the other hand, $t_{\text{FD}} \xrightarrow{d} 0$ if v_{it} is $I(0)$, under the null. In view of this and given that the order of integration of v_{it} is not known in practice, it is natural to consider alternative robust test procedures.

2.3.3. *The FE-FGLS estimator*

As shown in Chapter 1, the GLS has a faster speed of convergence than both the FE and FD estimators, no matter the error term and regressor are stationary or nonstationary. Baltagi *et al.* (2011) further show that the t-test statistic for $H_0 : \beta = \beta_0$ based on the GLS estimator is always $N(0,1)$ as $(n, T) \to \infty$. A critical assumption for the GLS estimator is that $E(\mu_i | x_{it}) = 0$. It is well known that when there is the correlation between the regressors and the individual effects, GLS suffers from omitted variable bias, while FD and FE wipe out this source of endogeneity and remain consistent. In the case of serial correlation, Baltagi *et al.* (2008) also suggest an FE-GLS estimator that uses the within transformation to wipe out the μ_i's and then runs GLS estimation to account for the serial correlation in the remainder error. As shown in Chapter 1, multiplying the PW transformation matrix $\mathbf{C}$ to Eq. (2.5) giving us

$$\mathbf{y}^* = \delta \iota^*_{nT} + \beta \mathbf{x}^* + u^* \tag{2.9}$$

where $\mathbf{y}^* = (I_n \otimes C)\mathbf{y}$,

$$\mathbf{x}^* = (I_n \otimes C)\mathbf{x} = \iota_n \otimes x^*_i$$

with $x^*_i = Cx_i$ and

$$\iota^*_{nT} = (I_n \otimes C)\iota_{nT} = (1 - \rho)(\iota_n \otimes \iota^\alpha_T)$$

using the fact that $C\iota_T = (1 - \rho)\iota^\alpha_T$, where $\iota^{\alpha'}_T = (\alpha, \iota'_{T-1})$ and

$$\alpha = \sqrt{(1 + \rho)/(1 - \rho)}.$$

The variance–covariance matrix of the transformed disturbance is

$$\Phi^* = E(u^* u^{*\prime}) = \sigma^2_\mu (1 - \rho)^2 (I_n \otimes \iota^\alpha_T \iota^{\alpha\prime}_T) + \sigma^2_\varepsilon (I_n \otimes I_T). \tag{2.10}$$

Premultiplying Eq. (2.9) by $\sigma_\varepsilon \Phi^{*-1/2}$, one gets

$$\sigma_\varepsilon \Phi^{*-1/2} \mathbf{y}^* = \sigma_\varepsilon \Phi^{*-1/2} \delta \iota^*_{nT} + \sigma_\varepsilon \Phi^{*-1/2} \beta \mathbf{x}^* + \sigma_\varepsilon \Phi^{*-1/2} u^*. \tag{2.11}$$

The OLS estimator of the transformed equation yields the GLS estimator $\hat{\beta}_{\text{GLS}}$. Now, to wipe out transformed individual effects, we premultiply Eq. (2.9) by $I_n \otimes E^\alpha_T$ instead. We get

$$(I_n \otimes E^\alpha_T)\mathbf{y}^* = (I_n \otimes E^\alpha_T)\mathbf{x}^* \beta + (I_n \otimes E^\alpha_T)v^* \tag{2.12}$$

using $E^\alpha_T \iota^\alpha_T = 0$. The OLS estimator of the transformed equation gives us the FE-GLS estimator, given by

$$\hat{\beta}_{\text{FE-GLS}} = \frac{\mathbf{x}^{*\prime}(I_n \otimes E^\alpha_T)\mathbf{y}^*}{\mathbf{x}^{*\prime}(I_n \otimes E^\alpha_T)\mathbf{x}^*}. \tag{2.13}$$

It is worth pointing out that the FE-GLS encompasses both the FE and FD estimators. To see this, note that (i) if $\rho = 0$, and there is no serial correlation in the remainder error, we have $C = I_T$, $\mathbf{x}^* = \mathbf{x}$, $\alpha = 1$, $\iota_T^\alpha = \iota_T$ and hence $E_T^\alpha = E_T$, where $E_T = I_T - \bar{J}_T$ and $\bar{J}_T$ is a $T \times T$ matrix of $1/T$. The FE-GLS estimator in Eq. (2.13) reduces to the FE estimator $\frac{\mathbf{x}'(I_n \otimes E_T)\mathbf{y}}{\mathbf{x}'(I_n \otimes E_T)\mathbf{x}}$.

(ii) Note also that $\bar{J}_T^\alpha$ can be rewritten as $\bar{J}_T^\alpha = l_T(l_T'l_T)^{-1}l_T'$, where

$$l_T = \sqrt{(1-\rho)}\iota_T^{\alpha'} = \sqrt{(1-\rho)}(\alpha, \iota_{T-1}') = (\sqrt{(1+\rho)}, \sqrt{(1-\rho)}\iota_{T-1}').$$

If $\rho = 1$, we have $l_T' = (\sqrt{2}, 0_{T-1}')$ and hence $\bar{J}_T^\alpha = \text{diag}(1, 0, \ldots, 0)$ and

$$E_T^\alpha = I_T - \bar{J}_T^\alpha = \begin{bmatrix} 0 & 0_{T-1}' \\ 0_{T-1} & I_{T-1} \end{bmatrix}.$$

Also, if $\rho = 0$, $\mathbf{C} = \begin{bmatrix} 0_T' \\ D \end{bmatrix}$ with

$$D = \begin{bmatrix} -1 & 1 & 0 & \cdots & 0 & 0 \\ \vdots & \vdots & \vdots & \ddots & \vdots & \vdots \\ 0 & 0 & 0 & -1 & 1 & 0 \\ 0 & 0 & 0 & 0 & -1 & 1 \end{bmatrix},$$

which is the well-known FD matrix. Hence

$$\mathbf{x}^* = \left(I_n \otimes \begin{bmatrix} 0_T' \\ D \end{bmatrix}\right) \mathbf{x}$$

and

$$[0_T \ D'] \begin{bmatrix} 0 & 0_{T-1}' \\ 0_{T-1} & I_{T-1} \end{bmatrix} \begin{bmatrix} 0_T' \\ D \end{bmatrix} = D'D.$$

The FE-GLS estimator in Eq. (2.13) reduces to the FD estimator $\frac{\mathbf{x}'(I_n \otimes D'D)\mathbf{y}}{\mathbf{x}'(I_n \otimes D'D)\mathbf{x}}$.

From Eq. (2.13), we have

$$\hat{\beta}_{\text{FE-GLS}} - \beta = \frac{F_2}{F_1}, \qquad (2.14)$$

where

$$F_1 = x_i^{*\prime} x_i^* - \frac{(\iota_T^{\alpha\prime} x_i^*)^2}{d^2}$$

and

$$F_2 = \frac{1}{n} \sum_{i=1}^{n} x_i^{*\prime} u_i^* - \frac{\iota_T^{\alpha\prime} x_i^*}{nd^2} \sum_{i=1}^{n} \iota_T^{\alpha\prime} u_i^*.$$

It is easy to show that

$$\text{Var}(\hat{\beta}_{\text{FE-GLS}}) = \frac{\sigma_e^2}{nF_1}.$$

Therefore,

$$t_{\text{FE-GLS}} = \frac{\hat{\beta}_{\text{FE-GLS}} - \beta}{\sqrt{\text{Var}(\hat{\beta}_{\text{FE-GLS}})}} = \frac{F_2/F_1}{\sqrt{\sigma_e^2/(nF_1)}} = \frac{\sqrt{n}F_2}{\sqrt{\sigma_e^2 F_1}}. \qquad (2.15)$$

Note that both the FE-GLS estimator of β and its corresponding t-statistic do not depend on σ_μ^2 or σ_α^2. With a consistent estimator $\hat{\rho}$, the corresponding FE-FGLS estimator $\hat{\beta}_{\text{FE-FGLS}}$ is obtained by replacing C and E_T^α by their corresponding estimators $\hat{C}$ and $\hat{E}_T^\alpha$. As suggested by Baltagi and Li (1991), an estimator of σ_e^2 can be obtained as

$$\hat{\sigma}_e^2 = \frac{1}{n(T-1)} \hat{u}^{*\prime} (I_n \otimes \hat{E}_T^\alpha) \hat{u}^*,$$

where $\hat{u}^*$ is an $nT \times 1$ vector of OLS residuals from the PW transformed regression using $\hat{\rho}$. The corresponding t-statistic based on the FE-FGLS estimator can be obtained from Eq. (2.15). The asymptotic properties are summarized in the following theorem.

Theorem 2.8. *Under Assumption 2.1, as $(n, T) \to \infty$,*

(1) *when $|\rho| < 1$, if $\hat{\rho} \overset{p}{\to} \rho$, we have*

$$t_{\text{FE-FGLS}} \overset{d}{\to} N(0, 1);$$

(2) *when $\rho = 1$, if $T(\hat{\rho} - 1) \overset{p}{\to} \kappa$, we have*

$$t_{\text{FE-FGLS}} \overset{d}{\to} N\left(0, \frac{(\kappa^2 - 3\kappa + 3)(\kappa^4 - 10\kappa^3 + 50\kappa^2 - 120\kappa + 120)}{10(\kappa^4 - 9\kappa^3 + 33\kappa^2 - 54\kappa + 36)}\right).$$

Theorem 2.8 implies that we need $\kappa = 0$ when $\rho = 1$. Otherwise $t_{\text{FE-FGLS}}$ does not converge to a $N(0,1)$. As shown in Eq. (1.18), the estimator of ρ suggested by Baltagi and Li (1991) is

$$\hat{\rho} = \frac{\sum_{i=1}^{n} \sum_{t=2}^{T} \hat{\nu}_{it} \hat{\nu}_{i,t-1}}{\sum_{i=1}^{n} \sum_{t=2}^{T} \hat{\nu}_{i,t-1}^2},$$

where $\hat{\nu}_{it}$ denotes the FE residual from Eq. (2.2) which is defined in Sec. 2. It can be obtained from a regression of $\hat{\nu}_{it}$ on $\hat{\nu}_{i,t-1}$. The asymptotic results for $\hat{\rho}$ are given in the following theorem.

Theorem 2.9. *Under Assumption* 2.1, *as* $(n,T) \to \infty$,

(1) *if* $|\rho| < 1$,

$$\sqrt{nT}\left(\hat{\rho} - \rho + \frac{1+\rho}{T}\right) \xrightarrow{d} N(0, 1 - \rho^2);$$

(2) *if* $\rho = 1$,

$$\sqrt{nT}\left(\hat{\rho} - 1 + \frac{3}{T}\right) \xrightarrow{d} N\left(0, \frac{51}{5}\right).$$

The limiting distribution of $\hat{\rho}$ in Theorem 2.9 is actually the same as Theorems 2 and 4 in Hahn and Kuersteiner (2002a) in a dynamic panel data model. Also, for $\rho = 1$, Theorem 2.9 is also the same as Theorem 2 in Kao (1999). As we can see from Theorem 2.9, when $|\rho| < 1$, there is an asymptotic bias $(1 + \rho)/T$ in $\hat{\rho}$, but it still implies $\hat{\rho} \xrightarrow{p} \rho$ as $(n,T) \to \infty$. When $\rho = 1$, $T(\hat{\rho} - 1)$ does not converge to zero in probability if there are individual effects in the model. Substituting $\kappa = -3$ into Theorem 2.8, one can verify that $\hat{\rho}$ suggested by Baltagi and Li (1991) leads to

$$t_{\text{FE-FGLS}} \xrightarrow{d} N\left(0, \frac{2989}{910}\right)$$

when $\rho = 1$. This limits the usefulness of the FE-GLS estimator when the error term is $I(1)$ and there are individual effects in the panel model. This difference is due to the fact that μ_i cannot be consistently estimated when the error term is $I(1)$; see Kao and Emerson (2004). To achieve

$$t_{\text{FE-FGLS}} \xrightarrow{d} N(0,1)$$

we need $\kappa = 0$. Therefore, when $|\rho| < 1$, a bias-corrected estimator of ρ is $\hat{\rho} + \frac{1+\hat{\rho}}{T}$ and when $\rho = 1$, a bias-corrected estimator of ρ is $\hat{\rho} + \frac{3}{T}$. Combining the two cases, Baltagi, Kao and Liu (2014) suggest a bias-corrected estimator of ρ as follows:

$$\tilde{\rho} = \begin{cases} \hat{\rho} + \frac{1+\hat{\rho}}{T} & \text{if } 1 - \hat{\rho} > \frac{3}{T}, \\ 1 & \text{if } 1 - \hat{\rho} \leq \frac{3}{T}. \end{cases}$$

The asymptotics for $\tilde{\rho}$ are given in the following theorem.

Theorem 2.10. *Under Assumption* 2.1, *as* $(n, T) \to \infty$,

(1) *if* $|\rho| < 1$,

$$\sqrt{nT}(\tilde{\rho} - \rho) \xrightarrow{d} N(0, 1 - \rho^2);$$

(2) *if* $\rho = 1$,

$$T(\tilde{\rho} - 1) \xrightarrow{p} 0.$$

Therefore, we have $t_{\text{FE-FGLS}} \xrightarrow{d} N(0, 1)$ *using* $\tilde{\rho}$ *for both* $|\rho| < 1$ *and* $\rho = 1$.

In this section, we have shown that the t-statistic based on FE-GLS is no longer robust if there are individual effects. Extra steps need to be taken to achieve the robustness when Eq. (2.2) includes individual effects.

2.4. Conclusion

This chapter has presented a number of inference procedures that can be used in the panel time trend models. The discussion focuses on four estimators, OLS, FE, FD and GLS, and corresponding t-statistics. We first demonstrate the advantage of using the large panel data for the estimation of autocorrelation parameter in a time trend regression. Further, we show that when the regression error is either stationary or nonstationary, the GLS is the preferred estimator. We discuss the t-statistic of the FGLS. In particular, the autocorrelation parameter in Baltagi and Li (1991) is asymptotically biased. Finally, we suggest a bias-corrected estimator and corresponding FGLS-based t-statistic which always converges to a standard normal random variable.

2.5. Technical Proofs

Proof of Theorems 2.3–2.5 can be found in Kao and Emerson (2004). Proof of Theorems 2.6–2.10 can be found in Baltagi *et al.* (2014).

2.6.   Exercises

(1) When an intercept is not included in the panel time trend model, Eq. (2.2) reduces to

$$y_{it} = \beta t + u_{it}.$$

The FE and FD estimators are not affected since the intercept will be canceled out by within or FD transformation together with individual effects. However, the OLS estimator $\widehat{\beta}_{\text{OLS}}$ in Eq. (2.4) becomes

$$\widehat{\beta}_{\text{OLS}} = \frac{\sum_{i=1}^{n} \sum_{t=1}^{T} t y_{it}}{\sum_{i=1}^{n} \sum_{t=1}^{T} t^2}$$

which is not as same as the FE estimator. Show that when an intercept is not included in the panel time trend model, different from Theorem 2.3, the OLS estimator has the following asymptotic results as $(n, T) \to \infty$:

(a) If $|\rho| < 1$,

$$\sqrt{n} T (\widehat{\beta}_{\text{OLS}} - \beta) \xrightarrow{d} N\left(0, \frac{9\sigma_\mu^2}{4}\right).$$

(b) If $\rho = 1$,

$$\sqrt{n T} (\widehat{\beta}_{\text{OLS}} - \beta) \xrightarrow{d} N\left(0, \left(\frac{6}{5} + \frac{9}{4}\pi\right)\sigma_e^2\right).$$

(2) When an intercept is not included in the panel time trend model, Eq. (2.5) reduces to

$$\mathbf{y} = \beta \mathbf{x} + u$$

and the GLS estimator $\widehat{\beta}_{\text{GLS}}$ in Eq. (2.6) correspondingly reduces to

$$\widehat{\beta}_{\text{GLS}} = (\mathbf{x}'\Phi^{-1}\mathbf{x})^{-1}(\mathbf{x}'\Phi^{-1}\mathbf{y})$$

where $\Phi^{-1} = I_n \otimes \Sigma^{-1}$,

$$\Sigma^{-1} = \left[\frac{1}{\sigma_e^2}\left(\mathbf{A}^{-1} - \frac{\sigma_\mu^2}{\sigma_e^2 + \theta\sigma_\mu^2}\mathbf{A}^{-1}\iota_T\iota_T'\mathbf{A}^{-1}\right)\right],$$

and $\theta = \iota_T'\mathbf{A}^{-1}\iota_T$.

(a) Use Kruskal's theorem (1968) to show that, when $|\rho| < 1$, GLS and OLS are not equivalent even asymptotically.

(b) When $\rho = 1$, show that $\hat{\beta}_{\text{GLS}}$ can be rewritten as

$$\hat{\beta}_{\text{GLS}} = \left(\sum_{i=1}^{n} \left(T - \frac{\sigma_\mu^2}{\sigma_e^2 + \sigma_\mu^2} \right) \right)^{-1} \left(\sum_{i=1}^{n} \left(y_{iT} - \frac{\sigma_\mu^2}{\sigma_e^2 + \sigma_\mu^2} y_{i1} \right) \right).$$

In particular, when $\frac{\sigma_\mu^2}{\sigma_e^2 + \sigma_\mu^2} = 1$, the GLS estimator $\hat{\beta}_{\text{GLS}}$ reduces to the FD estimator.

(c) When $\rho = 1$, with the initial condition in Assumption 2.1, show that when an intercept is not included in the panel time trend model, the GLS estimator has the following asymptotic results as $(n, T) \to \infty$:

   (i) If $|\rho| < 1$,

$$\sqrt{nT^3}(\hat{\beta}_{\text{GLS}} - \beta) \xrightarrow{d} N \left(0, \frac{12\sigma_e^2}{(1 - \rho)^2} \right).$$

   This is the same as in Theorem 2.5.

   (ii) If $\rho = 1$,

$$\sqrt{nT}(\hat{\beta}_{\text{GLS}} - \beta) \xrightarrow{d} N \left(0, \left[1 + \left(1 - \frac{\sigma_\mu^2}{\sigma_e^2 + \sigma_\mu^2} \right)^2 \pi \right] \sigma_e^2 \right).$$

   This is different from Theorem 2.5. In this case, the limiting distribution of the GLS estimator depends on the variance component, $\frac{\sigma_\mu^2}{\sigma_e^2 + \sigma_\mu^2}$ and the parameter that governs the variance of the initial error, π. The FD estimator is the most efficient when $\rho = 1$. The GLS is less efficient than FD unless $\frac{\sigma_\mu^2}{\sigma_e^2 + \sigma_\mu^2} = 1$ or $\pi = 0$.

(3) In the panel time trend model in Eq. (2.2), if $\rho = 1 + c/T$ with $c < 0$, the error term v_{it} follows a local-to-unit or a nearly $I(1)$ process. With the initial condition in Assumption 2.1, show that as $(n, T) \to \infty$,

   (a) $\sqrt{nT}(\hat{\beta}_{\text{OLS}} - \beta) \xrightarrow{d} N(0, R_0\sigma_e^2);$
   (b) $\sqrt{nT}(\hat{\beta}_{\text{FE}} - \beta) \xrightarrow{d} N(0, R_1\sigma_e^2);$
   (c) $\sqrt{nT}(\hat{\beta}_{\text{FD}} - \beta) \xrightarrow{d} N(0, [S_c(1) + (1 - e^c)S_c(\pi)]\sigma_e^2);$

(d) $\sqrt{nT}(\widehat{\beta}_{\text{GLS}} - \beta) \xrightarrow{d} N(0, \frac{9}{(c^2-3c+3)^2}R_2\sigma_e^2)$, where

$$S_c(\pi) = \frac{1}{-2c}(1 - e^{2c\pi}),$$

$$R_0 = \text{Var}\left[3\int_0^1 sW_c(s)ds\right] + \text{Var}\left[\widetilde{W}_c(\pi)3\int_0^1 se^{sc}ds\right],$$

$$R_1 = \text{Var}\left\{12\int_0^1\left(s - \frac{1}{2}\right)W_c(s)ds\right\}$$
$$+ \text{Var}\left\{12\widetilde{W}_c(\pi)\int_0^1\left(s - \frac{1}{2}\right)e^{sc}\widetilde{W}_c(\pi)ds\right\},$$

$$R_2 = \text{Var}\left\{[W_c(1) - (1 - e^c)\widetilde{W}_c(\pi)]\right.$$
$$\left. + c^2\int_0^1 s[W_c(s) + e^{sc}\widetilde{W}_c(\pi)]ds - c[W_c(1) + e^c\widetilde{W}_c(\pi)]\right\}.$$

(4) Vogelsang and Nawaz (2017) consider

$$y_{1t} = \mu_1 + \beta_1 t + u_{1t}$$

and

$$y_{2t} = \mu_2 + \beta_2 t + u_{2t},$$

where u_{1i} and u_{2i} are mean zero covariance stationary processes. Assume

$$\frac{1}{\sqrt{T}}\sum_{t=1}^{[Tr]}\begin{bmatrix}u_{1t}\\u_{2t}\end{bmatrix} \xrightarrow{d} \Lambda W(r),$$

where $r \in [0,1]$, $W(r)$ is a 2×1 vector of independent standard Brownian motion, and Λ is not necessarily diagonal allowing for correlation between u_{1t} and u_{2t}. Suppose that $\beta_2 \neq 0$ and we are interested in estimating the parameter $\theta = \frac{\beta_1}{\beta_2}$, which is the ratio of trend slopes. Define $\delta = \mu_1 - \theta\mu_2$ and $\varepsilon_t(\theta) = u_{1t} - \theta u_{2t}$. Then we can write

$$y_{1t} = \delta + \theta y_{2t} + \varepsilon_t(\theta)$$

and

$$\widehat{\theta} = \frac{\sum_{t=1}^T(y_{2t} - \bar{y}_2)(y_{1t} - \bar{y}_1)}{\sum_{t=1}^T(y_{2t} - \bar{y}_2)^2},$$

where $\overline{y}_1 = \frac{1}{T}\sum_{t=1}^{T} y_{1t}$ and $\overline{y}_2 = \frac{1}{T}\sum_{t=1}^{T} y_{2t}$. If $\beta_2 = \overline{\beta}_2$ is a nonzero constant, which is fixed with respect to T, show that

$$T^{3/2}(\widehat{\theta} - \theta) \xrightarrow{d} N\left(0, \frac{12\lambda_\theta^2}{\overline{\beta}_2}\right),$$

where λ_θ^2 is the long-run variance of $\varepsilon_t(\theta)$, i.e., $\lambda_\theta^2 = [1, -\theta]\Lambda\Lambda'[1, -\theta]'$.

(5) Vogelsang and Franses (2005) consider

$$y_{it} = \mu_i + \beta_i t + u_{it}.$$

Let $y_t = (y_{1t}, \ldots, y_{nt})'$ and $\beta = (\beta_1, \ldots, \beta_n)'$. The OLS of β is

$$\widehat{\beta} = \frac{\sum_{t=1}^{T}(t - \overline{t})y_t}{\sum_{t=1}^{T}(t - \overline{t})^2}.$$

Explain why OLS is the same as seemingly unrelated regression (SUR) and is asymptotically equivalent to GLS. Furthermore, let $u_t = (u_{1t}, \ldots, u_{nt})'$. Assume

$$\frac{1}{\sqrt{T}} \sum_{t=1}^{[Tr]} u_t \xrightarrow{d} \Lambda W_n(r),$$

where $W_n(r)$ is an $n \times 1$ vector of standard independent Brownian motions. Show that as $T \to \infty$,

$$T^{3/2}(\widehat{\beta} - \beta) \xrightarrow{d} N(0, 12\Omega),$$

where $\Omega = \Lambda\Lambda'$. What happens if we let $(n, T) \to \infty$?

(6) Xu and Yang (2015) consider

$$y_t = \alpha + \beta t + u_t$$

and

$$u_t = \rho u_{t-1} + e_t$$

with $e_t = \sigma_t \varepsilon_t$. Let

$$\rho = \rho_T = 1 + \frac{c}{T^h} \in (-1, 1),$$

where $c < 0$ and $h \geq 0$. Assume ε_t is an MDS with $E(\varepsilon_t^2) = 1$. Let $\sigma_t = g(\frac{t}{T})$. We consider four estimators: (i) OLS estimator, $\widehat{\beta}_{\text{OLS}}$;

(ii) FD estimator, $\widehat{\beta}_{\mathrm{FD}}$, obtained by applying OLS to

$$\triangle y_t = \beta + \triangle u_t$$

for $2 \leq t \leq T$; (iii) the Cochrane–Orcutt estimator, $\widehat{\beta}_{\mathrm{CC}}$, obtained by applying OLS to

$$y_t - \rho y_{t-1} = \alpha(1-\rho) + \beta[t - \rho(t-1)] + e_t$$

together with the first observation

$$y_1 = \alpha + \beta + u_1$$

and (iv) the generalized Cochrane–Orcutt estimator, $\widehat{\beta}_{\mathrm{GCC}}$, obtained by applying OLS

$$\frac{y_t - \rho y_{t-1}}{\sigma_t} = \frac{\alpha(1-\rho)}{\sigma_t} + \frac{\beta[t - \rho(t-1)]}{\sigma_t} + \varepsilon_t$$

together with the first observation

$$\frac{y_1}{\sigma_1} = \frac{\alpha}{\sigma_1} + \frac{\beta}{\sigma_1} + \frac{u_1}{\sigma_1}.$$

Show that if $h > 1$ as $T \to \infty$,

$$\sqrt{T}(\widehat{\beta}_{\mathrm{OLS}} - \beta) \xrightarrow{d} N\left(0, 36 \int s^2(1-s)^2 g^2\right),$$

$$\sqrt{T}(\widehat{\beta}_{\mathrm{FD}} - \beta) \xrightarrow{d} N\left(0, \int g^2\right),$$

$$\sqrt{T}(\widehat{\beta}_{\mathrm{CC}} - \beta) \xrightarrow{d} N\left(0, \int g^2\right),$$

$$\sqrt{T}(\widehat{\beta}_{\mathrm{GCC}} - \beta) \xrightarrow{d} N\left(0, \left(\int g^{-2}\right)^{-1}\right).$$

Furthermore, what happens if $h < 1$ and $h = 1$, respectively?

Chapter 3

Estimation of Change Points in Stationary and Nonstationary Regressors and Error Term

Testing and estimation of change points have been widely studied in econometrics. The focus of this chapter is to test and estimate for possible changes in the slope parameter of panel regression models. In Sec. 3.1, we discuss the spurious break in time-series. It is known that there is a tendency to spuriously estimate a break point in the middle of the sample when the errors follow an $I(1)$ process, even though a break point does not actually exist, e.g., Bai (1998). In Sec. 3.2, we discuss estimation of a change point when it does not exist. Baltagi, Kao, and Liu (2017) consider the spurious break in a panel data regression model where the error terms are either stationary or nonstationary. Here the spurious break may still exist even with large panels. As a solution, an FD estimator is proposed. In Sec. 3.3, we discuss spurious break when a change point exists. The results in Bai (1997) for the time-series, Feng, Kao, and Lazarova (2009) for a homogeneous panel data model, and Baltagi, Feng, and Kao (2016) for a heterogeneous panel data model are discussed and compared. In Sec. 3.4, we further discuss a few extensions. We discuss change point estimation in a trend model, a model with a stationary or nonstationary regressor and/or error term, and a model with common factors. Sec. 3.5 compares OLS and FGLS-based Wald-tests in Emerson and Kao (2001) and Baltagi, Kao, and Liu (2019). Sec. 3.6 concludes.

3.1. Spurious Break

3.1.1. *Spurious break in time-series*

Consider the following time-series regression with an unknown change point at k_0, e.g., Bai (1997),

$$y_t = \begin{cases} x_t'\beta_1 + u_t & \text{for } t = 1,\ldots,k_0, \\ x_t'\beta_2 + u_t & \text{for } t = k_0 + 1,\ldots,T. \end{cases}$$

It can be rewritten as

$$y_t = x_t'\beta + x_t'\delta \cdot 1\{t > k_0\} + u_t, \tag{3.1}$$

where $\delta = \beta_2 - \beta_1$ and $1(\cdot)$ is the indicator function. If $\delta \neq 0$, there is a change at k_0 where $k_0 = [\tau_0 T]$ for some $\tau_0 \in (0,1)$. If $\delta = 0$, there is no change in the model and hence $k_0 = [\tau_0 T]$ for $\tau_0 = 0$ or 1. Our interest is to estimate the change point k_0 or τ_0. Let $\hat{\beta}_1(k)$ be the OLS estimator of β_1 based on the first k observations and $\hat{\beta}_2(k)$ be the OLS estimator of β_2 based on the last $T - k$ observations, i.e.,

$$\hat{\beta}_1(k) = \left(\sum_{t=1}^{k} x_t x_t'\right)^{-1} \sum_{t=1}^{k} x_t y_t$$

and

$$\hat{\beta}_2(k) = \left(\sum_{t=k+1}^{T} x_t x_t'\right)^{-1} \sum_{t=k+1}^{T} x_t y_t.$$

The sum of squared residuals (SSR) for k is defined as

$$\text{SSR}(k) = \sum_{t=1}^{k} [y_t - x_t'\hat{\beta}_1(k)]^2 + \sum_{t=k+1}^{T} [y_t - x_t'\hat{\beta}_2(k)]^2.$$

The least squares (LS) estimator $\hat{k}$ is defined as follows:

$$\hat{k} = \arg \min_{1 \leq k \leq T} \text{SSR}(k)$$

and hence $\hat{\tau} = \hat{k}/T$. Because $\sum_{t=1}^{T} u_t^2$ does not depend on k, it is equivalent to denoting

$$\hat{k} = \arg \max_{1 \leq k \leq T} M(k),$$

where

$$M(k) = \sum_{t=1}^{T} u_t^2 - \text{SSR}(k)$$

$$= \left(\sum_{t=1}^{k} x_t u_t \right)' \left(\sum_{t=1}^{k} x_t x_t' \right)^{-1} \left(\sum_{t=1}^{k} x_t u_t \right)$$

$$+ \left(\sum_{t=k+1}^{T} x_t u_t \right)' \left(\sum_{t=k+1}^{T} x_t x_t' \right)^{-1} \left(\sum_{t=k+1}^{T} x_t u_t \right).$$

If both x_t and u_t are stationary, we would expect that $\hat{\tau}$ is consistent. However, Nunes, Kuan, and Newbold (1995) point out that when the error term is $I(1)$ there is a tendency to estimate a break point in the middle of the sample, even though a break point does not actually exist. This is called the "spurious break". For simplicity, let us consider only one regressor and without the intercept. Assume x_t and u_t are nonstationary, i.e.,

$$x_t = x_{t-1} + \varepsilon_t$$

and

$$u_t = u_{t-1} + e_t,$$

where ε_t and e_t are independent white noise with variances σ_ε^2 and σ_e^2, respectively. Clearly,

$$\frac{1}{T^2} \sum_{t=1}^{k} x_t^2 \overset{d}{\to} Q(\tau) = \sigma_\varepsilon^2 \int_0^\tau W_\varepsilon^2$$

and

$$\frac{1}{T^2} \sum_{t=1}^{k} x_t u_t \overset{d}{\to} G(\tau) = \sigma_\varepsilon \sigma_e \int_0^\tau W_e W_\varepsilon,$$

where W_e and W_ε are independent Brownian motions. The following theorem is taken from Bai (1998).

Theorem 3.1. *When there is no break point, for $\tau_0 = 0$ or 1,*

$$\hat{\tau} \overset{d}{\to} \arg\max M^*(\tau)$$

as $(n, T) \to \infty$, where

$$M^*(\tau) = \frac{G(\tau)^2}{Q(\tau)} + \frac{(G(1) - G(\tau))^2}{Q(1) - Q(\tau)}.$$

With probability 1,

$$M^*(0) = M^*(1) \leq M^*(\tau)$$

for every $0 < \tau < 1$.

Proof. First note that

$$\frac{1}{T^2}M(k) = \frac{\left(\frac{1}{T^2}\sum_{t=1}^{k}x_t u_t\right)^2}{\frac{1}{T^2}\sum_{t=1}^{k}x_t^2} + \frac{\left(\frac{1}{T^2}\sum_{t=k+1}^{T}x_t u_t\right)^2}{\frac{1}{T^2}\sum_{t=k+1}^{T}x_t^2} \xrightarrow{d} M^*(\tau),$$

where

$$M^*(\tau) = \frac{G(\tau)^2}{Q(\tau)} + \frac{(G(1) - G(\tau))^2}{Q(1) - Q(\tau)}.$$

For an arbitrary vector z and an arbitrary projection matrix P, we have

$$z'Pz \le z'z.$$

Apply this inequality to $\frac{1}{T^2}M(k)$ to obtain

$$\frac{1}{T^2}M(k) \le \frac{1}{T^2}\sum_{t=1}^{T}u_t^2$$

for all $k \in [1, T]$. Because $\frac{1}{T^2}\sum_{t=1}^{T}u_t^2$ does not depend on k, and it has a limit σ_e^2, $\frac{1}{T^2}M(k)$ is uniformly bounded in probability. Thus its limit, $M^*(\tau)$, is uniformly bounded in probability for $\tau \in (0, 1)$, i.e.,

$$\sup_{\tau \in (0,1)} M^*(\tau) = O_p(1).$$

Furthermore, the first term in $\frac{1}{T^2}M(k)$ is

$$\frac{\left(\frac{1}{T^2}\sum_{t=1}^{k}x_t u_t\right)^2}{\frac{1}{T^2}\sum_{t=1}^{k}x_t^2} \le \frac{1}{T^2}\sum_{t=1}^{k}u_t^2,$$

which converges to zero in probability for any given k or for $k = [\tau T]$ with $\tau \to 0$. It follows that $\frac{G(\tau)^2}{Q(\tau)} \to 0$ in probability as $\tau \to 0$. Thus the limit of $M^*(\tau)$ when $\tau \to 0$, $M^*(0)$ should be defined as

$$M^*(0) = \frac{G(1)^2}{Q(1)}.$$

To prove the inequality $M^*(0) \le M^*(\tau)$, it is equivalent to showing that

$$\frac{G(1)^2}{Q(1)} - \frac{G(\tau)^2}{Q(\tau)} - \frac{(G(1) - G(\tau))^2}{Q(1) - Q(\tau)} \le 0.$$

This is implied by Lemma 1 in Bai (1998) that for arbitrary positive definite matrices A and B with

$$A > B(p \times p)$$

and arbitrary vectors x and y $(p \times 1)$, we have

$$x'A^{-1}x - y'B^{-1}y - (x - y)'(A - B)^{-1}(x - y) \le 0.$$

Similarly, we can also show that

$$M^*(1) \le M^*(\tau).$$

This completes the proof. □

When the error term u_t is $I(0)$, a similar limiting process $M^*(\tau)$ can be obtained. However, a crucial difference is that $M^*(\tau) \to \infty$ as $\tau \to 0$ or 1. For an $I(1)$ error term, Theorem 3.1 implies that the maximum value of $M^*(\tau)$ will not be attained at 0 or 1. Correspondingly, with a spurious break k, it is easy to derive that

$$\hat{\beta}_1(k) - \beta_1 = \frac{\frac{1}{T^2}\sum_{t=1}^{k} x_t u_t}{\frac{1}{T^2}\sum_{t=1}^{k} x_t^2} \xrightarrow{d} \frac{\sigma_e \int_0^\tau W_e W_\varepsilon}{\sigma_\varepsilon \int_0^\tau W_\varepsilon^2}$$

and

$$\hat{\beta}_2(k) - \beta_2 = \frac{\frac{1}{T^2}\sum_{t=k+1}^{T} x_t u_t}{\frac{1}{T^2}\sum_{t=k+1}^{T} x_t^2} \xrightarrow{d} \frac{\sigma_e \int_\tau^1 W_e W_\varepsilon}{\sigma_\varepsilon \int_\tau^1 W_\varepsilon^2}$$

so that

$$\hat{\delta}(k) - \delta = (\hat{\beta}_2(k) - \beta_2) - (\hat{\beta}_1(k) - \beta_1) \xrightarrow{d} \frac{\sigma_e \int_\tau^1 W_e W_\varepsilon}{\sigma_\varepsilon \int_\tau^1 W_\varepsilon^2} - \frac{\sigma_e \int_0^\tau W_e W_\varepsilon}{\sigma_\varepsilon \int_0^\tau W_\varepsilon^2},$$

which is a random variable. Hence $\hat{\delta}(k)$ is not consistent when x_{it} and u_{it} are nonstationary. Let us illustrate the spurious change problem in time-series data using the following example in R.

Example 3.1.

```
> # write a function
> func.Break <- function(k, reg=FALSE){
+    reg1 <- lm(y.t[1:k]~x.t[1:k])
+    reg2 <- lm(y.t[(k+1):T.obs]~x.t[(k+1):T.obs])
+    SSR <- sum(reg1$residuals^2) + sum(reg2$residuals^2)
+    if(reg==TRUE){
+      result <- list(reg1=reg1, reg2=reg2, SSR=SSR)
+    }else{
+      result <- list(SSR=SSR)
+    }
+    return(result)
+ }
```

```
> # time series
> set.seed(1234)
> T.obs <- 50
> x.t <- cumsum(rnorm(T.obs))
> y.t <- cumsum(rnorm(T.obs))
> SSR.t <- rep(NA,T.obs)
> for (k in 10:(T.obs-10)){
+   SSR.t[k] <- func.Break(k)$SSR
+ }
> khat.t <- order(SSR.t)[1]
> khat.t

[1] 18

> reg.t <- func.Break(khat.t, reg=TRUE)
> summary(reg.t$reg1)

Call:
lm(formula = y.t[1:k] ~ x.t[1:k])

Residuals:
    Min      1Q  Median      3Q     Max
-1.8592 -0.7277  0.1475  0.7945  1.7648

Coefficients:
            Estimate Std. Error t value Pr(>|t|)
(Intercept)  -4.3959     0.5323  -8.259 3.66e-07 ***
x.t[1:k]     -0.7956     0.1321  -6.022 1.78e-05 ***
---
Signif. codes:  0 '***' 0.001 '**' 0.01 '*' 0.05 '.' 0.1 ' ' 1

Residual standard error: 1.151 on 16 degrees of freedom
Multiple R-squared:  0.6939,   Adjusted R-squared:  0.6747
F-statistic: 36.27 on 1 and 16 DF,  p-value: 1.776e-05

> summary(reg.t$reg2)

Call:
lm(formula = y.t[(k + 1):T.obs] ~ x.t[(k + 1):T.obs])
```

```
Residuals:
    Min       1Q   Median       3Q      Max
-2.0044 -0.5648   0.0141   0.5802   3.2998

Coefficients:
                    Estimate Std. Error t value Pr(>|t|)
(Intercept)          2.55149    0.52695   4.842 3.64e-05 ***
x.t[(k + 1):T.obs]  -0.04967    0.03921  -1.267    0.215
---
Signif. codes:  0 '***' 0.001 '**' 0.01 '*' 0.05 '.' 0.1 ' ' 1

Residual standard error: 1.258 on 30 degrees of freedom
Multiple R-squared:  0.05078,    Adjusted R-squared:  0.01913
F-statistic: 1.605 on 1 and 30 DF,  p-value: 0.215
```

In the time-series example above, the sample size is set as $T = 50$. The two random walks y.t and x.t are simulated by taking the cumulative sum of two sets of random numbers using command cumsum. Because y.t and x.t are independent, there is not a structural change in the model at all. However, the estimated change date is 18. The coefficients of slope for the parts before and after the change date are -0.7956 and -0.0496, respectively. Their difference is pretty large.

3.1.2. *Spurious break in panel data*

Consider the following panel regression with a change point at k_0:

$$y_{it} = \begin{cases} x'_{it}\beta_1 + u_{it} & \text{for } t = 1, \ldots, k_0, \\ x'_{it}\beta_2 + u_{it} & \text{for } t = k_0 + 1, \ldots, T. \end{cases}$$

or

$$y_{it} = x'_{it}\beta + x'_{it}\delta \cdot 1\{t > k_0\} + u_{it}.$$

Similar to time-series, $\hat{\beta}_1(k)$ and $\hat{\beta}_2(k)$ can be obtained as

$$\hat{\beta}_1(k) = \left(\sum_{i=1}^{n}\sum_{t=1}^{k} x_{it}x'_{it}\right)^{-1}\left(\sum_{i=1}^{n}\sum_{t=1}^{k} x_{it}y_{it}\right)$$

and

$$\hat{\beta}_2(k) = \left(\sum_{i=1}^{n}\sum_{t=k+1}^{T} x_{it}x'_{it}\right)^{-1}\left(\sum_{i=1}^{n}\sum_{t=k+1}^{T} x_{it}y_{it}\right).$$

The SSR for k is

$$\text{SSR}(k) = \sum_{i=1}^{n}\sum_{t=1}^{k}(y_{it} - x_{it}'\hat{\beta}_1(k))^2 + \sum_{i=1}^{n}\sum_{t=k+1}^{T}(y_{it} - x_{it}'\hat{\beta}_2(k))^2.$$

An estimator of k can be obtained by minimizing $\text{SSR}(k)$, i.e.,

$$\hat{k} = \arg\min_{1 \le k \le T}\text{SSR}(k)$$

and hence $\hat{\tau} = \hat{k}/T$. As shown in Theorem 6 of Baltagi *et al.* (2017), the spurious break may still exist in large panel data. In other words, there is a tendency to spuriously estimate a break point in the middle of the sample when the errors follow an $I(1)$ process, even though a break point does not actually exist. We will show this in later sections. However, using the estimated change point $\hat{k}$, the coefficients β and δ can be still consistently estimated. To see this, let us still consider the case of one regressor without a constant for simplicity. Assume x_{it} and u_{it} are nonstationary for all i, i.e.,

$$x_{it} = x_{i,t-1} + \varepsilon_{it}$$

and

$$u_{it} = u_{i,t-1} + e_{it},$$

where ε_{it} and e_{it} are independent white noise with variances σ_ε^2 and σ_e^2, respectively. Now

$$\frac{1}{T^2}\sum_{t=1}^{k} x_{it}^2 \xrightarrow{d} \sigma_\varepsilon^2 \int_0^\tau W_{\varepsilon i}^2$$

and

$$\frac{1}{T^2}\sum_{t=1}^{k} x_{it} u_{it} \xrightarrow{d} \sigma_\varepsilon \sigma_e \int_0^\tau W_{ei} W_{\varepsilon i},$$

where W_{ei} and $W_{\varepsilon i}$ are independent Brownian motions for all i.

For a break k, it is easy to derive that

$$\sqrt{n}(\hat{\beta}_1(k) - \beta_1) = \frac{\frac{1}{\sqrt{n}T^2}\sum_{i=1}^{n}\sum_{t=1}^{k} x_{it} u_{it}}{\frac{1}{nT^2}\sum_{i=1}^{n}\sum_{t=1}^{k} x_{it}^2} \xrightarrow{d} \frac{\frac{1}{\sqrt{n}}\sum_{i=1}^{n}\sigma_e \int_0^\tau W_{ei} W_{\varepsilon i}}{\frac{1}{n}\sum_{i=1}^{n}\sigma_\varepsilon \int_0^\tau W_{\varepsilon i}^2}$$

as $T \to \infty$, and hence

$$\sqrt{n}(\hat{\beta}_1(k) - \beta_1) \xrightarrow{d} \frac{N\left(0, \frac{\tau^4}{6}\sigma_e^2\right)}{\frac{\tau^2}{2}} = N\left(0, \frac{2}{3}\sigma_e^2\right)$$

as $(n, T) \to \infty$. Similarly,

$$\sqrt{n}(\hat{\beta}_2(k) - \beta_2) = \frac{\frac{1}{\sqrt{n}T^2}\sum_{i=1}^{n}\sum_{t=k+1}^{T} x_{it} u_{it}}{\frac{1}{nT^2}\sum_{i=1}^{n}\sum_{t=k+1}^{T} x_{it}^2} \xrightarrow{d} \frac{\frac{1}{\sqrt{n}}\sum_{i=1}^{n}\sigma_e \int_{\tau}^{1} W_{ei}W_{\varepsilon i}}{\frac{1}{n}\sum_{i=1}^{n}\sigma_\varepsilon \int_{\tau}^{1} W_{\varepsilon i}^2}$$

$$= O_p(1)$$

as $T \to \infty$, and hence

$$\sqrt{n}(\hat{\beta}_2(k) - \beta_2) \xrightarrow{d} \frac{N\left(0, \frac{(1-\tau)^2\left(1+2\tau+3\tau^2\right)}{6}\sigma_e^2\right)}{\frac{1-\tau^2}{2}}$$

$$= N\left(0, \frac{2\left(1 + 2\tau + 3\tau^2\right)}{3\left(1 + \tau\right)^2}\sigma_e^2\right) = O_p(1)$$

as $(n, T) \to \infty$. So that

$$\sqrt{n}(\hat{\delta}(k) - \delta) = \sqrt{n}(\hat{\beta}_2(k) - \beta_2) - \sqrt{n}(\hat{\beta}_1(k) - \beta_1) = O_p(1),$$

which implies that $\hat{\delta}(k)$ is $\sqrt{n}$-consistent. This intuition is the same as in Kao (1999). Therefore, the essence of using the large panel data is that, although the change point k cannot be identified, the change magnitude δ can still be identified. Let us illustrate the spurious change problem in the panel data using the following example in R.

Example 3.2.

```
> func.PanelBreak <- function(k, reg=FALSE){
+    reg1 <- lm(c(y.p[1:k,])~c(x.p[1:k,]))
+    reg2 <- lm(c(y.p[(k+1):T.obs,])~c(x.p[(k+1):T.obs,]))
+    SSR <- sum(reg1$residuals^2) + sum(reg2$residuals^2)
+    if(reg==TRUE){
+       result <- list(reg1=reg1, reg2=reg2, SSR=SSR)
+    }else{
+       result <- list(SSR=SSR)
+    }
+    return(result)
+ }
```

```
> # panel data
> set.seed(1234)
> T.obs <- 50
> n.obs <- 50
> nT.obs <- n.obs * T.obs
> y.p <- apply(matrix(rnorm(nT.obs), T.obs, n.obs),2,cumsum)
> x.p <- apply(matrix(rnorm(nT.obs), T.obs, n.obs),2,cumsum)
> SSR.p <- rep(NA,T.obs)
> for (k in 1:(T.obs-1)){
+    SSR.p[k] <- func.PanelBreak(k)$SSR
+ }
> khat.p <- order(SSR.p)[1]
> khat.p

[1] 39

> reg.p <- func.PanelBreak(khat.p, reg=TRUE)
> summary(reg.p$reg1)

Call:
lm(formula = c(y.p[1:k, ]) ~ c(x.p[1:k, ]))

Residuals:
    Min       1Q   Median       3Q      Max
-15.0218  -2.6609   0.0435   2.5182  13.6434

Coefficients:
              Estimate Std. Error t value Pr(>|t|)
(Intercept)   -0.02606    0.10303  -0.253 0.800332
c(x.p[1:k, ])  0.08820    0.02618   3.368 0.000771 ***
---
Signif. codes:  0 '***' 0.001 '**' 0.01 '*' 0.05 '.' 0.1 ' ' 1

Residual standard error: 4.548 on 1948 degrees of freedom
Multiple R-squared: 0.00579,    Adjusted R-squared: 0.00528
F-statistic: 11.34 on 1 and 1948 DF,  p-value: 0.0007714

> summary(reg.p$reg2)

Call:
lm(formula = c(y.p[(k + 1):T.obs, ]) ~ c(x.p[(k + 1):T.obs, ]))

Residuals:
    Min       1Q   Median       3Q      Max
-22.5208  -2.8488   0.7336   3.8297  15.1886

Coefficients:
```

```
                        Estimate Std. Error t value Pr(>|t|)
(Intercept)             -0.035819   0.286417  -0.125    0.901
c(x.p[(k + 1):T.obs, ])  0.008537   0.048603   0.176    0.861

Residual standard error: 6.684 on 548 degrees of freedom
Multiple R-squared:  5.629e-05, Adjusted R-squared:  -0.001768
F-statistic: 0.03085 on 1 and 548 DF,  p-value: 0.8606
```

In the panel data example above, we have $n = 50$ and $T = 50$. We still find a spurious change date at 39. However, the coefficients of the slope for the parts before and after the change date are 0.0882 and 0.0085, respectively. Their difference is very small.

3.2.   When a Break Point Does Not Exist

Baltagi *et al.* (2017) consider the following panel regression with a change point at k_0:

$$y_{it} = \begin{cases} \alpha_1 + \beta_1 x_{it} + u_{it} & \text{for } t = 1, \ldots, k_0, \\ \alpha_2 + \beta_2 x_{it} + u_{it} & \text{for } t = k_0 + 1, \ldots, T. \end{cases} \tag{3.2}$$

where x_{it} and u_{it} are assumed to be AR(1) processes for all i, i.e.,

$$x_{it} = \lambda x_{i,t-1} + \varepsilon_{it} \tag{3.3}$$

and

$$u_{it} = \rho u_{i,t-1} + e_{it} \tag{3.4}$$

where ε_{it} and e_{it} are independent white noise with variances σ_ε^2 and σ_e^2, respectively, with $-1 < \lambda \leq 1$ and $-1 < \rho \leq 1$. In this section, we discuss the consistency of the break fraction estimate when there is no break point, i.e., $\delta = 0$.

3.2.1.   *OLS estimator*

Theorem 3.2. *In the time-series case and when $\tau_0 = 0$ or 1, as $T \to \infty$, we have the following results:*

(a) *When $|\rho| < 1$ and $|\lambda| < 1$,*

$$\hat{\tau}_{\text{OLS}} \xrightarrow{p} \{0, 1\}.$$

(b) *When $\rho = 1$ and $|\lambda| < 1$,*

$$\hat{\tau}_{\text{OLS}} \xrightarrow{d} \arg\max_{\tau \in [\underline{\tau}, \bar{\tau}]} \frac{1}{\tau(1-\tau)} \left[\int_\tau^1 W_e - (1-\tau) \int_0^1 W_e \right]^2.$$

(c) *When $|\rho| < 1$ and $\lambda = 1$,*

$$\hat{\tau}_{\text{OLS}} \xrightarrow{p} \{0, 1\}.$$

(d) *When $\lambda = \rho = 1$,*

$$\hat{\tau}_{\text{OLS}} \xrightarrow{d} \arg \max_{\tau \in [\underline{\tau}, \bar{\tau}]} S(\tau)' F(\tau)^{-1} S(\tau),$$

where

$$F(\tau) = P(\tau) - P(\tau) P(0)^{-1} P(\tau),$$

$$S(\tau) = \begin{pmatrix} \sigma_e \int_{\underline{\tau}}^1 W_e \\ \sigma_\varepsilon \sigma_e \int_{\underline{\tau}}^1 W_e W_\varepsilon \end{pmatrix} - P(\tau) P(0)^{-1} \begin{pmatrix} \sigma_e \int_0^1 W_e \\ \sigma_\varepsilon \sigma_e \int_0^1 W_e W_\varepsilon \end{pmatrix},$$

and

$$P(\tau) = \begin{pmatrix} 1 - \tau & \sigma_\varepsilon \int_{\underline{\tau}}^1 W_\varepsilon \\ \sigma_\varepsilon \int_{\underline{\tau}}^1 W_\varepsilon & \sigma_\varepsilon^2 \int_{\underline{\tau}}^1 W_\varepsilon^2 \end{pmatrix}.$$

Theorem 3.2 implies that $\hat{\tau}_{\text{OLS}}$ is consistent when $|\rho| < 1$, but not consistent when $\rho = 1$ in time-series. When $|\rho| < 1$, as discussed in Nunes *et al.* (1995), $\hat{\tau}_{\text{OLS}}$ converges to 0 or 1 when a break point does not exist. However, when $\rho = 1$, Nunes *et al.* (1995) and Bai (1998) show that there is a tendency to spuriously estimate a break point in the middle of the sample when the error term follows an $I(1)$ process, even though a break point does not actually exist. For the panel data case, we have the following theorem.

Theorem 3.3. *For $\tau_0 = 0$ or 1,*

$$\hat{\tau}_{\text{OLS}} \xrightarrow{d} \arg \max M^*(\tau)$$

as $(n, T) \to \infty$, where

$$M^*(\tau) = R'(\tau) Q^{-1}(\tau) R(\tau) + [R(1) - R(\tau)]' [Q(1) - Q(\tau)]^{-1} [R(1) - R(\tau)]$$

in which $Q(\tau)$ and $R(\tau)$ are defined below.

(a) *If $|\rho| < 1$ and $|\lambda| < 1$,*

$$Q(\tau) = \begin{pmatrix} \tau & 0 \\ 0 & \frac{\tau \sigma_\varepsilon^2}{1 - \lambda^2} \end{pmatrix},$$

$$Q(1) - Q(\tau) = \begin{pmatrix} 1-\tau & 0 \\ 0 & \frac{(1-\tau)\sigma_\varepsilon^2}{1-\lambda^2} \end{pmatrix},$$

$$R(\tau) = N\left(0, \sigma_\varepsilon^2 \sigma_e^2 \begin{pmatrix} \tau & 0 \\ 0 & \frac{\tau}{(1-\rho\lambda)^2} \end{pmatrix}\right),$$

and

$$R(1) - R(\tau) = N\left(0, \sigma_\varepsilon^2 \sigma_e^2 \begin{pmatrix} 1-\tau & 0 \\ 0 & \frac{1-\tau}{(1-\rho\lambda)^2} \end{pmatrix}\right).$$

With probability 1, $M^*(\tau) < M^*(0)$ *and* $M^*(\tau) < M^*(1)$ *for every* $0 < \tau < 1$.

(b) *If* $\rho = 1$ *and* $|\lambda| < 1$,

$$Q(\tau) = \begin{pmatrix} \tau & 0 \\ 0 & \frac{\tau\sigma_\varepsilon^2}{1-\lambda^2} \end{pmatrix},$$

$$Q(1) - Q(\tau) = \begin{pmatrix} 1-\tau & 0 \\ 0 & \frac{(1-\tau)\sigma_\varepsilon^2}{1-\lambda^2} \end{pmatrix},$$

$$R(\tau) = N\left(0, \sigma_\varepsilon^2 \sigma_e^2 \begin{pmatrix} \frac{k\tau^2}{3} & 0 \\ 0 & \frac{\tau^2}{2(1-\lambda)^2} \end{pmatrix}\right),$$

and

$$R(1) - R(\tau) = N\left(0, \sigma_\varepsilon^2 \sigma_e^2 \begin{pmatrix} \frac{(T-k)(1-\tau)(1+2\tau)}{3} & 0 \\ 0 & \frac{(1-\tau)(1+\tau)}{2(1-\lambda)^2} \end{pmatrix}\right).$$

With probability 1, $M^*(0) < M^*(\tau) < M^*(1)$ *for every* $0 < \tau < 1$.

(c) *If* $|\rho| < 1$ *and* $\lambda = 1$,

$$Q(\tau) = \begin{pmatrix} \tau & 0 \\ 0 & \frac{\tau^2\sigma_\varepsilon^2}{2} \end{pmatrix},$$

$$Q(1) - Q(\tau) = \begin{pmatrix} 1-\tau & 0 \\ 0 & \frac{(1-\tau^2)\sigma_\varepsilon^2}{2} \end{pmatrix},$$

$$R(\tau) = N\left(0, \sigma_\varepsilon^2 \sigma_e^2 \begin{pmatrix} \tau & 0 \\ 0 & \frac{\tau^2}{2(1-\rho)^2} \end{pmatrix}\right),$$

and

$$R\left(1\right) - R\left(\tau\right) = N\left(0, \sigma_\varepsilon^2 \sigma_e^2 \begin{pmatrix} 1 - \tau & 0 \\ 0 & \frac{1-\tau^2}{2(1-\rho)^2} \end{pmatrix}\right).$$

With probability 1, $M^*(\tau) < M^*(0)$ *and* $M^*(\tau) < M^*(1)$ *for every* $0 < \tau < 1$.

(d) *If* $\rho = \lambda = 1$,

$$Q\left(\tau\right) = \begin{pmatrix} \tau & 0 \\ 0 & \frac{\tau^2 \sigma_\varepsilon^2}{2} \end{pmatrix},$$

$$Q\left(1\right) - Q\left(\tau\right) = \begin{pmatrix} 1 - \tau & 0 \\ 0 & \frac{(1-\tau^2)\sigma_\varepsilon^2}{2} \end{pmatrix},$$

$$R\left(\tau\right) = N\left(0, \sigma_\varepsilon^2 \sigma_e^2 \begin{pmatrix} \frac{\tau^3}{3} & 0 \\ 0 & \frac{\tau^4}{6} \end{pmatrix}\right),$$

and

$$R\left(1\right) - R\left(\tau\right) = N\left(0, \sigma_\varepsilon^2 \sigma_e^2 \begin{pmatrix} \frac{(1-\tau)^2(1+2\tau)}{3} & 0 \\ 0 & \frac{(1-\tau)^2(1+2\tau+3\tau^2)}{6} \end{pmatrix}\right).$$

With probability 1, $M^*(\tau) > M^*(0)$ *and* $M^*(\tau) > M^*(1)$ *for every* $0 < \tau < 1$.

First, Theorem 3.3 shows that when there is no break point in the model, $\hat{\tau}_{\text{OLS}} \overset{p}{\to} \{0,1\}$ if $|\rho| < 1$, whether $|\lambda| < 1$ or $\lambda = 1$. Secondly, $\hat{\tau}_{\text{OLS}} \overset{p}{\to} 1$ if $\rho = 1$ and $|\lambda| < 1$. The empirical distribution of $\hat{k}$ is not symmetric and the highest probability mass of $\hat{k}$ occurs at the right tail. This is because the signal x_{it} is a stationary $I(0)$ process and the error term u_{it} is a nonstationary $I(1)$ process when $\rho = 1$ and $|\lambda| < 1$. The error term dominates the signal and we are actually checking if there is a break in the error term. And of course, the answer is no. For an $I(1)$ process, the variation increases as t increases. Hence at the right tail where k is close to T, it looks more like a jump. Finally, when there is no break in the model and $\rho = \lambda = 1$, the spurious break problem that is found in Nunes *et al.* (1995) and Bai (1998) in the time-series case also exists in the large panel data case. This is consistent with the findings by Hsu and Lin (2011).

Since the spurious break problem still exists in large panel data if both x_{it} and u_{it} are nonstationary $I(1)$, Baltagi *et al.* (2017) suggest using an FD estimator. Different from the results in Theorem 3.3, the spurious break problem will not happen if we use the FD-based estimator of τ. Hence the FD-based estimator is robust whether a break point exists or not.

3.2.2. *FD-based estimator*

In time-series as shown in Theorem 3.2, the OLS-based change point estimator is inconsistent when $\rho = 1$. Nunes *et al.* (1995) and Bai (1998) show that there is a tendency to spuriously estimate a break point in the middle of the sample using the OLS-based estimator when the error term follows an $I(1)$ process, even though a break point does not exist. This spurious break problem can be resolved by using the FD-based estimator.

Theorem 3.4. *In the time-series case and as $T \to \infty$, for $\tau_0 = 0$ or 1, we have $\hat{\tau}_{\text{FD}} \xrightarrow{p} \{0, 1\}$.*

Similarly, the FD-based change point estimator $\hat{\tau}_{\text{FD}}$ is also consistent in the panel data case.

Theorem 3.5. *For $\tau_0 = 0$ or 1, we have $\hat{\tau}_{\text{FD}} \xrightarrow{p} \{0, 1\}$ as $(n, T) \to \infty$.*

Theorem 3.5 shows that $\hat{\tau}_{\text{FD}}$ always converges to 0 or 1.

3.3. When a Break Point Exists

3.3.1. *Multiple regressions in time-series*

Bai (1997) considers the following multiple regression model with a change point at k_0:

$$y_t = \begin{cases} x_t'\beta + u_t, & t = 1, \ldots, k_0 \\ x_t'\beta + z_t'\delta + u_t, & t = k_0 + 1, \ldots, T \end{cases} \tag{3.5}$$

where x_t is $p \times 1$ and $z_t = R'x_t$ denotes a $q \times 1$ subvector of x_t with $R' = (0_{q \times (p-q)}, I_q)$. I_q is a $q \times q$ identity matrix with $q \leq p$. The case where $q < p$ denotes a partial change model, while the case where $q = p$ is for a pure change model. δ denotes the slope jump. As a special case, when $x_t = 1$, it reduces to the mean shift model in Bai (1994). We aim to estimate the parameters β, δ and the change point k_0. Let $Y = (y_1', \ldots, y_T')'$, $X = (x_1', \ldots, x_T')'$, $Z_0 = (0, \ldots, 0, z'_{k_0+1}, \ldots, z_T')'$, and $U = (u_1', \ldots, u_T')'$ denote the stacked data over the time periods observed. Using these notations,

Eq. (3.5) can be written in matrix form

$$Y = X\beta + Z_0\delta + U.$$

For any possible change point k, we define matrices $Z_k = (0, \ldots, 0, z'_{k+1}, \ldots, z'_T)'$. The OLS estimators of slope parameters, which depend on k, are

$$\begin{pmatrix} \hat{\beta}(k) \\ \hat{\delta}(k) \end{pmatrix} = \begin{bmatrix} X'X \; X'Z_k \\ Z'_k X \; Z'_k Z_k \end{bmatrix}^{-1} \begin{bmatrix} X'Y \\ Z'_k Y \end{bmatrix}.$$

Hence,

$$\mathrm{SSR}(k) = (Y - X\hat{\beta}(k) - Z_k\hat{\delta}(k))'(Y - X\hat{\beta}(k) - Z_k\hat{\delta}(k)).$$

Let SSR be the sum of squared residuals for the case of no break, i.e., $k_0 = T$. Define V

$$(k) = \mathrm{SSR} - \mathrm{SSR}(k) = \hat{\delta}(k)'(Z_k M Z_k)\hat{\delta}(k)$$

with

$$M = I - X(X'X)^{-1}X'.$$

Since SSR does not depend on k, we have

$$\hat{k} = \arg \min_{1 \leq k \leq T} \mathrm{SSR}(k) = \arg \max_{1 \leq k \leq T} V(k).$$

There are several assumptions made in Bai (1997); in particular, Assumption A3 in Bai (1997).

Assumption 3.1. The matrices

$$\frac{1}{j} \sum_{t=1}^{j} x_t x'_t, \; \frac{1}{j} \sum_{t=T-j+1}^{T} x_t x'_t, \; \frac{1}{j} \sum_{t=k_0-j+1}^{k_0} x_t x'_t \; \text{and} \; \frac{1}{j} \sum_{t=k_0+1}^{k_0+j} x_t x'_t$$

have minimum eigenvalues bounded away from zero in probability for all large j. That is, there exists $\lambda > 0$ such that for every $\epsilon > 0$, there exists j_0 such that $P(\lambda_j > \lambda) > 1 - \epsilon$ for all $j > j_0$, where λ_j denotes the minimum eigenvalue for each of the above matrices. For simplicity, we assume these matrices are invertible when $j \geq p$. In addition, these four matrices have stochastically bounded norms uniformly in j. That is, for example, $\sup_{j \geq 1} \frac{1}{j} \sum_{t=1}^{j} x_t x_t'$ is stochastically bounded.

This assumption requires that there is enough data around the change point and at the beginning and at the end of the sample so that the change point can be identified. The latter half of the assumption is typically implied by the strong LLN for the sequence of $\{x_t x_t'\}$. The following theorem is taken from the Proposition 1 of Bai (1997).

Theorem 3.6. *Suppose Assumptions A1–A6 of Bai (1997) hold. Let $\delta = \delta_T$. If δ_T is fixed or $\delta_T \to 0$ but $T^{\frac{1}{2}-\alpha}\delta_T \to \infty$ for some $\alpha \in (0, \frac{1}{2})$, we have*

$$\hat{k} - k_0 = O_p\left(\frac{1}{\delta_T^2}\right).$$

Proof. Note that

$$V(k) - V(k_0) = \hat{\delta}(k)'(Z_k'MZ_k)\hat{\delta}(k) - \hat{\delta}(k_0)'(Z_0'MZ_0)\hat{\delta}(k_0),$$

where

$$\hat{\delta}(k) = (Z_k'MZ_k)^{-1}Z_k'MY = (Z_k'MZ_k)^{-1}Z_k'MZ_0\delta_T + (Z_k'MZ_k)^{-1}Z_k'MU$$

and

$$\hat{\delta}(k_0) = \delta_T + (Z_0'MZ_0)^{-1}Z_0'MU.$$

We can decompose the difference $V(k) - V(k_0)$ into terms with and without error U, respectively. To be specific, we have

$$V(k) - V(k_0) = -|k_0 - k|G(k) + H(k),$$

where

$$G(k) = \begin{cases} \dfrac{\delta_T'[Z_0'MZ_0 - Z_0'MZ_k(Z_k'MZ_k)^{-1}Z_k'MZ_0]\delta_T}{|k_0 - k|} & \text{for } k \neq k_0, \\ \delta_T'\delta_T & \text{for } k = k_0, \end{cases}$$

and

$$H(k) = 2\delta_T'Z_0'MZ_k(Z_k'MZ_k)^{-1}Z_k'MU - 2\delta_T'Z_0'MU$$
$$+ U'MZ_k(Z_k'MZ_k)^{-1}Z_k'MU - U'MZ_0(Z_0'MZ_0)^{-1}Z_0'MU.$$

$$(3.6)$$

Because

$$V(k) - V(k_0) \geq 0$$

by definition, it suffices to show that for each $\epsilon > 0$, there exists $C < \infty$, such that

$$P\left(\sup_{k \in K(C)} V(k) \geq V(k_0)\right) < \varepsilon,$$

where

$$K(C) = \left\{k : |k - k_0| \geq C\delta_T^{-2} \text{ and } \eta T \leq k \leq (1 - \eta)T\right\}$$

for a small number $\eta > 0$. Notice that

$$P\left(\sup_{k \in K(C)} V(k) \geq V(k_0)\right) \leq P\left(\sup_{k \in K(C)} \frac{H(k)}{|k_0 - k|} \geq \inf_{k \in K(C)} G(k)\right).$$

Lemma A.1 in Bai (1997) shows that there exists $\lambda > 0$ such that for every $\epsilon > 0$, there exists $C < \infty$, such that

$$\inf_{|k_0 - k| > C} G(k) \geq \lambda \delta_T^2$$

with probability at least $1 - \epsilon$. By generalizing the Hájek–Rényi inequality, Bai (1997) also shows

$$\frac{H(k)}{|k_0 - k|} = o_p(1)$$

uniformly on $K(C)$ for large C. This completes the proof. □

3.3.2. *Multiple regressions in homogeneous panel data*

Feng *et al.* (2009) consider a structural break model in a homogeneous panel data, which can be written as

$$y_{it} = \begin{cases} x_{it}'\beta + u_{it}, & t = 1, \ldots, k_0, \\ x_{it}'\beta + z_{it}'\delta + u_{it}, & t = k_0 + 1, \ldots, T, \end{cases}$$

where x_{it} is a $p \times 1$ vector of explanatory variables and $z_{it} = R'x_{it}$ denotes a $q \times 1$ subvector of x_{it} with $R' = (0_{q \times (p-q)}, I_q)$. I_q is the $q \times q$ identity matrix with $q \leq p$. The case where $q < p$ denotes a partial change model, while the case where $q = p$ is for a pure change model. Next, let us introduce the following assumptions.

Assumption 3.2. We assume x_{it} and u_{it} are i.i.d. random variables that are mutually independent for all $i = 1, \ldots, n$ and $t = 1, \ldots, T$. We also assume $E(u_{it}) = 0$, $E(x_{it}x_{it}') = \Sigma$, $E(u_{it}^2) = \sigma^2$, $E\|x_{it}\|^4 < \infty$ and $E(u_{it}^4) < \infty$.

Assumption 3.3. The matrices

$$\frac{1}{nj}\sum_{i=1}^{n}\sum_{t=1}^{j}x_{it}x_{it}', \qquad \frac{1}{nj}\sum_{i=1}^{n}\sum_{t=T-j+1}^{T}x_{it}x_{it}', \qquad \frac{1}{nj}\sum_{i=1}^{n}\sum_{t=k_0-j+1}^{k_0}x_{it}x_{it}'$$

and $\quad\dfrac{1}{nj}\displaystyle\sum_{i=1}^{n}\sum_{t=k_0+1}^{k_0+j}x_{it}x_{it}'$

have minimum eigenvalues bounded away from zero in probability for large n or both large n and j. In addition, these matrices are stochastically bounded uniformly in j for large n.

Assumption 3.4. Let $Q = E(z_{it}z_{it}')$ and $\Omega = E(z_{it}z_{it}'u_{it}^2)$. For both fixed and large T, we assume:

(a)

$$\frac{1}{nk_0}\sum_{i=1}^{n}\sum_{t=1}^{k_0}z_{it}z_{it}' \xrightarrow{p} Q,$$

$$\frac{1}{n(T-k_0)}\sum_{i=1}^{n}\sum_{t=k_0+1}^{T}z_{it}z_{it}' \xrightarrow{p} Q;$$

(b)

$$\frac{1}{\sqrt{nk_0}}\sum_{i=1}^{n}\sum_{t=1}^{[rk_0]}z_{it}u_{it} \xrightarrow{d} B_1(r),$$

$$\frac{1}{\sqrt{n(T-k_0)}}\sum_{i=1}^{n}\sum_{t=k_0+1}^{k_0+[r(T-k_0)]}z_{it}u_{it} \xrightarrow{d} B_2(r)$$

as $n \to \infty$, where $B_1(r)$ and $B_2(r)$ are Brownian motions with a variance matrix $r\Omega$.

Assumption 3.2 is assumed for simplicity and can be relaxed. Assumption 3.3 is the identification condition, which means lots of information around the change point is needed. In a special case of $j = 1$, it turns out to be a regularity condition in a linear multiple regression model. Compared to the assumption in time-series case (e.g., A3 in Bai 1997), in which enough data around the change point across time period is required, Assumption 3.3 is more realistic and easier to be satisfied when n is large. That is an advantage of using panel data for identification. Assumption 3.4 assumes that joint limit LLN and CLT hold as $(n, T) \to \infty$. However, for fixed T, we still assume Assumption 3.4 holds as $n \to \infty$. Similar to Assumption 3.3, for fixed T Assumption 3.4 is equivalent to the regularity condition in the linear multiple regression model. From this point of view, it makes more sense to derive asymptotic properties locally around the change point for panel data model with large n than the time-series setting. The following theorem is taken from the Proposition 1 of Feng *et al.* (2009).

Theorem 3.7. *Under Assumptions* 3.2–3.4, *we have* $\hat{k} - k_0 = O_p(\frac{1}{n\|\delta^2\|})$.

Proof. Similar to the proof of Theorem 3.6, we have $V(k) - V(k_0) = -n|k_0 - k|G(k) + H(k)$, where

$$
G(k) = \begin{cases} \dfrac{\delta_T'[Z_0'MZ_0 - Z_0'MZ_k(Z_k'MZ_k)^{-1}Z_k'MZ_0]\delta_T}{n|k_0 - k|} & \text{for } k \neq k_0, \\ \delta_T'\delta_T & \text{for } k = k_0, \end{cases}
$$

and $H(k)$ is the same defined as in Eq. (3.6). Same as in the proof of Theorem 3.6, Theorem 3.7 can be proved if we can show

$$
P\left(\sup_{k \in K(C)} \frac{H(k)}{|k_0 - k|} \geq \inf_{k \in K(C)} G(k)\right) < \varepsilon
$$

where

$$
K(C) = \left\{k : |k - k_0| \geq \frac{C}{n\|\delta\|^2}\right\}.
$$

Similarly, it can be further shown that $\inf n|k_0 - k| > CG(k) > 0$ with probability at least $1 - \epsilon$. By generalizing the Hájek–Rényi inequality, Bai (1997) also shows $\frac{H(k)}{n|k_0 - k|} = o_p(1)$ uniformly on $K(C)$ for large C. This completes the proof. $\square$

Different from Theorem 3.6, the proof above does not rely on Hájek–Rényi inequality. For any $k \in K(C)$ with large C, we can regard $n|k_0 - k|$ as a big number, which justifies applying an LLN. Even if k or $|k_0 - k|$ is small, the product $n|k_0 - k|$ is still big enough when n is large. Therefore, the result holds uniformly. That is the difference between panel data setting and time-series models in Bai (1994) and Bai (1997).

The intuition behind Theorems 3.6 and 3.7 is quite interesting but straightforward. Consider the figure below. In a time-series model, the change point k_0 is assumed to be unbounded, increasing with the sample size T. Even with a lot of observations nearby, k_0 cannot be consistently estimated. Only the break fraction $\tau_0 = k_0/T$ is identifiable, i.e., estimated consistently. However, in the panel data case, lots of observations around k_0 in the time dimension are not necessary. Instead, if a lot of individuals in each period are observed, then the change break can be identified and estimated consistently. Thus, the existence of the structural change is detectable even in the short panel. In this sense, when $k_0 = 5$, for instance, $\tau_0 = k_0/T \to 0$, the discussion above implies that the true change point is still identifiable. That is, the conventional assumption $\tau_0 \in (0,1)$ is not necessary for the panel data setting. Bai (2010) points out this in a mean shift panel data model.

(a) Time-series data	(b) Large panel data

Besides, the consistency of the estimator of k_0 in panel data has a different meaning. For fixed T, the fixed k_0 can be regarded as a parameter. Proposition 1 shows that as $n \to \infty$, $\hat{k} \xrightarrow{p} k_0$. For large T, k_0 increases with T, however, the distance between the estimate and the true value vanishes, i.e., $\hat{k} - k_0 \xrightarrow{p} 0$ as $(n, T) \to \infty$.

3.3.3. *Multiple regressions in heterogeneous panel data*

Baltagi *et al.* (2016) consider a structural break model in a heterogeneous panel data, which can be written as

$$y_{it} = \begin{cases} x'_{it}\beta_i + u_{it}, & t = 1, \ldots, k_0, \\ x'_{it}\beta_i + z'_{it}\delta_i + u_{it}, & t = k_0 + 1, \ldots, T. \end{cases} \tag{3.7}$$

In vector form

$$Y_i = X_i \beta_i + Z_{0i} \delta_i + U_i.$$

For a possible change point k, we define matrices

$$Z_{ik} = \left(0, \ldots, 0, z'_{i,k+1}, \ldots, z'_{iT}\right)'.$$

Now $\hat{\beta}_i(k)$ and $\hat{\delta}_i(k)$ can be obtained by

$$\begin{pmatrix} \hat{\beta}_i(k) \\ \hat{\delta}_i(k) \end{pmatrix} = \begin{pmatrix} X'_i X_i & X'_i Z_{ik} \\ Z'_{ik} X_i & Z'_{ik} Z_{ik} \end{pmatrix}^{-1} \begin{pmatrix} X'Y \\ Z'_{ik} Y \end{pmatrix}.$$

The corresponding SSR is

$$\mathrm{SSR}_i(k) = [Y_i - X_i \hat{\beta}_i(k) - Z_{ik} \hat{\delta}_i(k)]' [Y_i - X_i \hat{\beta}_i(k) - Z_{ik} \hat{\delta}_i(k)]$$

for $i = 1, \ldots, n$. Given that the structural break occurs at a common date for all cross-sectional units in the panel setup, the least squares (LS) estimator of k_0 is

$$\hat{k} = \arg \min_{1 \le k \le T-1} \sum_{i=1}^{n} \pi_i \, \mathrm{SSR}_i(k), \tag{3.8}$$

where weights $\pi_i \in (0, 1)$ and $\sum_{i=1}^{n} \pi_i = 1$. The weights are allowed for the possibility of different magnitudes across series such as different variances. When $n = 1$, $\hat{k}$ defined in Eq. (3.8) boils down to the change point estimator considered by Bai (1997) in a time-series setting, with $\hat{k} - k_0 = O_p(1)$ for large T. In time-series models, only the break fraction $\tau_0 = k_0/T$, instead of k_0 itself, can be consistently estimated. In a multivariate time-series setup, Bai, Lumsdaine, and Stock (1998) show that the width of the confidence interval of the estimated change point decreases as the number of time-series increases. This implies that cross-sectional observations with common breaks improve the accuracy of the estimated change point. In fact, Bai (2010) shows that the LS estimator of the change point is consistent in a panel mean-shift model, i.e., $\hat{k} - k_0 = o_p(1)$. A similar result is also obtained by Kim (2011) in a panel deterministic time trend model. In our heterogeneous panel regression model, Eq. (3.8) combines the information from each series by summing up $\mathrm{SSR}_i(k)$. With a large n, $\hat{k}$ uses more information provided by the multiple time-series sharing a common break. Baltagi *et al.* (2016) show the following asymptotic property of $\hat{k}$.

Theorem 3.8. *Under Assumptions 1–6 (or 7) in Baltagi, Feng and Kao (2016), we have* $\lim_{(n,T) \to \infty} P(\hat{k} = k_0) = 1$.

Consequently, the panel data estimator $\hat{k}$ is more accurate than the time-series estimator and achieves consistency, i.e., $\hat{k} - k_0 \xrightarrow{p} 0$ as $(n, T) \to \infty$. Given the estimated change point $\hat{k}$, the corresponding estimator of the slopes $\hat{\beta}_i(\hat{k})$ and $\hat{\delta}_i(\hat{k})$ can be obtained.

3.4. Extensions

3.4.1. *Change point estimation in time trend model*

3.4.1.1.   Time trend model in time-series

Perron and Zhu (2005) consider the following panel data time trend model with a structural change:

$$y_t = \mu + d_t + u_t,$$

where

$$d_t = \beta t + \gamma DT$$

and

$$DT = 1(t > k_0)(t - k_0)$$

for a change point $k_0 = [\lambda_0 T]$ for some $\lambda_0 \in (0, 1)$. Let $Y = (y_1, \ldots, y_T)'$,

$$DT(k) = 1(t > k)(t - k)$$

and

$$x_t(k)' = (1, t, DT(k)),$$

and

$$P(k) = x_t(k)[x_t(k)'x_t(k)]x_t(k)'$$

is the projection matrix constructed using $x_t(k)$. The SSR for k is

$$\text{SSR}(k) = Y'(I - P(k))Y.$$

Define

$$\hat{k} = \arg\min_{1 \le k \le T} \text{SSR}(k)$$

and hence $\hat{\tau} = \hat{k}/T$. As shown in Theorem 3 of Perron and Zhu (2005), $\hat{\tau}$ is a consistent estimator of τ_0 no matter u_t is $I(0)$ or $I(1)$.

Theorem 3.9. *As $T \to \infty$, we have the following conditions:*

(1) *If u_t is $I(0)$, $\hat{\tau} - \tau_0 = O_p(\frac{1}{T^{3/2}})$,*
(2) *If u_t is $I(1)$, $\hat{\tau} - \tau_0 = O_p(\frac{1}{\sqrt{T}})$.*

As shown in Theorem 3.10, if u_t is $I(0)$,

$$\hat{\tau} - \tau_0 = O_p\left(\frac{1}{T^{3/2}}\right)$$

is equivalent to

$$\hat{k} - k_0 = O_p\left(\frac{1}{\sqrt{T}}\right).$$

The break date estimate is consistent as $T \to \infty$. However, if u_t is $I(1)$,

$$\hat{\tau} - \tau_0 = O_p\left(\frac{1}{\sqrt{T}}\right)$$

is equivalent to $\hat{k} - k_0 = O_p(\sqrt{T})$. The break date estimate is hence inconsistent. Perron and Zhu (2005) also consider other time trend models with a structural change. In Eq. (3.9), d_t is of the forms

$$d_t = \beta t + \gamma DT + \theta DU$$

and

$$d_t = \beta t + \theta DU,$$

where $DU = 1(t > k_0)$. As shown in Perron and Zhu (2005), the break fraction converges at a faster rate when the intercept shift regressor is absent.

3.4.1.2. Time trend model in panel data

Kim (2011, 2014) extend the time-series model in Perron and Zhu (2005) to the panel model. Consider the following panel time trend model with a structural change:

$$y_{it} = d_{it} + u_{it}, \tag{3.9}$$

where

$$d_{it} = \mu_i + \beta_i t + \gamma_i DT,$$

and

$$DT = 1(t > k)(t - k)$$

for a change point $k = [\lambda T]$ for some $\lambda \in (0, 1)$. The error term u_{it} could be either $I(0)$ or $I(1)$. Similar to the time-series case, a common deterministic trend break in panels is estimated by minimizing the SSR. Kim (2011) derives the following results for Eq. (3.9).

Theorem 3.10. *Assume $(n, T) \to \infty$, we have the following conditions:*

(1) *If u_{it} is $I(0)$,*

$$\hat{k} - k_0 = O_p\left(\frac{1}{\sqrt{nT}}\right).$$

(2) *If u_{it} is $I(1)$,*

$$\hat{\tau} - \tau_0 = O_p\left(\frac{1}{\sqrt{nT}}\right),$$

i.e.,

$$\hat{k} - k_0 = O_p\left(\sqrt{\frac{T}{n}}\right).$$

As shown in Theorem 3.10, if u_{it} is $I(0)$, the break date estimate is consistent as both n and T are large. Even if T is fixed, the break date estimate is still consistent. However, if u_{it} is $I(1)$, the break date estimate is inconsistent unless $\frac{T}{n} \to 0$. Kim (2011) also considers other panel time trend model with a structural change. In Eq. (3.9), d_{it} is of the forms

$$d_{it} = \mu_i + \beta_i t + \gamma_i DT + \theta_i DU$$

and

$$d_{it} = \mu_i + \beta_i t + \theta_i DU,$$

where $DU = 1(t > k)$. As shown in Kim (2011), the form of the break, that is, whether it is only a slope change or a slope change combined with an intercept shift, affects the convergence rate and the form of the limiting distribution of the break date estimate.

3.4.2. *Panel model with stationary or nonstationary regressor and error term*

Baltagi *et al.* (2017) consider the case when a change point exists. For the model in Eq. (3.2), let us assume $\beta_2 - \beta_1 \neq 0$. This assumption ensures that we have a one-time break in the systematic part and that the pre- and post-break samples are not asymptotically negligible which is a standard assumption needed to derive any meaningful asymptotic result. In general, for any x_{it} with nonzero mean θ, the model in Eq. (3.2) can be rewritten as

$$y_{it} = \begin{cases} (\alpha_1 + \beta_1\theta) + \beta_1(x_{it} - \theta) + u_{it} & \text{for } t = 1, \ldots, k_0, \\ (\alpha_2 + \beta_2\theta) + \beta_2(x_{it} - \theta) + u_{it} & \text{for } t = k_0 + 1, \ldots, T, \end{cases}$$

where the new regressor is zero mean again. From the equation above, we can see that a change in the slope implies a change in the intercept, as long as the initial regressor x_{it} has a nonzero mean. Following Feng *et al.* (2009), the magnitude of the break $\beta_2 - \beta_1$ is assumed to be fixed.

3.4.2.1. Stationary or nonstationary regressor and error term in time-series

The following theorem shows that $\hat{\tau}_{\mathrm{OLS}}$ may not be always consistent in the time-series case.

Theorem 3.11. *Assume* $\beta_2 - \beta_1 \neq 0$. *In the time-series case for* $\tau_0 \in (0,1)$ *and as* $T \to \infty$, *we have the following results:*

(a) *When* $|\rho| < 1$ *and* $|\lambda| < 1$,

$$\hat{\tau}_{\mathrm{OLS}} \xrightarrow{p} \tau_0.$$

(b) *When* $\rho = 1$ *and* $|\lambda| < 1$,

$$\hat{\tau}_{\mathrm{OLS}} \xrightarrow{d} \arg\max_{\tau \in [\underline{\tau}, \bar{\tau}]} \frac{1}{\tau(1-\tau)} \left[\int_\tau^1 W_e - (1-\tau) \int_0^1 W_e \right]^2.$$

(c) *When* $|\rho| < 1$ *and* $\lambda = 1$,

$$\hat{\tau}_{\mathrm{OLS}} \xrightarrow{p} \tau_0.$$

(d) *When* $\lambda = \rho = 1$,

$$\hat{\tau}_{\mathrm{OLS}} \xrightarrow{d} \arg\max_{\tau \in [\underline{\tau}, \bar{\tau}]} [\tilde{F}(\tau, \tau_0) + S(\tau)]' F(\tau)^{-1} [\tilde{F}(\tau, \tau_0) + S(\tau)],$$

where

$$F(\tau) = P(\tau) - P(\tau)P(0)^{-1}P(\tau),$$

$$\tilde{F}(\tau, \tau_0) = \begin{cases} [P(0) - P(\tau)]\, P(0)^{-1} P(\tau_0) \begin{pmatrix} 0 \\ \beta_2 - \beta_1 \end{pmatrix} & \text{if } \tau \leq \tau_0, \\[2mm] P(\tau)P(0)^{-1} [P(0) - P(\tau_0)] \begin{pmatrix} 0 \\ \beta_2 - \beta_1 \end{pmatrix} & \text{if } \tau > \tau_0, \end{cases}$$

$$S(\tau) = \begin{pmatrix} \sigma_e \int_\tau^1 W_e \\ \sigma_\varepsilon \sigma_e \int_\tau^1 W_e W_\varepsilon \end{pmatrix} - P(\tau)P(0)^{-1} \begin{pmatrix} \sigma_e \int_0^1 W_e \\ \sigma_\varepsilon \sigma_e \int_0^1 W_e W_\varepsilon \end{pmatrix},$$

and

$$P(\tau) = \begin{pmatrix} 1 - \tau & \sigma_\varepsilon \int_\tau^1 W_\varepsilon \\ \sigma_\varepsilon \int_\tau^1 W_\varepsilon & \sigma_\varepsilon^2 \int_\tau^1 W_\varepsilon^2 \end{pmatrix}.$$

Theorem 3.11 indicates that $\hat{\tau}_{\text{OLS}}$ is consistent when $|\rho| < 1$ but inconsistent when $\rho = 1$ if there is a break in the time-series case. To be more specific, when $|\rho| < 1$ and $|\lambda| < 1$, this verifies with the findings in Nunes *et al.* (1995). When $|\rho| < 1$ and $\lambda = 1$, as discussed in Bai (1996), both $\hat{\tau}_{\text{OLS}}$ and $\hat{k}_{\text{OLS}}$ are consistent in this cointegration model. When $\rho = 1$ and $|\lambda| < 1$, $\hat{\tau}_{\text{OLS}}$ converges to a function that does not depend on the true value of the break fraction τ_0. Similarly, when $\rho = \lambda = 1$, $\hat{\tau}_{\text{OLS}}$ converges to a function that includes

$$\tilde{F}(\tau, \tau_0)' F(\tau)^{-1} \tilde{F}(\tau, \tau_0)$$

and

$$S(\tau)' F(\tau)^{-1} S(\tau).$$

One can show that the function

$$\tilde{F}(\tau, \tau_0)' F(\tau)^{-1} \tilde{F}(\tau, \tau_0)$$

will be maximized at τ_0, but the function

$$S(\tau)' F(\tau)^{-1} S(\tau)$$

does not depend on τ_0 at all. This implies that $\hat{\tau}_{\text{OLS}}$ is inconsistent when $\rho = 1$, whether $|\lambda| < 1$ or $\lambda = 1$. Overall, using the relationship that $\hat{\tau}_{\text{OLS}} = \hat{k}_{\text{OLS}}/T$, we know that $\hat{k}_{\text{OLS}}$ is inconsistent except in a cointegration model. In fact, if the magnitude of the break δ is fixed, the asymptotic distribution of $\hat{k}_{\text{OLS}} - k_0$ depends upon the underlying distribution of the regressors and the error term, e.g., Picard (1985) and Bai (1997). This difficulty can be overcome using large panel data.

3.4.2.2. Stationary or nonstationary regressor and error term in panel data

As shown in Bai (2010), the consistency of $\hat{k}_{\text{OLS}}$ can be established in a mean shift panel model. The theorem below extends Bai (2010)'s results to the case where the regressor and the error term are allowed to be $I(0)$ or $I(1)$ processes.

Theorem 3.12. *Assume $\beta_2 - \beta_1 \neq 0$. For $\tau_0 \in (0, 1)$ and as $(n, T) \to \infty$, we have the following results:*

(a) *When $|\rho| < 1$ and $|\lambda| < 1$, $\hat{k}_{\text{OLS}} - k_0 = O_p(\frac{1}{n})$.*
(b) *When $\rho = 1$ and $|\lambda| < 1$, $\hat{k}_{\text{OLS}} - k_0 = O_p(\frac{T}{n})$ if $\frac{T}{n} \to 0$.*

(c) *When* $|\rho| < 1$ *and* $\lambda = 1$, $\hat{k}_{\text{OLS}} - k_0 = O_p(\frac{1}{nT})$.

(d) *When* $\lambda = \rho = 1$, $\hat{k}_{\text{OLS}} - k_0 = O_p(\frac{1}{nT})$.

Theorem 3.12 shows that the consistency of $\hat{k}_{\text{OLS}}$ can be achieved even for a fixed δ, as long as n is large. That is, large cross-sectional dimension will create enough information to identify the true change point over time. Unlike the time-series setup, for fixed δ, $\hat{k}_{\text{OLS}}$ is consistent with the convergence speed of n when $|\rho| < 1$ and $|\lambda| < 1$. However, when $\rho = 1$ and $|\lambda| < 1$, consistency of $\hat{k}_{\text{OLS}}$ needs $\frac{T}{n} \to 0$. When $\lambda = 1$, no matter whether $|\rho| < 1$ or $\rho = 1$, $\hat{k}_{\text{OLS}}$ is consistent with nT convergence speed. This is because when $|\rho| < 1$ and $\lambda = 1$, x_{it} is an $I(1)$ process. That is, the signal is strong enough to dominate the $I(0)$ error term. When $\lambda = \rho = 1$, large n helps to reduce the noise caused by the $I(1)$ error term as in the panel spurious regression (e.g., Kao, 1999). Since $\hat{\tau}_{\text{OLS}} = \hat{k}_{\text{OLS}}/T$, the fraction estimate $\hat{\tau}_{\text{OLS}}$ is always consistent with a convergence speed of at least n. Comparing this result with that in Theorem 3.11, it is clear that $\hat{\tau}_{\text{OLS}}$ in a panel data setting is robust to different values of λ and ρ. This highlights the difference between the results in the panel data case and those in the time-series case. With the estimator $\hat{k}$, the asymptotic of $\hat{\gamma}_{\hat{k}_{\text{OLS}}} = \hat{\gamma}(\hat{k}_{\text{OLS}})$ and $\hat{\delta}_{\hat{k}_{\text{OLS}}} = \hat{\delta}(\hat{k}_{\text{OLS}})$ can be established.

3.4.3. *Change point estimation in panel data models with common factors*

Recently, change point estimation has been extended to panel data models with common factors. For example, Horváth and Husková (2012) and Horváth, Husková, Rice, and Wang (2017) extend panel mean-shift model in Bai (2010) by allowing common factors. Similarly, Kim (2011, 2014) also consider the case where time trend model contains common factors. As shown in Kim (2011), the amount of correlation in both the time and cross-sectional spans affects the rate of convergence. The strong correlation in any of the time and cross-sectional span results in a slower rate of convergence. Especially the strong cross-sectional dependence generated by the common factors makes the rate of convergence the same as the univariate case and thus eliminates the benefit of the panel data.

In a multiple regression, Baltagi *et al.* (2016) further extend the model in Eq. (3.7) into

$$y_{it} = \begin{cases} x_{it}'\beta_i + \gamma_i'f_t + u_{it}, & t = 1, \ldots, k_0, \\ x_{it}'\beta_i + z_{it}'\delta_i + \gamma_i'f_t + u_{it}, & t = k_0 + 1, \ldots, T, \end{cases} \tag{3.10}$$

where f_t is an $m \times 1$ vector of unobserved factors and γ_i is the corresponding loading vector. Typically, f_t and λ_i are assumed to satisfy the standard assumptions in the literature such as: $E(f_t f_t') = \Sigma_F$ and Σ_F is positive definite and

$$\left\| \frac{1}{n} \Lambda' \Lambda - \Sigma_\Lambda \right\| \to 0$$

for some positive definite matrix Σ_Λ, where $\| \cdot \|$ is the Frobenius norm.

When the regressors x_{it} are uncorrelated with the unobservable factors f_t, Baltagi, Kao, and Wang (2017) show that the estimated change point $\hat{k}$ could be estimated as if the factors were known. Under their assumptions, we still have $\hat{k} - k_0 = O_p(1)$ as $(n, T) \to \infty$. This result confirms the results in Kim (2011) for the current regression setup, i.e., when cross-sectional dependence is strong, more series do not increase the accuracy of the change point estimator. To recover consistency, we will use estimated factors as extra regressors to control for cross-sectional dependence. Nevertheless, $\hat{k} - k_0 = O_p(1)$ is good enough to estimate the factor space. It can be verified that with $O_p(1)$ estimation error, results in Song (2013) remain the same. Once the estimated factors are available and incorporated in the model as extra regressors, the consistency of the OLS estimator can be recovered.

When the regressors x_{it} are allowed to be correlated with the unobservable factors f_t, Baltagi *et al.* (2016) assume

$$x_{it} = \Gamma_i' f_t + v_{it}.$$

If f_t were observable, it could be treated as a regressor, and this correlation can be removed using a partitioned regression. However, f_t are unobservable in practice. To proceed, Baltagi *et al.* (2016) follow Common Correlated Effects (CCE) of Pesaran (2006) using the cross-sectional averages of y_{it} and x_{it} as proxies for f_t. Combining (3.7) and (3.10) yield

$$\underset{(p+1) \times 1}{w_{it}} = \begin{pmatrix} y_{it} \\ x_{it} \end{pmatrix} = \underset{(p+1) \times m}{C_i(k_0)'} \underset{m \times 1}{f_t} + \underset{(p+1) \times 1}{u_{it}(k_0)},$$

where

$$\underset{m \times (p+1)}{C_i(k_0)} = (\gamma_i, \Gamma_i) \begin{pmatrix} 1 & 0 \\ \beta_i(k_0) & I_p \end{pmatrix}$$

and

$$u_{it}(k_0) = \begin{pmatrix} \varepsilon_{it} + v_{it}' \beta_i(k_0) \\ v_{it} \end{pmatrix}.$$

Let $\bar{w}_t = \sum_{i=1}^{n} \theta_i w_{it}$ be the cross-sectional averages of w_{it} using weights θ_i, $i = 1, \ldots, n$. In particular,

$$\bar{w}_t = \bar{C}(k_0)' f_t + \bar{u}_t(k_0),$$

where

$$\bar{C}(k_0) = \sum_{i=1}^{n} \theta_i C_i(k_0)$$

and

$$\bar{u}_t(k_0) = \sum_{i=1}^{n} \theta_i u_{it}(k_0).$$

When $\bar{C}(k_0)$ is of full rank, f_t can be written as

$$f_t = [\bar{C}(k_0)\bar{C}(k_0)']^{-1}\bar{C}(k_0)(\bar{w}_t - \bar{u}_t(k_0))$$

so that

$$f_t - [\bar{C}(k_0)\bar{C}(k_0)']^{-1}\bar{C}(k_0)\bar{w}_t \xrightarrow{p} 0. \qquad (3.11)$$

This suggests that it is asymptotically valid to use $\bar{w}_t$ as observable proxies for f_t. Let $\bar{W} = (\bar{w}_1, \bar{w}_2, \ldots, \bar{w}_T)'$ denote the $T \times (p+1)$ matrix of cross-sectional averages. Denote the $T \times T$ matrix M_w by

$$M_w = I_T - \bar{W}(\bar{W}'\bar{W})^{-1}\bar{W}'.$$

Thus, similar to the result $M_f F = 0$, by (3.11) it is expected that the terms involving $M_w F$ are ignorable asymptotically as $n \to \infty$. Define $\tilde{Y}_i = M_w Y_i$, $\tilde{X}_i = M_w X_i$, $\tilde{Z}_{0i} = M_w Z_{0i}$ and $\tilde{Z}_{ik} = M_w Z_{ik}$. Given k,

$$\tilde{b}_i(k) = \begin{pmatrix} \tilde{\beta}_i(k) \\ \tilde{\delta}_i(k) \end{pmatrix}$$

can be estimated by OLS. The resulting SSR is

$$\widetilde{\mathrm{SSR}}_i(k) = [\tilde{Y}_i - \tilde{X}_i\tilde{\beta}_i(k) - \tilde{Z}_{ik}\tilde{\delta}_i(k)]'[\tilde{Y}_i - \tilde{X}_i\tilde{\beta}_i(k) - \tilde{Z}_{ik}\tilde{\delta}_i(k)]$$

for $i = 1, \ldots, n$. Baltagi *et al.* (2016) suggest to estimate k_0 as

$$\tilde{k} = \arg\min_{1 \leq k \leq T-1} \sum_i \pi_i \widetilde{\mathrm{SSR}}_i(k),$$

where π_i are weights. As shown in Baltagi *et al.* (2016), we have

$$\lim_{(n,T)\to\infty} P(\tilde{k} = k_0) = 1. \qquad (3.12)$$

Given the change point estimator $\tilde{k}$, the CCE estimator of the slope coefficients $\tilde{b}_i(\tilde{k})$ can be obtained. With the consistency of $\tilde{k}$, the asymptotic result of $\tilde{b}_i$ can be established as

$$\sqrt{T}(\tilde{b}_i - b_i) \xrightarrow{d} N(0, \Sigma_{\tilde{\mathbb{X}},i}^{-1} \Sigma_{\tilde{\mathbb{X}}\tilde{u},i} \Sigma_{\tilde{\mathbb{X}},i}^{-1}),$$

where

$$\Sigma_{\tilde{\mathbb{X}},i} = p \lim_{T\to\infty} \frac{1}{T} \tilde{\mathbb{X}}_{0i}' \tilde{\mathbb{X}}_{0i}$$

and

$$\Sigma_{\tilde{\mathbb{X}}\tilde{u},i} = p \lim_{T\to\infty} \frac{1}{T} \tilde{\mathbb{X}}_{0i}' \Sigma_{u,i} \tilde{\mathbb{X}}_{0i}$$

with $\tilde{\mathbb{X}}_{0i} = (\tilde{X}_i, \tilde{Z}_{0i})$ for $i = 1, \ldots, n$.

3.5. Testing for the Change Point

Testing for the change point in a panel time trend model has been considered by Emerson and Kao (2001, 2002) and Baltagi *et al.* (2019). Consider a panel data model with homogeneous coefficients of the time trend:

$$y_{it} = \delta + \beta_t t + \mu_i + \nu_{it}, \tag{3.13}$$

where δ and β_t are unknown parameters, μ_i are the unobservable individual effects and

$$\nu_{it} = \rho \nu_{i,t-1} + e_{it}$$

with $-1 < \rho \leq 1$. When there is a change point at k,

$$\beta_t = \begin{cases} \beta_1 & \text{for } t = 1, \ldots, k, \\ \beta_2 & \text{for } t = k+1, \ldots, T. \end{cases}$$

3.5.1. *OLS-based Wald statistic*

To test the null hypothesis is $H_0 : \beta_1 = \beta_2$, Emerson and Kao (2001) derive the Wald statistic based on OLS estimators as

$$\mathrm{W}_{\mathrm{OLS}}(k) = \frac{(\widehat{\beta}_{1k} - \widehat{\beta}_{2k})^2}{\hat{\sigma}_v^2 \left[\frac{1}{\sum_{i=1}^{n} \sum_{t=1}^{k}(t-\bar{t}_{1k})^2} + \frac{1}{\sum_{i=1}^{n} \sum_{t=k+1}^{T}(t-\bar{t}_{2k})^2} \right]} \tag{3.14}$$

where

$$\widehat{\beta}_{1k} = \frac{\sum_{i=1}^{n} \sum_{t=1}^{k}(t - \bar{t}_{1k})y_{it}}{\sum_{i=1}^{n} \sum_{t=1}^{k}(t - \bar{t}_{1k})^2},$$

$$\widehat{\beta}_{2k} = \frac{\sum_{i=1}^{n} \sum_{t=k+1}^{T}(t - \bar{t}_{2k})y_{it}}{\sum_{i=1}^{n} \sum_{t=k+1}^{T}(t - \bar{t}_{2k})^2},$$

$$\bar{t}_{1k} = \tfrac{1}{k}\sum_{t=1}^{k} t, \ \bar{t}_{2k} = \tfrac{1}{T-k}\sum_{t=k+1}^{T} t,$$

$$\hat{\sigma}_v^2 = \sum_{i=1}^{n}\sum_{t=1}^{T}(\nu_{it} - \bar{\nu}_i)$$

and

$$\bar{\nu}_i = \sum_{t=1}^{T} \nu_{it}.$$

The asymptotic distribution of the Wald statistic under $H_0 : \gamma = 0$ is shown in Emerson and Kao (2001).

Theorem 3.13. *Assume* $(n, T) \to \infty$.

(1) *If* $|\rho| < 1$, *then*

$$\frac{(1-\rho)^2\sigma_v^2}{3\sigma_e^2}\mathrm{W}_{\mathrm{OLS}}(k)$$

$$\xrightarrow{d} \left\{ \frac{P(r)(1-r)^3 - r^3[P(1) - P(r) + W(r) - rW(1)]}{[r^3(1-r)^3[(1-r)^3 + r^3]]^{\frac{1}{2}}} \right\}^2$$

where

$$P(r) = rW(r) - 2\int_0^r W(s)ds.$$

(2) *If* $\rho = 1$, *then*

$$\frac{\sigma_v^2}{3T^2\sigma_e^2}\mathrm{W}_{\mathrm{OLS}}(k)$$

$$\xrightarrow{d} \left\{ \frac{Q(r)(1-r)^3 - [Q(1) - Q(r) - r\int_0^1 W(s)ds + \int_0^r W(s)ds]r^3}{[r^3(1-r)^3[(1-r)^3 + r^3]]^{1/2}} \right\}^2$$

where

$$Q(r) = 2\int_0^r s[W(s) + \widetilde{W}(\pi)]ds - r\int_0^r [W(s) + \widetilde{W}(\pi)]ds$$

and $\widetilde{W}(\pi)$ *is a different Brownian motion from* $W(s)$.

From Theorem 3.13, these imply that, under the null, $\mathrm{W}_{\mathrm{OLS}}(k) = O_p(1)$ when ν_{it} is $I(0)$ and $\mathrm{W}_{\mathrm{OLS}}(k) \to \infty$ when ν_{it} is $I(1)$. This is not surprising since $\hat{\sigma}_v^2 = O_p(T)$, i.e., σ_v^2 is not identified when ν_{it} is $I(1)$. In view of this and given that the order of integration of ν_{it} is not known in practice, it is natural to consider a robust test procedure.

3.5.2. FGLS-based Wald statistic

In a time-series model, Perron and Yabu (2009b) suggest a GLS procedure using a super-efficient estimate of the autoregressive parameters as a robust test. Following Perron and Yabu (2009b), Baltagi *et al.* (2019) propose a robust test using the FE-FGLS estimator for the panel data model discussed in Baltagi *et al.* (2014) and modify for structural change. The model in Baltagi *et al.* (2019) is

$$y_{it} = \delta + \beta t + \gamma DT + \mu_i + v_{it}, \tag{3.15}$$

where

$$DT = 1(t > k)(t - k)$$

for a change point k and

$$v_{it} = \rho v_{it-1} + e_{it}$$

with $|\rho| \leq 1$. The null hypothesis of interest is $H_0 : \gamma = 0$. Rewrite Eq. (3.15) in matrix form

$$y = \delta \iota_{nT} + Z'\Psi + u, \tag{3.16}$$

where $u = Z_\mu \mu + v$, μ is an $n \times 1$ vector of μ_i, v is an $nT \times 1$ vector of v_{it}, $Z_\mu = I_n \otimes \iota_T$, y is an $nT \times 1$ vector of y_{it}, $Z = \iota_n \otimes Z_i$ and $Z_i = (x_i, DT_i)$ where x_i is a $T \times 1$ vector of $(1, 2, \ldots, T)'$ and DT_i is a $T \times 1$ vector of $(0, \ldots, 0, 1, \ldots, T - k)'$. ι_{nT} is a vector of ones of dimension nT. $\Psi = (\beta, \gamma)'$. Define $R = (0, 1)$, the null hypothesis H_0 can be rewritten into $R\Psi = 0$. As shown in Sec. 2.3.3, the FE-GLS estimator of Ψ is given by

$$\hat{\Psi}_{\text{FE-GLS}} = [Z^{*\prime}(I_n \otimes E_T^\alpha)Z^*]^{-1}Z^{*\prime}(I_n \otimes E_T^\alpha)y^* \tag{3.17}$$

and

$$\hat{\Psi}_{\text{FE-GLS}} - \Psi = F_1^{-1}F_2, \tag{3.18}$$

where

$$F_1 = Z_i^{*\prime}E_T^\alpha Z_i^* = Z_i^{*\prime}Z_i^* - \frac{1}{d^2}Z_i^{*\prime}\iota_T^\alpha \iota_T^{\alpha\prime}Z_i^*$$

and

$$F_2 = \frac{1}{n}Z^{*\prime}(I_n \otimes E_T^\alpha)v^* = \frac{1}{n}\sum_{i=1}^{n}Z_i^{*\prime}v_i^* - Z_i^{*\prime}\iota_T^\alpha \frac{1}{n}\sum_{i=1}^{n}\iota_T^{\alpha\prime}v_i^*$$

with

$$E_T^\alpha = I_T - \bar{J}_T^\alpha,$$

$$\bar{J}_T^\alpha = \iota_T^\alpha \iota_T^{\alpha\prime}/d^2,$$

$$d^2 = \iota_T^{\alpha\prime} \iota_T^\alpha = \alpha^2 + T - 1,$$

$$\sigma_\alpha^2 = \sigma_e^2 + \theta\sigma_\mu^2$$

and

$$\theta = d^2(1-\rho)^2.$$

Therefore, the Wald statistic of the FE-GLS estimator is

$$\mathrm{W}_{\text{FE-GLS}}(k)$$

$$= [R(\hat{\Psi}_{\text{FE-GLS}} - \Psi)]'[R\ \text{Var}(\hat{\Psi}_{\text{FE-GLS}})R']^{-1}[R(\hat{\Psi}_{\text{FE-GLS}} - \Psi)]$$

$$= n\sigma_e^{-2}(RF_1^{-1}F_2)'(RF_1^{-1}R')^{-1}(RF_1^{-1}F_2). \tag{3.19}$$

The Wald statistic based on the FE-GLS depends on ρ. With a consistent estimator $\hat{\rho}$, the corresponding FE-FGLS estimator $\mathrm{W}_{\text{FE-GLS}}(k)$ is obtained by replacing C and E_T^α by their corresponding estimators $\hat{C}$ and $\hat{E}_T^\alpha$. As suggested by Baltagi and Li (1991), an estimator of σ_e^2 can be obtained as

$$\hat{\sigma}_e^2 = \frac{1}{n(T-1)}\hat{u}^{*\prime}(I_n \otimes \hat{E}_T^\alpha)\hat{u}^*,$$

where $\hat{u}^*$ is an $nT \times 1$ vector of OLS residuals from the PW transformed regression using $\hat{\rho}$. The corresponding Wald-statistic based on the FE-FGLS estimator can be obtained from Eq. (3.19). Baltagi *et al.* (2019) show asymptotic properties of $\mathrm{W}_{\text{FE-GLS}}(k)$ using an estimator $\hat{\rho}$, which are summarized in the following theorem.

Theorem 3.14. *For a fixed n, as $T \to \infty$, we have the following conditions:*

(1) *When $|\rho| < 1$, if $\hat{\rho} \xrightarrow{p} \rho$,*

$$\mathrm{W}_{\text{FE-GLS}}(k) \xrightarrow{d} \frac{3}{\lambda^3(1-\lambda)^3}$$

$$\left\{ \frac{1}{\sqrt{n}} \sum_{i=1}^n [H_i^0(\lambda) - (1+2\lambda)(1-\lambda)^2 H_i^0(0)] \right\}^2,$$

where

$$H_i^0(\lambda) = \int_\lambda^1 (r-\lambda)dW_i - \frac{(1-\lambda)^2}{2}W_i(1)$$

and

$$H_i^0(0) = \int rdW_i - \frac{1}{2}W_i(1).$$

(2) *When $\rho = 1$, if $T(\hat{\rho} - 1) \xrightarrow{p} \kappa$,*

$$W_{\text{FE-GLS}}(k) \xrightarrow{d} \frac{1}{\Lambda_{11}^2 (\Lambda_{11}\Lambda_{22} - \Lambda_{12}^2)}$$

$$\left\{ \frac{1}{\sqrt{n}} \sum_{i=1}^{n} [\Lambda_{11} H_i^1(\kappa, \lambda) - \Lambda_{12} \tilde{H}_i^1(\kappa, 0)] \right\}^2$$

where

$$\Lambda_{11} = \frac{1}{12}\kappa^2 - \frac{1}{2}\kappa + 1, \quad \Lambda_{12} = \frac{(1-\lambda)^2(2\lambda+1)}{12}\kappa^2 - \frac{1-\lambda}{2}\kappa + 1 - \lambda,$$

$$\Lambda_{22} = \frac{(1-\lambda)^3}{3}\kappa^2 - (1-\lambda)^2\kappa + 1 - \lambda + \frac{(1-\lambda)^2\kappa[-(1-\lambda)\kappa + 2]^2}{4(2-\kappa)},$$

$$H_i^1(\kappa, \lambda) = \int_\lambda^1 dW_i - \frac{\kappa^2}{2} \int_\lambda^1 (r-\lambda)^2 dW_i$$

$$+ \frac{\kappa^2(1-\lambda)}{2-\kappa} \left[-\frac{\kappa(1-\lambda)}{2} + 1 \right] \int r \, dW_i$$

$$- \frac{\kappa(1-\lambda)}{2-\kappa} \left[-\frac{\kappa(1-\lambda)}{2} + 1 \right] W_i(1)$$

and

$$\tilde{H}_i^1(\kappa, 0) = -\frac{\kappa^2}{2} \int r^2 dW_i + \frac{\kappa^2}{2} \int r \, dW_i + \left(\frac{3\kappa}{2} + 1 \right) W_i(1).$$

Theorem 3.14 implies that $W_{\text{FE-GLS}}(k)$ converges to a $\chi^2(1)$ when $|\rho| < 1$. However, when $|\rho| = 1$, the distribution of $W_{\text{FE-GLS}}(k)$ depends on κ. This distribution becomes a $\chi^2(1)$ only if $\kappa = 0$. In other words, in order to make the Wald statistics robust to both $|\rho| < 1$ and $|\rho| = 1$, the estimator of ρ needs to be consistent when $\rho < 1$; and satisfy the condition

$$T(\hat{\rho} - 1) \xrightarrow{p} 0$$

when $\rho = 1$. As shown in Eq. (1.18), the estimator of ρ suggested by Baltagi and Li (1991) is

$$\hat{\rho} = \frac{\sum_{i=1}^{n} \sum_{t=2}^{T} \hat{\nu}_{it} \hat{\nu}_{i,t-1}}{\sum_{i=1}^{n} \sum_{t=2}^{T} \hat{\nu}_{i,t-1}^2},$$

where

$$\hat{\nu}_{it} = (y_{it} - \bar{y}_i) - \hat{\beta}_{\text{FE}}(t - \bar{t})$$

is the within residual in (3.16). As discussed in Theorem 2.9, Baltagi *et al.* (2014) show that if $|\rho| < 1$,

$$\sqrt{nT}\left(\hat{\rho} - \rho + \frac{1+\rho}{T}\right) \xrightarrow{d} N(0, 1 - \rho^2).$$

However, if $\rho = 1$,

$$\sqrt{nT}\left(\hat{\rho} - 1 + \frac{3}{T}\right) \xrightarrow{d} N\left(0, \frac{51}{5}\right)$$

as $(n, T) \to \infty$. Theorem 3.14 implies that when $\rho = 1$ and $\kappa = -3$, using $\hat{\rho}$ suggested by Baltagi and Li (1991), $\frac{RV^{-1}B\Xi B'V^{-1}R'}{RVR'}$ is a function of λ. It means that the Wald statistic $\mathrm{W_{FE\text{-}GLS}}(k)$ does not converge to a chi-squared distribution using $\hat{\rho}$ when $\rho = 1$. Therefore, when $|\rho| < 1$, a bias-corrected estimator of ρ is $\hat{\rho} + \frac{1+\hat{\rho}}{T}$. When $\rho = 1$, a bias-corrected estimator of ρ is $\hat{\rho} + \frac{3}{T}$. Combining the two cases, Baltagi *et al.* (2014) suggest a bias-corrected estimator of ρ as follows:

$$\tilde{\rho} = \begin{cases} \hat{\rho} + \frac{1+\hat{\rho}}{T} & \text{if } 1 - \hat{\rho} > \frac{3}{T}, \\ 1 & \text{if } 1 - \hat{\rho} \le \frac{3}{T}. \end{cases}$$

As shown in Baltagi *et al.* (2014), if $|\rho| < 1$, then

$$\sqrt{nT}(\tilde{\rho} - \rho) \xrightarrow{d} N(0, 1 - \rho^2).$$

However, if $\rho = 1$,

$$T(\tilde{\rho} - 1) \xrightarrow{p} 0$$

as $(n, T) \to \infty$. This bias-corrected estimator $\tilde{\rho}$ satisfies the condition $\kappa = 0$ when $\rho = 1$ without changing the asymptotic distribution when $|\rho| < 1$. From Theorem 3.14, we have the following corollary.

Corollary 3.1. *For $\tilde{\rho}$, we have*

$$\mathrm{W_{FE\text{-}FGLS}}(k) \xrightarrow{d} G(r) \sim \chi^2(1)$$

for both $|\rho| < 1$ and $\rho = 1$ as $(n, T) \to \infty$, where

$$G(r) = \begin{cases} \frac{3}{\lambda^3(1-\lambda)^3}[H^0(\lambda) - (1 + 2\lambda)(1 - \lambda)^2 H^0(0)]^2 & \text{if } |\rho| < 1, \\ \frac{1}{\lambda(1-\lambda)}[\lambda W(1) - W(\lambda)]^2 & \text{if } \rho = 1, \end{cases}$$

with

$$H^0(\lambda) = \int_\lambda^1 (r - \lambda)dW - \frac{(1-\lambda)^2}{2}W(1)$$

and

$$H^0(0) = \int r\,dW - \frac{1}{2}W(1).$$

3.6. Conclusion

In this chapter, we discuss the estimation and inference of the change point in a panel regression not knowing whether the regressor and error term are stationary or nonstationary. The spurious break is discussed in the time-series and panel data models. We show that the spurious break may be avoided using a large panel. In a homogeneous panel model, we consider the change point estimation using the OLS and FD estimators. We recommend the FD-based estimator of the change point, since the FD-based estimator of the change point is robust to stationary or nonstationary regressors and error term, no matter whether a change point is present or not. The heterogeneous panel data model and the time trend model are also discussed in this chapter.

3.7. Technical Proofs

Proof of Theorems 3.2–3.5 and Theorems 3.11–3.12 can be found in Baltagi *et al.* (2017). Proof of Theorem 3.6 can be found in Bai (1997). Proof of Theorem 3.7 can be found in Feng *et al.* (2009). Proof of Theorem 3.8 can be found in Baltagi *et al.* (2016). Proof of Theorem 3.13 can be found in Emerson and Kao (2001). Proof of Theorem 3.14 can be found in Baltagi *et al.* (2019). Proof of Theorem 3.6 can be found in Bai (1997). Proof of Theorem 3.9 can be found in Perron and Zhu (2005). Proof of Theorem 3.10 can be found in Kim (2011).

3.8. Exercises

(1) Bai (1994) considers the following time-series regression with a possible change point at k_0 in the slope parameter,

$$
y_t = \begin{cases} \mu_1 + u_t & \text{for } t = 1, \dots, k_0, \\ \mu_2 + u_t & \text{for } t = k_0 + 1, \dots, T, \end{cases}
$$

where μ_1 and μ_2 are unknown parameters. For simplicity, we assume that the error term u_t is an independent white noise process with variance σ^2. Rewrite the change point as $k_0 = [\tau_0 T]$. Our interest is to estimate the change point k_0, or equivalently, τ_0. Let

$$
\hat{\mu}_1(k) = \frac{1}{k} \sum_{t=1}^{k} y_t
$$

and

$$\hat{\mu}_2(k) = \frac{1}{T-k} \sum_{t=k+1}^{T} y_t.$$

Correspondingly, the SSR for k can be defined as

$$\text{SSR}(k) = \sum_{t=1}^{k}[y_t - \hat{\mu}_1(k)]^2 + \sum_{t=k+1}^{T}[y_t - \hat{\mu}_2(k)]^2$$

$$= \sum_{t=1}^{T}(y_t - \bar{y})^2 - TV_k^2,$$

where

$$V_k = \left[\frac{k(T-k)}{T^2}\right]^{1/2}[\hat{\mu}_2(k) - \hat{\mu}_1(k)].$$

An estimator of k can be obtained by

$$\hat{k} = \arg\min_{1\le k\le T}\text{SSR}(k) = \arg\max_{1\le k\le T}|V_k|.$$

Let $d = k/T$, $\tau = k_0/T$ and $\lambda = \mu_2 - \mu_1$. Answer the following questions from Bai (1994).

(a) Verify Eq. (10) in Bai (1994)

$$|V_k| - |V_{k_0}| \le |V_k - EV_k| + |V_{k_0} - EV_{k_0}| + |EV_k| - |EV_{k_0}|.$$

(b) Verify Eq. (13) in Bai (1994)

$$EV_k = \frac{1-\tau}{1-d}[d(1-d)]^{1/2}\lambda > 0 \quad \text{for } k \le k_0.$$

(c) Verify Eq. (14) in Bai (1994)

$$|EV_{k_0}| - |EV_k| = \lambda\frac{\tau-d}{1-d}\left[\left(\frac{\tau}{1-\tau}\right)^{1/2} + \left(\frac{d}{1-d}\right)^{1/2}\right]^{-1}.$$

(d) Verify the line above Eq. (15) in Bai (1994)

$$V_k - EV_k$$
$$= \frac{1}{\sqrt{T}}\left(\frac{k}{T}\right)^{1/2}\frac{1}{\sqrt{T-k}}\sum_{t=k+1}^{T}u_t - \frac{1}{\sqrt{T}}\left(1 - \frac{k}{T}\right)^{1/2}\frac{1}{\sqrt{k}}\sum_{t=1}^{k}u_t.$$

(2) Bai (2010) considers the following panel regression with a change point at k_0 in the shift parameter:

$$y_{it} = \begin{cases} \mu_{i1} + u_{it} & \text{for } t = 1, \ldots, k_0, \\ \mu_{i2} + u_{it} & \text{for } t = k_0 + 1, \ldots, T, \end{cases}$$

where y_{it} is the dependent variable. For simplicity, we assume that the error term u_{it} is an independent white noise process with variance σ^2. Rewrite the change point as $k_0 = [\tau_0 T]$, where τ_0 is the fraction of the change point which is within the range 0 and 1. As discussed in Bai (2010), "Theoretically, common break is a more restrictive assumption than the random breaks of Joseph and Wolfson (1993). Nevertheless, when break points are indeed common, as a result of common shocks or policy shift affecting every individual, imposing the constraint gives a more precise estimation. Computationally, the common break model is much simpler. Furthermore, even if each series has its own break point, the common break method can be considered as estimating the mean of the random break points, which can be useful." Our interest is to estimate the change point k_0, or equivalently, τ_0. Let $\hat{\mu}_{i1}(k) = \frac{1}{k}\sum_{t=1}^{k} y_{it}$ and $\hat{\mu}_{i2}(k) = \frac{1}{T-k}\sum_{t=k+1}^{T} y_{it}$. Correspondingly, the SSR for the ith equation for k can be defined as

$$\text{SSR}_i(k) = \sum_{t=1}^{k}[y_{it} - \hat{\mu}_{i1}(k)]^2 + \sum_{t=k+1}^{T}[y_{it} - \hat{\mu}_{i2}(k)]^2$$

and hence the total SSR across all equations is defined as

$$\text{SSR}(k) = \sum_{i=1}^{n} \text{SSR}_i(k).$$

An estimator of k can be obtained by minimizing $\text{SSR}(k)$, i.e.,

$$\hat{k} = \arg\min_{1 \leq k \leq T} \text{SSR}(k).$$

(a) Assumption 2 in Bai (2010) is

$$\lim_{n \to \infty} n^{-1/2} \sum_{i=1}^{n} (\mu_{i2} - \mu_{i1})^2 = \infty.$$

Bai (2010) points out that "the condition does not require every series to have a break". Explain the reason why it is true.

(b) In the univariate case, i.e., $n = 1$, assuming $\mu_2 - \mu_1$ is fixed, Eq. (6) in Bai (2010) shows the limiting distribution of $\hat{k}$ as

$$\hat{k} - k_0 \overset{d}{\to} \arg\max_l V(l),$$

where $V(0) = 0$,

$$V(l) = (\mu_2 - \mu_1)^2 |l| - 2(\mu_2 - \mu_1) \sum_{s=-l+1}^{0} u_s$$

for $l = -1, -2, \ldots$, and

$$V(l) = (\mu_2 - \mu_1)^2 l - 2(\mu_2 - \mu_1) \sum_{s=1}^{l} u_s$$

for $l = 1, 2, \ldots$. Verify this result.

(c) In the univariate case, i.e., $n = 1$, assuming $v_T = \mu_2 - \mu_1 \to 0$ and $T v_T^2 \to \infty$, Eq. (7) in Bai (2010) shows the limiting distribution of $\hat{k}$ as

$$(v_T^2 / \sigma^2)(\hat{k} - k_0) \overset{d}{\to} \arg\min_r [-|r| + 2W(r)],$$

where σ^2 is the long-run variance of u_t, that is, the spectral density at frequency zero multiplied by 2π; $W(r)$ is a two-sided Brownian motion on the real line. Explain the statement "the long-run variance is the spectral density at frequency zero multiplied by 2π."

(d) Bai (2010) states on p. 82 that "we assume

$$\lim_{n\to\infty} \sum_{i=1}^{n} (\mu_{i2} - \mu_{i1})^2 = \lambda > 0$$

for some $\lambda < \infty$. Roughly speaking, this implies that the magnitude of break in each equation is small." Explain.

(e) Assuming $\mu_{i2} - \mu_{i1} = n^{-1/2} \Delta_i$ with

$$\lim_{n\to\infty} \sum_{i=1}^{n} (\mu_{i2} - \mu_{i1})^2 = \lim_{n\to\infty} n^{-1} \sum_{i=1}^{n} \Delta_i^2 = \lambda,$$

Lemma 4.1 in Bai (2010) shows that $\hat{k} - k_0 = O_p(1)$. In particular, Bai (2010) states that "The $O_p(1)$ in the lemma is genuine in the sense that it is not $o_p(1)$. Thus, due to small magnitude of breaks, $\hat{k}$ does not collapse to k_0, leading to a nondegenerate distribution." Explain.

(3) The following questions are based on Bai (1997). In the following model:

$$Y = X\beta + Z_0\delta + U$$

for any possible change point k, we define matrices, the OLS estimators of slope parameters, which depend on k, are

$$\begin{pmatrix} \hat{\beta}_k \\ \hat{\delta}_k \end{pmatrix} = \begin{bmatrix} X'X & X'Z_k \\ Z_k'X & Z_k'Z_k \end{bmatrix}^{-1} \begin{bmatrix} X'y \\ Z_k'y \end{bmatrix}.$$

Hence,

$$\text{SSR}(k) = (Y - X\hat{\beta}_k - Z_k\hat{\delta}_k)'(Y - X\hat{\beta}_k - Z_k\hat{\delta}_k).$$

Plug in the estimate $\hat{k}$, we obtain the estimates of slope parameters $(\hat{\beta}_{\hat{k}}', \hat{\delta}_{\hat{k}}')'$. Let SSR be the sum of squared residuals for the case of no break, i.e., $k_0 = T$. Define

$$V(k) = \text{SSR} - \text{SSR}(k) = \hat{\delta}_k'(Z_k M Z_k)\hat{\delta}_k$$

with $M = I - X(X'X)^{-1}X'$, since SSR does not depend on k.

(a) For the structure change model in Eq. (3.5), Eq. (5) in Bai (1997) shows that $\hat{k}$ can be expressed as

$$\hat{k} = \arg\max_{1 \le k \le T} \hat{\delta}_k'(Z_k M Z_k)\hat{\delta}_k, \qquad (3.20)$$

where $Z_k = (0, \dots, 0, z_{k+1}', \dots, z_T')'$ and $\hat{\delta}_k$ is the OLS estimator of δ for a possible change point k. Consider a pure structural change case where $z_t = x_t$, the model in Eq. (3.5) reduces to

$$y_t = \begin{cases} x_t'\beta_1 + u_t, & t = 1, \dots, k_0, \\ x_t'\beta_2 + u_t, & t = k_0 + 1, \dots, T. \end{cases}$$

Verify that the expression of $\hat{k}$ in Eq. (3.20) correspondingly reduced to

$$\hat{k} = \arg\max_k \{(\hat{\beta}_1 - \hat{\beta}_2)'[(X_1'X_1)^{-1} + (X_2'X_2)^{-1}]^{-1}(\hat{\beta}_1 - \hat{\beta}_2)\}$$

where $\hat{\beta}_1$ and $\hat{\beta}_2$ are the OLS estimators of β_1 and β_2 for a possible change point k. X_1 and X_2 are matrix notations of x_t' before and after the change point k, respectively.

(b) Bai (1997) states

$$\hat{\delta}_k = (Z_2'MZ_2)^{-1}(Z_2'MZ_0)\delta_T + (Z_2'MZ_2)^{-1}Z_2'M\varepsilon$$

on p. 560. Verify this result.

(c) For $H(k)$ that is defined in Eq. (3.6), in order to verify

$$\frac{1}{T} \sup_k |H_T(k)| = O_p\left(\frac{1}{\sqrt{T}} \log T\right) = o_p(1),$$

we first need to show the following:

(i) For each fixed k, show that

$$H_T(k) = O_p(\sqrt{T}).$$

(ii) From (i) we know that $\frac{1}{T} H_T(k) \xrightarrow{p} 0$ for a fixed k. However, this is not enough. Prove that the maximum value of $H_T(k)$ taken over all possible k grows at a slower rate than T.

(iii) Divided by T, the first term of the RHS of $H_T(k)$ can be written as

$$2\delta' \frac{1}{\sqrt{T}} \frac{1}{\sqrt{T}} (Z_0' M Z_2)(Z_2' M Z_2)^{-1/2} (Z_2' M Z_2)^{-1/2} Z_2 M \varepsilon.$$

Show that

$$\sup_k \|(Z_2' M Z_2)^{-1/2} Z_2 M \varepsilon\| = O_p(\sqrt{\log T}).$$

(iv) Show that

$$\sup_k \frac{1}{\sqrt{T}} (Z_0' M Z_2)(Z_2' M Z_2)^{-1/2} = O_p(1).$$

(v) Show that the second term of $H_T(k)$ is

$$\delta' Z_0' M \varepsilon = O_p(\sqrt{T}).$$

(vi) Show that the third term of $H_T(k)$ is

$$\sup_k \varepsilon' M Z_2 (Z_2' M Z_2)^{-1} Z_2' M \varepsilon = O_p(\log T).$$

(vii) Show the last term of $H_T(k)$ is $O_p(1)$.

(viii) Show that

$$\frac{1}{T} \sup_k |H_T(k)| = O_p\left(\frac{1}{\sqrt{T}} \log T\right).$$

(4) As shown in Theorem 3.12, $\hat{k}_{\text{OLS}}$ has faster speed so that $\hat{\gamma}_{\hat{k}_{\text{OLS}}}$ and $\hat{\delta}_{\hat{k}_{\text{OLS}}}$ have the same distributions as $\hat{\gamma}_{k_0}$ and $\hat{\delta}_{k_0}$. Theorem 3 in Baltagi *et al.* (2017) shows that the asymptotic distributions of $\hat{\gamma}_{\hat{k}_{\text{OLS}}}$ and $\hat{\delta}_{\hat{k}_{\text{OLS}}}$ can be established as if the change points were known. To be specific, let us define $D_{nT} = \begin{pmatrix} nT & 0 \\ 0 & nT^2 \end{pmatrix}$. With the estimator $\hat{k}$, the asymptotic of $\hat{\gamma}_{\hat{k}_{\text{OLS}}} = \hat{\gamma}(\hat{k}_{\text{OLS}})$ and $\hat{\delta}_{\hat{k}_{\text{OLS}}} = \hat{\delta}(\hat{k}_{\text{OLS}})$ can be established. Assume $\beta_2 - \beta_1 \neq 0$. As $(n, T) \to \infty$, prove the following results:

(a) When $|\rho| < 1$ and $|\lambda| < 1$,

$$
\begin{pmatrix} \sqrt{nT}(\hat{\gamma}_{\hat{k}_{\mathrm{OLS}}} - \gamma) \\ \sqrt{nT}(\hat{\delta}_{\hat{k}_{\mathrm{OLS}}} - \delta) \end{pmatrix}
$$

$$
\xrightarrow{d} N\left(0, \sigma_e^2 \begin{pmatrix} \frac{1}{\tau_0} & 0 & -\frac{1}{\tau_0} & 0 \\ 0 & \frac{(1-\lambda^2)^2}{\tau_0(1-\lambda\rho)^2\sigma_\varepsilon^2} & 0 & -\frac{(1-\lambda^2)^2}{\tau_0(1-\lambda\rho)^2\sigma_\varepsilon^2} \\ -\frac{1}{\tau_0} & 0 & \frac{1}{\tau_0(1-\tau_0)} & 0 \\ 0 & -\frac{(1-\lambda^2)^2}{\tau_0(1-\lambda\rho)^2\sigma_\varepsilon^2} & 0 & \frac{(1-\lambda^2)^2}{\tau_0(1-\tau_0)(1-\lambda\rho)^2\sigma_\varepsilon^2} \end{pmatrix}\right).
$$

(b) When $\rho = 1$ and $|\lambda| < 1$,

$$
\begin{pmatrix} T^{-1}D_{nT}^{1/2}(\hat{\gamma}_{\hat{k}_{\mathrm{OLS}}} - \gamma) \\ T^{-1}D_{nT}^{1/2}(\hat{\delta}_{\hat{k}_{\mathrm{OLS}}} - \delta) \end{pmatrix}
$$

$$
\xrightarrow{d} N\left(0, \sigma_e^2 \begin{pmatrix} \frac{1}{3}\tau_0 & 0 & \frac{1}{6}\tau_0 & 0 \\ 0 & \frac{(\lambda+1)^2}{2\sigma_\varepsilon^2} & 0 & -\frac{(\lambda+1)^2}{2\sigma_\varepsilon^2} \\ \frac{1}{6}\tau_0 & 0 & \frac{1}{3} & 0 \\ 0 & -\frac{(\lambda+1)^2}{2\sigma_\varepsilon^2} & 0 & \frac{(\lambda+1)^2}{\sigma_\varepsilon^2(1-\tau_0)} \end{pmatrix}\right).
$$

(c) When $|\rho| < 1$ and $\lambda = 1$,

$$
\begin{pmatrix} D_{nT}^{1/2}(\hat{\gamma}_{\hat{k}_{\mathrm{OLS}}} - \gamma) \\ D_{nT}^{1/2}(\hat{\delta}_{\hat{k}_{\mathrm{OLS}}} - \delta) \end{pmatrix}
$$

$$
\xrightarrow{d} N\left(0, \sigma_e^2 \begin{pmatrix} \frac{1}{\tau_0} & 0 & -\frac{1}{\tau_0} & 0 \\ 0 & \frac{2}{\tau_0^2(1-\rho)^2\sigma_\varepsilon^4} & 0 & -\frac{2}{\tau_0^2(1-\rho)^2\sigma_\varepsilon^4} \\ -\frac{1}{\tau_0} & 0 & \frac{1}{\tau_0(1-\tau_0)} & 0 \\ 0 & -\frac{2}{\tau_0^2(1-\rho)^2\sigma_\varepsilon^4} & 0 & \frac{2}{\tau_0^2(1-\tau_0^2)(1-\rho)^2\sigma_\varepsilon^4} \end{pmatrix}\right).
$$

(d) When $\lambda = \rho = 1$,

$$
\begin{pmatrix} T^{-1}D_{nT}^{1/2}(\hat{\gamma}_{\hat{k}_{\mathrm{OLS}}} - \gamma) \\ T^{-1}D_{nT}^{1/2}(\hat{\delta}_{\hat{k}_{\mathrm{OLS}}} - \delta) \end{pmatrix}
$$

$$
\xrightarrow{d} N\left(0, \sigma_e^2 \begin{pmatrix} \frac{1}{3}\tau_0 & 0 & \frac{1}{6}\tau_0 & 0 \\ 0 & \frac{2}{3\sigma_\varepsilon^4} & 0 & -\frac{2(1-\tau_0)}{3(1+\tau_0)\sigma_\varepsilon^4} \\ \frac{1}{6}\tau_0 & 0 & \frac{1}{3} & 0 \\ 0 & -\frac{2(1-\tau_0)}{3(1+\tau_0)\sigma_\varepsilon^4} & 0 & \frac{4}{3(1+\tau_0)^2\sigma_\varepsilon^4} \end{pmatrix}\right).
$$

(5) Similar to Question 4, Baltagi *et al.* (2017) show that the FD-based estimator $\hat{k}_{\mathrm{FD}}$ is always n-consistent, no matter whether the regressor and error term are stationary or nonstationary. Since $\hat{k}_{\mathrm{FD}}$ has a faster

convergence speed than $\sqrt{n}$ consistency of the slope parameters, the asymptotic of $\tilde{\gamma}_{2,\hat{k}_{\text{FD}}} = \tilde{\gamma}_2(\hat{k}_{\text{FD}})$ and $\tilde{\delta}_{2,\hat{k}_{\text{FD}}} = \tilde{\delta}_2(\hat{k}_{\text{FD}})$ can be established as if the change points were known. Theorem 9 in Baltagi *et al.* (2017) shows the following asymptotic results: Assume $\beta_2 - \beta_1 \neq 0$. As $(n, T) \to \infty$, we have

$$\sqrt{nT} \begin{pmatrix} \tilde{\gamma}_{2,\hat{k}_{\text{FD}}} - \gamma_2 \\ \tilde{\delta}_{2,\hat{k}_{\text{FD}}} - \delta_2 \end{pmatrix} \xrightarrow{d} N\left(0, \frac{\omega}{\psi^2}\begin{pmatrix} 1 & 1 - \tau_0 \\ 1 - \tau_0 & 1 - \tau_0 \end{pmatrix}\right),$$

where

$$\psi = \left[1 + (\lambda - 1)^2 \sum_{j=0}^{\infty} \lambda^{2j}\right]\sigma_\varepsilon^2$$

and

$$\omega = \left\{\left[1 + (\lambda - 1)(\rho - 1)\sum_{j=0}^{\infty}(\rho\lambda)^j\right]^2 \right.$$
$$\left. + \left[\sum_{j=0}^{\infty}(\rho\lambda)^j\right]^2 \sum_{r=1}^{\infty}[(\rho - 1)^2\rho^{2(r-1)} + (\lambda - 1)^2\lambda^{2(r-1)}]\right\}\sigma_\varepsilon^2\sigma_e^2.$$

It implies that the convergence speed of $\tilde{\gamma}_{2\hat{k}_{\text{FD}}}$ and $\tilde{\delta}_{2\hat{k}_{\text{FD}}}$ is always $\sqrt{nT}$, whether the regressor and the error term are stationary or non-stationary. Prove the results above.

(6) Emerson and Kao (2001) also suggest another estimator to test $H_0 : \gamma = 0$ for the model in Eq. (3.13). Consider the estimator to be the recursive OLS

$$\widehat{\beta}_k = \frac{\sum_{i=1}^{n}[\sum_{t=1}^{k}(t - \bar{t}_k)y_{it}]}{\sum_{i=1}^{n}\sum_{t=1}^{k}(t - \bar{t}_k)^2},$$

where $\bar{t}_k = \frac{1}{k}\sum_{t=1}^{k}t$. Following Ploberger, Krämer, and Kontrus (1989) and Chu and White (1992), the null hypothesis is rejected if $\widehat{\beta}_k$ fluctuate too much, i.e., the null hypothesis is rejected if $\max i = 1, \ldots, k|\widehat{\beta}_k - \widehat{\beta}_T|$ is too large. Prove the following result in Emerson and Kao (2001): As $(n, T) \to \infty$,

(a) if $|\rho| < 1$,

$$\sqrt{NT^3}\frac{1 - \rho}{6\sigma_\varepsilon}\left(\frac{k}{T}\right)^3(\widehat{\beta}_k - \widehat{\beta}_T) \xrightarrow{d} P(r) - r^3 P(1);$$

(b) if $\rho = 1$,

$$\sqrt{NT} \frac{1}{6\sigma_\varepsilon} \left(\frac{k}{T}\right)^3 (\widehat{\beta}_k - \widehat{\beta}_T) \overset{d}{\to} Q(r) - r^3 Q(1)$$

where $P(r)$ and $Q(r)$ are given in Theorem 3.13.

(7) Horváth and Husková (2012) consider

$$X_{it} = \mu_i + \delta_i I\{t > t_0\} + e_{it}, \tag{3.21}$$

where $E(e_{it}) = 0$ for all i and t. According to the (3.21), μ_i changes to $\mu_i + \delta_i$ in case of panel i at time t_0. The parameter t_0, the time of change, is unknown. Both T and n are assumed to be large. Here we wish to test that the location parameter μ_i will not change during the observation period, i.e., $H_0 : \delta_i = 0$ for all $1 \le i \le n$. Define

$$V_{nT}(r) = \frac{1}{\sqrt{n}} \sum_{i=1}^{n} \left\{ \frac{1}{\sigma_i^2} Z_{T,i}^2(r) - \frac{[Tr](T - [Tr])}{T^2} \right\}$$

for $0 \le r \le 1$, where $[\cdot]$ denotes the integer part,

$$Z_{T,i}(r) = \frac{1}{\sqrt{T}} \left(S_{T,i}(r) - \frac{[Tr]}{T} S_{T,i}(1) \right)$$

with

$$S_{T,i}(r) = \sum_{i=1}^{[Tr]} X_{it}$$

and σ_i^2 is a suitably chosen standardization constant. Show that under the null,

$$V_{nT}(r) \overset{d}{\to} G(r),$$

where $G(r)$ is a Gaussian process with

$$E[G(r)] = 0$$

and

$$E[G(r)G(s)] = 2r^2(1 - s)^2$$

with $0 \le r \le s \le 1$. Spell out the conditions you need.

(8) Horváth *et al.* (2017) consider the following panel data model:
$$X_{it} = \mu_i + \delta_i I\{t > t_0\} + \lambda_i f_t + e_{it},$$
where $E(e_{it}) = 0$ for all i and t. f_t denotes the common factor with loadings λ_i and δ_i denotes the change in the mean that occurs at the common and unknown change point t_0. Our estimator for t_0 is defined of the maximum of the sum of the CUSUM
$$\widehat{t}_{nT} = \arg\max_{1<t<T} \sum_{i=1}^{n} (S_i(t) - \frac{t}{T} S_i(T))^2,$$
where
$$S_i(t) = \sum_{s=1}^{t} X_{is}.$$
Define $\Delta_{nT} = \sum_{i=1}^{n} \delta_i^2$, $\Gamma_{nT} = \sum_{i=1}^{n} \lambda_i^2$ and $\Sigma_{nT} = \sum_{i=1}^{n} \delta_i \lambda_i$. Suppose $\frac{T\Delta_{nT}}{n} \to \infty$ and $\frac{\Gamma_{nT}}{\sqrt{T\Delta_{nT}}} \to 0$. Show that
$$P(\widehat{t}_{nT} = t_0) \to 1$$
as $(n, T) \to \infty$ and spell out the conditions you need.

(9) Aue and Horváth (2013) consider the following signal-plus-noise model:
$$y_t = \mu_t + \varepsilon_t,$$
where μ_t is the signal and ε_t is the noise with $E(\varepsilon_t) = 0$ and $E(\varepsilon_t^2) = \sigma^2$. We are interested in testing the null hypothesis of constant means $H_0 : \mu_1 = \cdots = \mu_T = \mu$. Define the CUSUM
$$Z_T(r) = \frac{1}{\sqrt{T}} \left(\sum_{t=1}^{[Tr]} y_t - \frac{[Tr]}{T} \sum_{t=1}^{T} y_t \right)$$
for $r \in [0, 1]$. Note that under the null,
$$Z_T(r) = \frac{1}{\sqrt{T}} \left(\sum_{t=1}^{[Tr]} \varepsilon_t - \frac{[Tr]}{T} \sum_{t=1}^{T} \varepsilon_t \right)$$
so that the value of CUSUM is then independent of the unknown but common mean μ. Assume
$$S_T(r) = \frac{1}{\sqrt{T}} \sum_{t=1}^{[Tr]} \varepsilon_t \xrightarrow{d} \sigma W(r),$$
where $W(r)$ is a standard Brownian motion. Show that
$$Z_T(r) \xrightarrow{d} \sigma B(r),$$
where
$$B(r) = W(r) - rW(1)$$
is a standard Brownian bridge.

(10) Chan, Horváth, and Husková (2013) consider a panel change point model

$$x_{it} = \mu_i + \delta_i 1\{t > k_0\} + \varepsilon_{it},$$

where $E(\varepsilon_{it}) = 0$ for all i and t and $E(\varepsilon_{it}^2) = \sigma_i^2$. We wish to test $H_0 : \delta_i = 0$ for all i. Define

$$H_{nT}(k) = \frac{1}{\sqrt{n}} \frac{T}{k(T-k)} \sum_{i=1}^{n} \left[\frac{1}{\sigma_i^2} \left(S_i(k) - \frac{k}{T} S_i(T) \right)^2 - \frac{k(T-k)}{T} \right]$$

with

$$S_i(k) = \sum_{t=1}^{k} \varepsilon_{it}.$$

Show that under the null,

$$\lim_{\min(n,T) \to \infty} P \left\{ \frac{A(\log T^2)}{\sqrt{2}} \max_{1 \le k < T} |H_{nT}(k)| \le t + D(\log T^2) \right\}$$
$$= \exp(-2e^{-t})$$

with

$$A(x) = \sqrt{2 \log x}$$

and

$$D(x) = 2 \log x + \frac{1}{2} \log \log x - \frac{1}{2} \log \pi.$$

(11) Xu (2015) considers a varying coefficient regression model

$$y_t = x_t' \beta_t + e_t,$$

where the error is $e_t = s_t v_t$. The process v_t is stationary and mixing with $E(v_t) = 0$, $E(v_t^2) = \gamma_0$, autocovariance γ_l $(l = 1, 2, \ldots)$ and the finite long-run variance

$$\lambda^2 = \gamma_0 + 2 \sum_{l=1}^{\infty} \gamma_l < \infty.$$

The regressor x_t and the parameter β_t are $k \times 1$. The first element of x_t is one. Assume $\beta_t = \beta(\frac{t}{T})$ and $s_t = s(\frac{t}{T})$. We are interested in testing the null hypothesis of constant means

$$H_0 : \beta_1 = \cdots = \beta_T = \beta.$$

Let

$$\widehat{e}_t = y_t - x_t'\widehat{\beta}$$

be the OLS residual under the null. Define the CUSUM statistic

$$Q = \max_{1 \le k \le T} Q(k),$$

where

$$Q(k) = \frac{|\frac{1}{\sqrt{T}} \sum_{t=1}^{k} \widehat{e}_t|}{\widehat{\omega}}$$

and

$$\widehat{\omega}^2 = \widehat{\phi}_0 + 2 \sum_{l=1}^{T-1} h\left(\frac{l}{k}\right) \widehat{\phi}_l$$

with

$$\widehat{\phi}_l = \frac{1}{T} \sum_{t=l+1}^{T} \widehat{e}_t \widehat{e}_{t-l}.$$

Here h is the kernel function and m is the truncation parameter. Show that under the null,

$$Q \xrightarrow{d} \sup_{0 \le r \le 1} |W(\zeta(r) - rW(1))|,$$

where

$$\zeta(r) = \frac{\int_0^r s^2}{\int_0^1 s^2}$$

and $W(\cdot)$ is the standard Brownian motion. Spell out the conditions you need.

(12) Kim, Oka, Estrada and Perron (2019) consider the following n-variate system:

$$y_{it} = \mu_i + \beta_i t + \sum_{j=1}^{m_i} \delta_{ij} b_t(k_{ij}^0) + u_{it},$$

where

$$b_t(k_{ij}^0) = 1(t \ge k_{ij}^0)(t - k_{ij}^0)$$

and k_{ij}^0 is the jth break date for the change (with magnitudes δ_{ij}) in the trend of the ith variable. The vector of break dates for ith variable is $k_i^0 = (k_{i1}^0, \ldots, k_{im_i}^0)'$ and k^0 is the vector of break dates for the entire system, $k^0 = (k_1^{0'}, \ldots, k_n^{0'})$. We let $m = \sum_{i=1}^n m_i$ denote the total number of breaks in the system. Hence, k^0 is an $m \times 1$ vector. For the ith variable, we have in matrix form

$$y_i = X(k_i^0)\theta_i + u_i,$$

where $X(k_i^0) = [c, \tau, b(k_{i1}^0), \ldots, b(k_{im_i}^0)]$ and $\theta = (\mu_i, \beta_i, \delta_{i1}, \ldots, \delta_{im_i})'$ with $c = (1, \ldots, 1)'$, $\tau = (1, \ldots, T)'$ and $b(k_{ij}^0) = (b_1(k_{ij}^0), \ldots, b_T(k_{ij}^0))'$. The entire system in matrix notation is

$$y = X^0\theta + u,$$

where $y = (y_1, \ldots, y_n)'$, $X^0 = \mathrm{diag}(X(k_1^0), \ldots, X(k_n^0))$, $\theta = (\theta_1', \ldots, \theta_n')$ and $u = (u_1', \ldots, u_n')'$. We are interested in the case where the number of breaks for each variable is known but the break dates are unknown. For a vector of generic break dates, we will have the notation without a "0" superscript. For a generic break date vector k and the corresponding regressor matrix X, the log-likelihood is

$$l(k, \theta, \Sigma) = -\frac{nT}{2}\log 2\pi - \frac{T}{2}\log|\Sigma| - \frac{1}{2}(y - X\theta)'(\Sigma^{-1} \otimes I_T)(y - X\theta).$$

Let $\widehat{\theta} = (\widehat{\theta}_1', \ldots, \widehat{\theta}_n')'$ and $\widehat{\Sigma}$ be the MLE for θ and Σ, which jointly solve

$$\widehat{\theta} = [X'(\widehat{\Sigma}^{-1}(k) \otimes I_T)X]^{-1}[X'(\widehat{\Sigma}^{-1}(k) \otimes I_T)y]$$

and

$$\widehat{\Sigma}(k) = \frac{1}{T}\widehat{U}_k'\widehat{U}_k$$

where

$$\widehat{U}_k = [y_1 - X(k_1)\widehat{\theta}_1, \ldots, y_n - X(k_n)\widehat{\theta}_n].$$

Thus, the maximized the log-likelihood is

$$l(k) = -\frac{nT}{2}(\log 2\pi + 1) - \frac{T}{2}\log|\widehat{\Sigma}(k)|.$$

Define $\lambda_{ij} = \frac{k_{ij}}{T}$, $\lambda_i = \frac{k_i}{T}$ and $\lambda = \frac{k}{T}$. Similarly, denote λ_{ij}^0, λ_i^0 and λ^0 as the true break fractions. We consider the null hypothesis $H_0 : R\lambda^0 = r$ and $H_a : R\lambda^0 \neq r$. Define the LR test statistic

$$LR = -2 \left[\max_{\lambda : R\lambda = r} l(\lambda) - \max_\lambda l(\lambda) \right].$$

Show that under the null hypothesis as $T \to \infty$, we have $LR \to \chi_q^2$, where $q = \text{rank}(R)$. Furthermore, what happens if $(n, T) \to \infty$?

(13) Seo and Shin (2016) consider dynamic panel threshold regression model

$$y_{it} = (1, x_{it}')\phi_1 1(q_{it} \leq \gamma) + (1, x_{it}')\phi_2 1(q_{it} > \gamma) + \varepsilon_{it},$$

where y_{it} is a scalar, x_{it} is a $k \times 1$ vector, and q_{it} is the transition variable, and γ is the threshold parameter. Let $\varepsilon_{it} = \alpha_i + v_{it}$. In FD form

$$\triangle y_{it} = \beta' \triangle x_{it} + \delta' X_{it}' 1_{it}(\gamma) + \triangle \varepsilon_{it},$$

where $\triangle$ is the FD operator, $\beta = (\phi_{12}, \ldots, \phi_{1,k_1+1})'$ is a $k_1 \times 1$ vector, $\delta = \phi_2 - \phi_1$ is a $(k_1 + 1) \times 1$ vector,

$$X_{it} = \begin{pmatrix} (1, x_{it}') \\ (1, x_{i,t-1}') \end{pmatrix}$$

is a $2 \times (k_1 + 1)$ matrix and

$$1_{it}(\gamma) = \begin{pmatrix} 1\{q_{it} > \gamma\} \\ -1\{q_{i,t-1} > \gamma\} \end{pmatrix}$$

is a 2×1 vector. Let $\theta = (\beta', \delta', \gamma)'$ and $\delta = \delta_n = \delta_0 n^{-\delta}$ with $0 \leq \alpha < \frac{1}{2}$. Choose $l \times 1$ vector of instrument variables $(z_{it_0}', \ldots, z_{iT}')$ for $2 < t_0 \leq T$ with $l \geq k$ such that $E(\triangle \varepsilon_{it} | z_{it}) = 0$ for $t = t_0, \ldots, T$. Let

$$\bar{g}_n = \frac{1}{n} \sum_{i=1}^n g_i(\theta),$$

where

$$g_i(\theta) = \begin{pmatrix} z_{it_0}(\triangle y_{i0} - \beta' \triangle x_{i0} - \delta' X_{i0}' 1_{i0}(\gamma)) \\ \vdots \\ z_{iT}(\triangle y_{iT} - \beta' \triangle x_{iT} - \delta' X_{iT}' 1_{iT}(\gamma)) \end{pmatrix}.$$

Assume $E(g_i(\theta)) = 0$ if and only if $\theta = \theta_0$. Let

$$g_i = g_i(\theta_0) = (z_{it_0}' \triangle \varepsilon_{it_0}, \ldots, z_{iT}' \triangle \varepsilon_{iT})'$$

and $\Omega = E(g_i g_i')$. Define $\widehat{\theta} = \arg\min_\theta \overline{J}_n(\theta)$ with

$$\overline{J}_n(\theta) = \overline{g}_n'(\theta) W_n \overline{g}_n(\theta),$$

where W_n is a positive definite matrix. Show that as $n \to \infty$,

$$\left(\sqrt{n} \begin{pmatrix} \widehat{\beta} - \beta_0 \\ \widehat{\delta} - \delta_0 \end{pmatrix} \atop n^{\frac{1}{2}-\alpha}(\widehat{\gamma} - \gamma_0) \right) \xrightarrow{d} N(0, (G'\Omega^{-1}G)^{-1})$$

for a full column rank G.

Chapter 4

Weak Instruments
in Panel Data Models

The issues of weak IV have attracted considerable attention; see Stock,
Wright, and Yogo (2002) for a survey. This chapter is based on Baltagi, Kao,
and Liu (2012). It is known that when IVs are weak, the 2SLS estimator
is inconsistent, as we will explain in Sec. 4.1. However, in the panel data
model with both large n and T, we show that the 2SLS is consistent. Hence
the large panel model with weak IV is identifiable.

In Sec. 4.1, we explain the findings of Staiger and Stock (1997) and
Baltagi *et al.* (2012). In Sec. 4.2, we consider a general panel model with
individual fixed effects. The asymptotics of the k-class estimator, Wald test
under weak identification, and testing for weak IV are discussed. Section
4.3 concludes the chapter.

4.1.   Weak IV Problem

4.1.1.   *Weak IV in cross-sectional data*

Let us illustrate the issues of the weak IV using the following simple regression model with endogenous regressors:

$$y = Y\beta + u \qquad (4.1)$$

and

$$Y = Z\Pi + V, \qquad (4.2)$$

where y is an $n \times 1$ vector and Y is an $n \times L$ matrix of endogenous variables,
Z is an $n \times K_2$ matrix of K_2 IVs, and β and Π are unknown parameters.

The error terms u and V are of dimensions $n \times 1$ and $n \times L$, respectively. Let u_i and V_i be the ith element of u and V, respectively. $(u_i, V_i')'$ are assumed to be i.i.d. $N(0, \Sigma)$, with the elements of Σ denoted by σ_{uu}, Σ_{Vu}, and Σ_{VV}. It is assumed throughout that $EZ_i(u_i, V_i') = 0$ for all i. The 2SLS estimator is

$$\widehat{\beta}_{2\text{SLS}} = \frac{Y'P_Z y}{Y'P_Z Y}$$

and hence

$$\widehat{\beta}_{2\text{SLS}} - \beta = \frac{Y'P_Z u}{Y'P_Z Y}.$$

Under regularity conditions, it is easy to show that

$$\frac{1}{n}Z'Z \xrightarrow{p} \Phi_{ZZ},$$

$$\frac{1}{\sqrt{n}}Z'u \xrightarrow{d} \Psi_{Zu},$$

and

$$\frac{1}{\sqrt{n}}Z'V \xrightarrow{d} \Psi_{ZV}$$

as $n \to \infty$. Therefore, if Π is a constant matrix, we have

$$\frac{1}{n}Z'Y = \frac{1}{n}Z'(Z\Pi + V) = \frac{1}{n}Z'Z\Pi + \frac{1}{\sqrt{n}}\left(\frac{1}{\sqrt{n}}Z'V\right) \xrightarrow{p} \Phi_{ZZ}\Pi$$

and hence

$$\sqrt{n}(\widehat{\beta}_{2\text{SLS}} - \beta) = \frac{\left(\frac{1}{n}Y'Z\right)\left(\frac{1}{n}Z'Z\right)^{-1}\left(\frac{1}{\sqrt{n}}Z'u\right)}{\left(\frac{1}{n}Y'Z\right)\left(\frac{1}{n}Z'Z\right)^{-1}\left(\frac{1}{n}Z'Y\right)}$$

$$\xrightarrow{d} \frac{(\Phi_{ZZ}\Pi)'\Phi_{ZZ}^{-1}\Psi_{Zu}}{(\Phi_{ZZ}\Pi)'\Phi_{ZZ}^{-1}(\Phi_{ZZ}\Pi)}$$

$$\sim N(0, \sigma_{uu}(\Pi'\Phi_{ZZ}\Pi)^{-1})$$

since Ψ_{Zu} follows a normal distribution $N(0, \sigma_{uu}\Phi_{ZZ})$. This implies that $\widehat{\beta}_{2\text{SLS}}$ is $\sqrt{n}$-consistent and asymptotically normally distributed. The strength of the IVs is measured by the concentration matrix

$$\Lambda_{Tn} = \Sigma_{VV}^{-1/2'}\Pi'Z'Z\Pi\Sigma_{VV}^{-1/2}.$$

When Π is a constant matrix, we have

$$\Lambda_n = \Sigma_{VV}^{-1/2\prime}\Pi'Z'Z\Pi\Sigma_{VV}^{-1/2} = n\left(\Sigma_{VV}^{-1/2\prime}\Pi'\frac{Z'Z}{n}\Pi\Sigma_{VV}^{-1/2}\right) = O_p(n)$$

since

$$\frac{Z'Z}{n} \xrightarrow{p} \Phi_{ZZ}.$$

However, Staiger and Stock (1997) point out that if the IV, Z, is weak, this asymptotic result does not hold. The following theorem is taken from Staiger and Stock (1997) where Π is assumed to be local to zero.

Theorem 4.1. *Let* $\Pi = \frac{C}{\sqrt{n}}$, *where* C *is a* $K_2 \times L$ *constant matrix. As* $n \to \infty$,

$$\widehat{\beta}_{2SLS} - \beta \xrightarrow{d} \frac{(\Phi_{ZZ}C + \Psi_{ZV})'\Phi_{ZZ}^{-1}\Psi_{Zu}}{(\Phi_{ZZ}C + \Psi_{ZV})'\Phi_{ZZ}^{-1}(\Phi_{ZZ}C + \Psi_{ZV})}.$$

Proof. First note that when $\Pi = \frac{C}{\sqrt{n}}$, we have

$$\frac{1}{\sqrt{n}}Z'Y = \frac{1}{\sqrt{n}}Z'(Z\Pi + V)$$

$$= \frac{1}{n}Z'ZC + \frac{1}{\sqrt{n}}Z'V \xrightarrow{d} \Phi_{ZZ}C + \Psi_{ZV}.$$

Together with

$$\frac{1}{n}Z'Z \xrightarrow{p} \Phi_{ZZ}$$

and

$$\frac{1}{\sqrt{n}}Z'u \xrightarrow{d} \Psi_{Zu}$$

we have

$$\widehat{\beta}_{2SLS} - \beta = \frac{\left(\frac{1}{\sqrt{n}}Y'Z\right)\left(\frac{1}{n}Z'Z\right)^{-1}\left(\frac{1}{\sqrt{n}}Z'u\right)}{\left(\frac{1}{\sqrt{n}}Y'Z\right)\left(\frac{1}{n}Z'Z\right)^{-1}\left(\frac{1}{\sqrt{n}}Z'Y\right)}$$

$$\xrightarrow{d} \frac{(\Phi_{ZZ}C + \Psi_{ZV})'\Phi_{ZZ}^{-1}\Psi_{Zu}}{(\Phi_{ZZ}C + \Psi_{ZV})'\Phi_{ZZ}^{-1}(\Phi_{ZZ}C + \Psi_{ZV})}. \qquad \square$$

Theorem 4.1 implies $\widehat{\beta}_{2SLS} - \beta = O_p(1)$. With weak IV, $\widehat{\beta}_{2SLS}$ is inconsistent. In this case, the strength of the IVs is

$$\Lambda_n = \Sigma_{VV}^{-1/2\prime}\Pi'Z'Z\Pi\Sigma_{VV}^{-1/2} = \Sigma_{VV}^{-1/2\prime}C'\frac{Z'Z}{n}C\Sigma_{VV}^{-1/2} = O_p(1)$$

since $\frac{Z'Z}{n} \overset{p}{\longrightarrow} \Phi_{ZZ}$. Let us illustrate the weak IV issue using the following example in R.

Example 4.1.

```
> library(MASS)
> library(AER)
> # Generate our cross-sectional data
> # y = 1 + 0.5*x + u
> # x = 1/sqrt(n)*z + v
> # z is the instrument variable. u and v are correlated.
> set.seed(1234)
> n.obs <- 50
> E <- mvrnorm(n.obs, c(0, 0), matrix(c(1,0.5,0.5,1),2,2))
> u <- E[,1]
> v <- E[,2]
> z <- rnorm(n.obs, mean=1, sd=1)
> x <- (1/sqrt(n.obs))*z + v
> y <- 1 + 0.5*x + rnorm(n.obs)
> # Run a TSLS regression
> tsls <- ivreg(y ~ x | z)
> summary(tsls)

Call:
ivreg(formula = y ~ x | z)


Residuals:
    Min       1Q   Median       3Q      Max
-3.22141 -0.93665 -0.06598  0.74784  3.97719


Coefficients:
            Estimate Std. Error t value Pr(>|t|)
(Intercept)   0.8847     0.2406   3.677 0.000595 ***
x            -0.4970     0.7034  -0.707 0.483270
---
Signif. codes:  0 '***' 0.001 '**' 0.01 '*' 0.05 '.' 0.1 ' ' 1

Residual standard error: 1.452 on 48 degrees of freedom
Multiple R-Squared: -0.3554,    Adjusted R-squared: -0.3837
Wald test: 0.4992 on 1 and 48 DF,  p-value: 0.4833
```

```
> # Let's check the first stage F-statistic
> summary(lm(x ~ z))$fstatistic[1]

    value
5.372719
```

In the example above, the variables are created as `y = 1+0.5*x+u` and `x = 1/sqrt(n)*z + v`. Error terms `u` and `v` are created from a multivariate normal distribution with 0.5 covariance using command `mvrnorm`. Hence the endogeneity problem exists since `x` and `u` are correlated. Note that the coefficient of the instrument `z` is `1/sqrt(n)`. In this example, the sample size is set as $n = 50$, which means the coefficient of the instrument `z` is 0.2. As we can see from the 2SLS regression results above, the estimated coefficient of the slope is -0.4970, which is negative and hence of opposite sign of the true value 0.5. The first stage F-statistic is 5.3727, which is less than the "rule-of-thumb" standard of 10. This is an indication of the weak IV problem.

4.1.2. *Weak IV in panel data*

Consider the following panel model:

$$y_t = Y_t \beta + u_t \tag{4.3}$$

and

$$Y_t = Z_t \Pi + V_t, \tag{4.4}$$

where y_t is an $n \times 1$ vector and Y_t is an $n \times L$ matrix of endogenous variables, Z_t is an $n \times K_2$ matrix of K_2 IVs. Other parameters are similarly defined as in the previous subsection. The following theorem is based on Baltagi *et al.* (2012).

Theorem 4.2. *Let* $\Pi = \frac{C}{\sqrt{n}}$, *where* C *is a* $K_2 \times L$ *constant matrix. As* $(n, T) \to \infty$,

$$\sqrt{T}(\widehat{\beta}_{2\text{SLS}} - \beta) \xrightarrow{d} N(0, \sigma_{uu}(C'\Phi_{ZZ}C)^{-1}).$$

Proof. First note that when $\Pi = \frac{C}{\sqrt{n}}$, we have

$$\frac{1}{T\sqrt{n}}Z'Y = \frac{1}{T\sqrt{n}}Z'(Z\Pi + V)$$

$$= \frac{1}{Tn}Z'ZC + \frac{1}{\sqrt{T}}\left(\frac{1}{\sqrt{Tn}}Z'V\right) \xrightarrow{d} \Phi_{ZZ}C.$$

Together with the results of

$$\frac{1}{n} Z'Z \xrightarrow{p} \Phi_{ZZ}$$

and

$$\frac{1}{\sqrt{n}} Z'u \xrightarrow{d} \Psi_{Zu},$$

we have

$$\sqrt{T}(\widehat{\beta}_{2\text{SLS}} - \beta) = \frac{\left(\frac{1}{T\sqrt{n}} Y'Z\right) \left(\frac{1}{Tn} Z'Z\right)^{-1} \left(\frac{1}{\sqrt{Tn}} Z'u\right)}{\left(\frac{1}{T\sqrt{n}} Y'Z\right) \left(\frac{1}{Tn} Z'Z\right)^{-1} \left(\frac{1}{T\sqrt{n}} Z'Y\right)}$$

$$\xrightarrow{d} \frac{(\Phi_{ZZ}C)' \Phi_{ZZ}^{-1} \Psi_{Zu}}{(\Phi_{ZZ}C)' \Phi_{ZZ}^{-1} (\Phi_{ZZ}C)}$$

$$\sim N(0, \sigma_{uu}(C'\Phi_{ZZ}C)^{-1})$$

since $\Psi_{Zu} \sim N(0, \sigma_{uu}\Phi_{ZZ})$. $\qquad\square$

Theorem 4.2 implies that $\widehat{\beta}_{2\text{SLS}}$ is $\sqrt{n}$-consistent in panel data and asymptotically normally distributed. In this panel data case, the strength of the IVs is

$$\Lambda_{Tn} = \Sigma_{VV}^{-1/2'}\Pi'Z'Z\Pi\Sigma_{VV}^{-1/2} = T\Sigma_{VV}^{-1/2'}C'\frac{Z'Z}{Tn}C\Sigma_{VV}^{-1/2} = O_p(T)$$

since $\frac{Z'Z}{Tn} \xrightarrow{p} \Phi_{ZZ}$. Hence Λ_{Tn} grows as T increases. Let us illustrate weak IV problem in the panel data using the following example in R.

Example 4.2.

```
> library(MASS)
> library(AER)
> # Generate our panel data, which is created as same as
> # in the cross-sectional example, i.e.,
> # y = 1 + 0.5*x + u
> # x = 1/sqrt(n)*z + v
> # z is the instrument variable. u and v are correlated.
> # However, these variables are created over another
    T dimension.
> set.seed(1234)
> T.obs <- 50
> n.obs <- 50
> nT.obs <- n.obs * T.obs
```

```
> E.p <- mvrnorm(nT.obs, c(0, 0), matrix(c(1,0.5,0.5,1),2,2))
> u.p <- E.p[,1]
> v.p <- E.p[,2]
> z.p <- rnorm(nT.obs, mean=1, sd=1)
> x.p <- (1/sqrt(n.obs))*z.p + v.p
> y.p <- 1 + 0.5*x.p + rnorm(nT.obs)
> # Run a TSLS regression
> tsls.p <- ivreg(y.p ~ x.p | z.p)
> summary(tsls.p)

Call:
ivreg(formula = y.p ~ x.p | z.p)

Residuals:
        Min         1Q      Median         3Q         Max
 -3.7579146  -0.6409686  -0.0004398   0.6665854   3.3790492

Coefficients:
            Estimate Std. Error t value Pr(>|t|)
(Intercept)  0.97070    0.02858  33.960  < 2e-16 ***
x.p          0.76978    0.14451   5.327 1.09e-07 ***
---
Signif. codes:  0 '***' 0.001 '**' 0.01 '*' 0.05 '.' 0.1 ' ' 1

Residual standard error: 1.002 on 2498 degrees of freedom
Multiple R-Squared: 0.1768, Adjusted R-squared: 0.1765
Wald test: 28.37 on 1 and 2498 DF,  p-value: 1.089e-07

> # Let's check the first stage F-statistic
> summary(lm(x.p ~ z.p))$fstatistic[1]

   value
48.97749
```

In the example of the panel data regression above, the variables are created as same as in the previous cross-sectional example. However, these variables are created over another dimension of T. As we can see from the panel data 2SLS regression results above, the estimated coefficient of the slope is 0.7698, which turns out to be positive and is close to the true value 0.5. The first stage F-statistic is 48.9775, which is pretty large now.

By adding information over time dimension, we do not suffer from the weak IV problem anymore.

4.2. A General Framework

Consider the following general panel data regression model with endogenous regressors:

$$y_t = Y_t\beta + X_t\gamma + \mu + u_t \qquad (4.5)$$

and

$$Y_t = Z_t\Pi + X_t\Gamma + \alpha + V_t, \qquad (4.6)$$

where y_t is an $n \times 1$ vector and Y_t is an $n \times L$ matrix of endogenous variables, X_t is an $n \times K_1$ matrix of K_1 exogenous regressors, Z_t is an $n \times K_2$ matrix of K_2 IVs, and β, γ, Π, and Γ are unknown parameters. μ and α denote the individual effects which are of dimensions $n \times 1$ and $n \times L$, respectively. The error terms u_t and V_t are of dimensions $n \times 1$ and $n \times L$, respectively. These $(u_t, V_t)'$ are assumed to be i.i.d. $N(0, \Sigma)$ across $t = 1, 2, \ldots, T$, with the elements of Σ denoted by σ_{uu}, Σ_{Vu}, and Σ_{VV}. Let $Z_{it}^* = [X_{it}, Z_{it}]$, $Y_{it}^* = [y_{it}, Y_{it}]$ and let $\Phi = EZ_{it}^{*\prime}Z_{it}^*$, partitioned so that

$$EX_{it}X_{it}' = \Phi_{XX},$$

$$EX_{it}Z_{it}' = \Phi_{XZ},$$

and

$$EZ_{it}Z_{it}' = \Phi_{ZZ}.$$

It is assumed throughout that

$$EZ_{it}^* (u_{it}, V_{it}') = 0$$

for all i and t. This i.i.d. assumption for the errors can be relaxed to allow for weak dependence across the time-series and cross-sectional dimensions at the expense of more complicated notation. Equation (4.5) is the structural equation and β is the parameter of interest. The reduced-form of Eq. (4.6) relates the endogenous regressors to the IVs. In matrix form,

$$y = Y\beta + X\gamma + \mu \otimes \iota_T + u \qquad (4.7)$$

and

$$Y = Z\Pi + X\Gamma + \alpha \otimes \iota_T + V \qquad (4.8)$$

where $y = (y_1', y_2', \ldots, y_T')'$ is an $nT \times 1$ vector, and Y, X, Z, u, and V are similarly defined.

To wipe out the individual effects, we left-multiply Eqs. (4.7) and (4.8) by the within transformation

$$Q = I_n \otimes E_T$$

with

$$E_T = I_T - \bar{J}_T,$$

$\bar{J}_T = J_T/T$ where J_T is a matrix of ones of dimension T and I_n is an identity matrix of dimension n. This yields

$$\tilde{y} = \tilde{Y}\beta + \tilde{X}\gamma + \tilde{u} \qquad (4.9)$$

and

$$\tilde{Y} = \tilde{Z}\Pi + \tilde{X}\Gamma + \tilde{V}, \qquad (4.10)$$

where $\tilde{y} = Qy$, and $\tilde{Y}$, $\tilde{X}$, $\tilde{Z}$, $\tilde{u}$, and $\tilde{V}$ are similarly defined. This wipes out the possible correlation between these individual effects and the regressors. It also wipes out time-invariant variables that may cause omission bias if not included in the model. Baltagi *et al.* (2012) model weak IVs by focusing on Π being local to zero which is analogous to the local-to-unity panel unit root literature as in Moon, Perron, and Phillips (2007).

Assumption 4.1. Let $\Pi = \frac{C}{\sqrt{nT^\delta}}$, where C is a $K_2 \times L$ constant matrix and $\delta \geq 0$.

Assumption 4.1 controls the relative magnitude of the IV strength, as measured by δ. When $\delta = 1/2$, it is the standard weak IV case introduced by Staiger and Stock (1997). When $\delta = 0$, it reduces to the weak IV case in Cai, Fang, and Li (2012). Following Staiger and Stock (1997), we assume the following.

Assumption 4.2. As $(n, T) \to \infty$,

(1) $\left(\frac{1}{Tn} \sum_{t=1}^{T} u_t' u_t, \frac{1}{Tn} \sum_{t=1}^{T} V_t' u_t, \frac{1}{Tn} \sum_{t=1}^{T} V_t' V_t \right) \xrightarrow{p} (\sigma_{uu}, \Sigma_{Vu}, \Sigma_{VV})$;

(2) $\frac{1}{Tn} \sum_{t=1}^{T} (\tilde{X}_t, \tilde{Z}_t)'(\tilde{X}_t, \tilde{Z}_t) \xrightarrow{p} \Phi \equiv \begin{pmatrix} \Phi_{XX} & \Phi_{XZ} \\ \Phi_{ZX} & \Phi_{ZZ} \end{pmatrix}$;

(3)

$$\left(\frac{1}{\sqrt{Tn}} \sum_{t=1}^{T} X_t' u_t, \frac{1}{\sqrt{Tn}} \sum_{t=1}^{T} Z_t' u_t, \frac{1}{\sqrt{Tn}} \sum_{t=1}^{T} X_t' V_t, \frac{1}{\sqrt{Tn}} \sum_{t=1}^{T} Z_t' V_t \right)$$

$$\xrightarrow{d} (\Psi_{Xu}, \Psi_{Zu}, \Psi_{XV}, \Psi_{ZV}),$$

where

$$\Psi = \left(\Psi'_{Xu}, \Psi'_{Zu}, \text{vec}\,(\Psi_{XV})', \text{vec}\,(\Psi_{ZV})'\right)' \sim N\left(0, \Sigma \otimes \Phi\right).$$

Assumption 4.2 implies that

$$\left(\frac{1}{Tn}\sum_{t=1}^{T} \tilde{u}'_t \tilde{u}_t, \frac{1}{Tn}\sum_{t=1}^{T} \tilde{V}'_t \tilde{u}_t, \frac{1}{Tn}\sum_{t=1}^{T} \tilde{V}'_t \tilde{V}_t\right) \xrightarrow{p} (\sigma_{uu}, \Sigma_{Vu}, \Sigma_{VV})$$

and

$$\left(\frac{1}{\sqrt{Tn}}\sum_{t=1}^{T} \tilde{X}'_t \tilde{u}_t, \frac{1}{\sqrt{Tn}}\sum_{t=1}^{T} \tilde{Z}'_t \tilde{u}_t, \frac{1}{\sqrt{Tn}}\sum_{t=1}^{T} \tilde{X}'_t \tilde{V}_t, \frac{1}{\sqrt{Tn}}\sum_{t=1}^{T} \tilde{Z}'_t \tilde{V}_t\right)$$
$$\xrightarrow{d} (\Psi_{Xu}, \Psi_{Zu}, \Psi_{XV}, \Psi_{ZV})$$

since $\frac{1}{T}\sum_{t=1}^{T} u_t \xrightarrow{p} 0$ and $\frac{1}{T}\sum_{t=1}^{T} V_t \xrightarrow{p} 0$. Following Staiger and Stock (1997), we define

$$\lambda = \Omega^{1/2} C \Sigma_{VV}^{-1/2},$$

where

$$\Omega = \Phi_{ZZ} - \Phi_{ZX}\Phi_{XX}^{-1}\Phi_{XZ}.$$

Also define

$$z_u = \Omega^{-1/2\prime}(\Psi_{Zu} - \Phi_{ZX}\Phi_{XX}^{-1}\Psi_{Xu})\sigma_{uu}^{-1/2}$$

and

$$z_V = \Omega^{-1/2\prime}(\Psi_{ZV} - \Phi_{ZX}\Phi_{XX}^{-1}\Psi_{XV})\Sigma_{VV}^{-1/2}.$$

The random variable $[z'_u, \text{vec}(z_V)']'$ is distributed as $N(0, \bar{\Sigma}\otimes I_{K_2})$, where

$$\bar{\Sigma} = \begin{pmatrix} 1 & \rho' \\ \rho & I_L \end{pmatrix} \tag{4.11}$$

with

$$\rho = \Sigma_{VV}^{-1/2\prime}\Sigma_{Vu}\sigma_{uu}^{-1/2}$$

and I_L is an identity matrix with dimension L.

4.2.1. *Within-group k-class panel data estimators*

Let $P_{\tilde{X}} = \tilde{X}(\tilde{X}'\tilde{X})^{-1}\tilde{X}'$ be the projection matrix on the space spanned by the columns of $\tilde{X}$ and $M_{\tilde{X}} = I - P_{\tilde{X}}$. Premultiplying Eqs. (4.7) and (4.8) by $M_{\tilde{X}}$, we get

$$\tilde{y}^\perp = \tilde{Y}^\perp \beta + \tilde{u}^\perp$$

and

$$\tilde{Y}^\perp = \tilde{Z}^\perp \Pi + V^\perp,$$

where the superscript "$\perp$" denotes the residuals from the projection on $\tilde{X}$, such as $\tilde{y}^\perp = M_{\tilde{X}}\tilde{y}$, $\tilde{Z}^\perp = M_{\tilde{X}}\tilde{Z}$, and $\tilde{Y}^\perp = M_{\tilde{X}}\tilde{Y}$. The within 2SLS (W2SLS) estimator of β is given by

$$\widehat{\beta}_{\text{W2SLS}} = [\tilde{Y}^{\perp\prime}(I - M_{\tilde{Z}^\perp})\tilde{Y}^\perp]^{-1}[\tilde{Y}^{\perp\prime}(I - M_{\tilde{Z}^\perp})\tilde{y}^\perp].$$

To be more general, we can consider the within-group k-class estimator of β, which is given by

$$\widehat{\beta}(k) = [\tilde{Y}^{\perp\prime}(I - kM_{\tilde{Z}^\perp})\tilde{Y}^\perp]^{-1}[\tilde{Y}^{\perp\prime}(I - kM_{\tilde{Z}^\perp})\tilde{y}^\perp]$$

for some choice of k. Note that the W2SLS estimator is a special case of the within-group k-class estimator when $k = 1$, i.e., $\widehat{\beta}_{\text{W2SLS}} = \widehat{\beta}(1)$. The within-group k-class estimator also includes the within-group Limited Information Maximum Likelihood (LIML) and the within-group bias-adjusted 2SLS (B2SLS) described in Donald and Newey (2001) as special cases. Advantages and disadvantages of k-class estimators have been summarized in Stock *et al.* (2002). Theorem 4.3 derives the asymptotic properties of this within-group k-class panel data estimator.

Theorem 4.3. *As $(n, T) \to \infty$, we have the following conditions*:

(1) *For $0 \le \delta < \frac{1}{2}$, joint with*

$$\kappa_{Tn} = T^{1/2+\delta}n(k-1) \xrightarrow{d} \kappa,$$

we have

$$T^{1/2-\delta}(\widehat{\beta}(k) - \beta) + \theta_{Tn} \xrightarrow{d} N(0, \sigma_{uu}(\Sigma_{VV}^{1/2\prime}\lambda'\lambda\Sigma_{VV}^{1/2})^{-1}),$$

where

$$\theta_{Tn} = \left[\frac{1}{T^{1-2\delta}}\tilde{Y}^{\perp\prime}(I - kM_{\tilde{Z}^\perp})\tilde{Y}^\perp\right]^{-1}\kappa_{Tn}\Sigma_{Vu}.$$

(2) *For* $\delta = \frac{1}{2}$, *joint with*

$$\kappa_{Tn} = Tn\,(k-1) \xrightarrow{d} \kappa,$$

we have

$$\widehat{\beta}\,(k) - \beta \xrightarrow{d} \sigma_{uu}^{1/2}\Sigma_{VV}^{-1/2}\Delta_1\,(\kappa),$$

where

$$\Delta_1\,(\kappa) = [(\lambda + z_V)'\,(\lambda + z_V) - \kappa I_{Tn}]^{-1}[(\lambda + z_V)'\,z_u - \kappa\rho].$$

(3) *For* $\frac{1}{2} < \delta < \infty$, *joint with*

$$\kappa_{Tn} = Tn\,(k-1) \xrightarrow{d} \kappa,$$

we have

$$\widehat{\beta}\,(k) - \beta \xrightarrow{d} \sigma_{uu}^{1/2}\Sigma_{VV}^{-1/2}\Delta_2\,(\kappa)$$

where

$$\Delta_2\,(\kappa) = [z_V'z_V - \kappa I_{Tn}]^{-1}\,[z_V'z_u - \kappa\rho].$$

Theorem 4.3 shows that $\widehat{\beta}\,(k)$ is consistent if $0 \le \delta < \frac{1}{2}$ and inconsistent if $\frac{1}{2} \le \delta < \infty$. As shown in Baltagi *et al.* (2012), the strength of the IVs is measured by the following concentration matrix:

$$
\begin{aligned}
\Lambda_{Tn} &= \Sigma_{VV}^{-1/2\prime}\Pi'\,\tilde{Z}^{\perp\prime}\,\tilde{Z}^{\perp}\Pi\Sigma_{VV}^{-1/2}\\
&= \frac{1}{T^{2\delta-1}}\Sigma_{VV}^{-1/2\prime}C'\,\frac{\tilde{Z}^{\perp\prime}\,\tilde{Z}^{\perp}}{Tn}C\Sigma_{VV}^{-1/2}\\
&= \frac{1}{T^{2\delta-1}}\Sigma_{VV}^{-1/2\prime}C'\,\Omega C\Sigma_{VV}^{-1/2} + o_p\,(1)\\
&= O_p(T^{1-2\delta}).
\end{aligned}
$$

Note that $T^{1-2\delta}$ can be interpreted as the rate at which Λ_{Tn} grows as T increases. Clearly, for consistency of the within-group k-class estimator, one needs $\Lambda_{Tn} \to \infty$ as $T^{1-2\delta} \to \infty$ which holds if $0 \le \delta < \frac{1}{2}$.

For the W2SLS estimator $\widehat{\beta}_{\text{W2SLS}}$ with $k = 1$, it follows that

$$T^{1/2+\delta}n\,(k-1) = 0$$

and

$$Tn\,(k-1) = 0.$$

Therefore, the W2SLS estimator satisfies the conditions of κ_{Tn} for the three cases considered in Theorem 4.3. For the B2SLS estimator with

$$k = nT/(nT - K_2 + 2),$$

it follows that

$$T^{1/2+\delta} n\,(k - 1) = (K_2 - 2)\,/T^{1/2-\delta} = o_p\,(1)$$

and

$$Tn\,(k - 1) = K_2 - 2 = O_p\,(1)\,.$$

Hence, the B2SLS estimator satisfies the conditions of κ_{Tn}, too. Theorem 3 in Baltagi *et al.* (2012) discusses the results of the LIML estimator.

4.2.2. *Wald test under weak identification*

Next, we consider testing the q linear restrictions $R\beta = r$, where R is $q \times L$. The standard formula for the Wald statistic, based on the within-group k-class estimator, is

$$W(k) = [R\hat{\beta}(k) - r]'$$
$$\times \{\hat{\sigma}_{uu}\,(k)\,R[\tilde{Y}^{\perp\prime}\,(I - kM_{\tilde{Z}\perp})\,\tilde{Y}^{\perp}]^{-1}R'\}^{-1}[R\hat{\beta}\,(k) - r],$$

where

$$\hat{\sigma}_{uu}\,(k) = \widehat{\tilde{u}}\,(k)'\,\widehat{\tilde{u}}(k)/(Tn - K_1 - L)$$

and

$$\widehat{\tilde{u}}\,(k) = \tilde{y} - \tilde{Y}\hat{\beta}\,(k) - \tilde{X}\hat{\gamma}\,(k) = \tilde{y}^{\perp} - \tilde{Y}^{\perp}\hat{\beta}\,(k)\,.$$

We then have the following theorem.

Theorem 4.4. *As $(n, T) \to \infty$, we have the following conditions:*

(1) *For $0 \le \delta < \frac{1}{2}$, joint with*

$$\kappa_{Tn} = T^{1/2+\delta} n\,(k - 1) \xrightarrow{d} \kappa,$$

we have

$$W(k) \xrightarrow{d} \chi^2(q, \Lambda),$$

which is a noncentral chi-squared distribution with q degrees of freedom and noncentrality parameter

$$\Lambda = \theta' R'[\sigma_{uu} R(\Sigma_{VV}^{1/2\prime}\lambda'\lambda\Sigma_{VV}^{1/2})^{-1}R']^{-1}R\theta,$$

where

$$\theta = \kappa(\Sigma_{VV}^{1/2\prime}\lambda'\lambda\Sigma_{VV}^{1/2})^{-1}\Sigma_{Vu}\,.$$

(2) *For* $\delta = \frac{1}{2}$, *joint with* $\kappa_{Tn} = Tn \, (k - 1) \xrightarrow{d} \kappa$, *we have*

$$W \, (k) \xrightarrow{d} \Delta_1' \, (\kappa) \, \Sigma_{VV}^{-1/2} R'$$
$$\times \{ S \, (\Delta_1 \, (\kappa)) \, R \{ \Sigma_{VV}^{1/2'} [(\lambda + z_V)' \, (\lambda + z_V) - \kappa I_{Tn}] \Sigma_{VV}^{1/2} \}^{-1} R' \}^{-1}$$
$$\times R \Sigma_{VV}^{-1/2} \Delta_1 \, (\kappa) \, .$$

(3) *For* $\frac{1}{2} < \delta < \infty$, *joint with* $\kappa_{Tn} = Tn \, (k - 1) \xrightarrow{d} \kappa$, *we have*

$$W \, (k) \xrightarrow{d} \Delta_2' \, (\kappa) \, \Sigma_{VV}^{-1/2} R'$$
$$\times \{ S \, (\Delta_2 \, (\kappa)) \, R \{ \Sigma_{VV}^{1/2'} [z_V' z_V - \kappa I_{Tn}] \Sigma_{VV}^{1/2} \}^{-1} R' \}^{-1}$$
$$\times R \Sigma_{VV}^{-1/2} \Delta_2 \, (\kappa) \, .$$

Note that for $0 \le \delta < \frac{1}{2}$, if $\kappa = 0$, then $\theta = 0$ and $\Lambda = 0$. Hence $W \, (k) \xrightarrow{d} \chi^2 \, (q)$ is a central chi-squared distribution with q degrees of freedom.

4.2.3. *Testing for weak IVs*

In this section, we discuss the testing of the null hypothesis that the set of IVs is weak against the alternative that they are strong. In this case, the IVs are defined to be strong if W2SLS inference is reliable for any linear combination of the coefficients. From the results in Theorems 4.3 and 4.4, weak IVs can produce inconsistent IV estimators and test of hypotheses with large size distortions, e.g., when $\frac{1}{2} \le \delta < \infty$. The Stock and Yogo (2005) test is based on the partial identification test statistic proposed by Cragg and Donald (1993). For our case, this statistic is $g_{\min}$, the smallest eigenvalue of the matrix analog of the F-statistic from the first stage regression of W2SLS, i.e.,

$$g_{\min} = \min \text{ eval } G_{Tn}$$

where

$$G_{Tn} = \frac{\widehat{\Sigma}_{VV}^{-1/2'} \tilde{Y}^{\perp'} P_{\tilde{Z}^{\perp}} \tilde{Y}^{\perp} \widehat{\Sigma}_{VV}^{-1/2}}{K_2} \tag{4.12}$$

with

$$\hat{\Sigma}_{VV} = \tilde{Y}' M_{\tilde{Z}} \tilde{Y} / \, (Tn - K_1 - K_2) \, .$$

A small $g_{\min}$ indicates that the IVs are weak. Baltagi et al. (2012) propose using the conservative critical value x in Stock and Yogo (2005), which satisfies the relationship

$$P\left(g_{\min} \leq x\right) \leq P\left(\chi^2\left(K_2, \delta_{\min}\right) \geq \nu x\right),$$

where $\delta_{\min}$ is the smallest eigenvalue of $\lambda' \lambda$, $\chi^2\left(\nu, \delta_{\min}\right)$ denotes the non-central chi-squared random variable with ν degrees of freedom and non-centrality parameter $\delta_{\min}$. Tables for critical values can be found in Stock and Yogo (2005).

4.3. Conclusion

In this chapter, we discuss k-class IV estimators and test statistics and study their asymptotics when IVs are weak in a large panel model. Cai *et al.* (2012) study this panel data model, but they let the degree of weakness of the IVs depend upon n^δ, where $\delta \geq 0$, and study the asymptotic properties of W2SLS and pivotal statistics for fixed T and $n \to \infty$. In contrast, Baltagi *et al.* (2012) let the degree of weakness of the IVs depend upon $\sqrt{n}T^\delta$ and study the asymptotic properties of k-class IV estimators and pivotal test statistics as both $(n, T) \to \infty$. Both papers argue that there are benefits using panel data in reducing the bias of W2SLS and k-class IV estimators in case of weak IVs. Following Stock *et al.* (2002), Baltagi *et al.* (2012) also discuss the Anderson–Rubin (AR) test of Anderson and Rubin (1949), the Lagrange multiplier (LM) test of Kleibergen (2002) and Moreira (2009), and the conditional likelihood ratio (CLR) test of Moreira (2003) but apply to the individual fixed effects panel data model. Cai *et al.* (2012) also study these tests for fixed T and $n \to \infty$.

4.4. Technical Proofs

Proof of Theorems 4.3 and 4.4 can be found in Baltagi, Kao and Liu (2012).

4.5. Exercises

(1) Hahn and Kuersteiner (2002b) study the model in Eqs. (4.1) and (4.2). However, different from Assumption 4.1, they assume $\Pi = n^{-\delta}C$, where C is a $K_2 \times L$ constant matrix and $\delta \geq 0$. Then, $\delta = 1/2$ reduces to the weak IVs case as addressed by Staiger and Stock (1997). When $0 < \delta < 1/2$, IVs are stronger and are called "nearly weak". When $\delta > 1/2$, IVs are weaker and are called "near nonidentified".

When $\delta = 1/2$, we have

$$\widehat{\beta}_{2SLS} - \beta \xrightarrow{d} \frac{(\Phi_{ZZ}C + \Psi_{ZV})' \Phi_{ZZ}^{-1} \Psi_{Zu}}{(\Phi_{ZZ}C + \Psi_{ZV})' \Phi_{ZZ}^{-1} (\Phi_{ZZ}C + \Psi_{ZV})},$$

which is shown in Theorem 4.1. Theorem 1 of Hahn and Kuersteiner (2002b) further shows that when $0 < \delta < 1/2$, we have

$$n^{1/2-\delta}(\widehat{\beta}_{2SLS} - \beta) \xrightarrow{d} N(0, \sigma_{uu}(C'\Phi_{ZZ}C)^{-1})$$

and when $\delta > 1/2$, we have

$$\widehat{\beta}_{2SLS} - \beta \xrightarrow{d} \frac{\Psi'_{ZV} \Phi_{ZZ}^{-1} \Psi_{Zu}}{\Psi'_{ZV} \Phi_{ZZ}^{-1} \Psi_{ZV}}$$

as $n \to \infty$. Verify these results.

(2) Cai *et al.* (2012) study the fixed effects panel data model in Eq. (4.5). However, different from Assumption 4.1, they assume $\Pi = n^{-\delta}C$, where C is a $K_2 \times L$ constant matrix and $\delta \geq 0$. Then, $0 < \delta < 1/2$ corresponds to the nearly weak case as defined in Hahn and Kuersteiner (2002b), $\delta = 1/2$ reduces to the weak IVs case as addressed by Staiger and Stock (1997), and $\delta > 1/2$ becomes the nearly nonidentified case as discussed in Hahn and Kuersteiner (2002b). Corollary 4 of Cai *et al.* (2012) shows that when $\delta > 1/2$ and $n^{\delta-1/2}(T-1)^{-1/2} \to 0$, we have

$$n^{\delta-1/2}(T-1)^{1/2}(\widehat{\beta}_{2SLS} - \beta) \xrightarrow{d} N(0, \sigma_{uu}(C'\Phi_{ZZ}C)^{-1})$$

as $(n, T) \to \infty$. Verify this result.

(3) Baltagi *et al.* (2012) derive the results of the LIML estimator, where $\hat{k}_{\text{LIML}}$ is the smallest root of the determinantal equation

$$|[\tilde{Y}^{\perp\prime}(I - \hat{k}_{\text{LIML}}M_{\tilde{Z}^{\perp}})\tilde{Y}^{\perp}]| = 0.$$

Prove the following results: under Assumptions 4.1 and 4.2, with $\bar{\Sigma}$ is defined in Eq. (4.11), we have

(a) For $0 \leq \delta < \frac{1}{2}$, $T^{2\delta}n(\hat{k}_{\text{LIML}} - 1) \xrightarrow{p} 0$.

(b) For $\delta = \frac{1}{2}$,

$$Tn(\hat{k}_{\text{LIML}} - 1) \xrightarrow{d} \kappa^*_{\text{LIML}},$$

where κ^*_{LIML} is the smallest root of the determinantal equation, $|\Xi_2 - \kappa\bar{\Sigma}| = 0$, where $\Xi_2 = \begin{pmatrix} z'_u z_u & z'_u (\lambda + z_V) \\ (\lambda + z_V)' z_u & (\lambda + z_V)' (\lambda + z_V) \end{pmatrix}$.

(c) For $\frac{1}{2} < \delta < \infty$,

$$Tn(\hat{k}_{\text{LIML}} - 1) \xrightarrow{d} \kappa^*_{\text{LIML}},$$

where κ^*_{LIML} is the smallest root of the determinantal equation, $|\Xi_3 - \kappa\bar{\Sigma}| = 0$, where

$$\Xi_3 = \begin{pmatrix} z'_u z_u & z'_u z_V \\ z'_V z_u & z'_V z_V \end{pmatrix}.$$

(4) Baltagi *et al.* (2012) derive the results of weak IV test statistic G_{Tn} in Eq. (4.12). Let $W(K, \Omega, \Upsilon)$ denote the Wishart distribution with K denoting the degrees of freedom, Ω denoting the covariance matrix, and Υ denoting the noncentrality matrix. Prove the following results: under Assumptions 4.1 and 4.2, we have

(a) For $0 \le \delta < \frac{1}{2}$, $\frac{1}{T^{1-2\delta}} K_2 G_{Tn} \xrightarrow{p} \lambda'\lambda$.

(b) For $\delta = \frac{1}{2}$, $K_2 G_{Tn} \xrightarrow{d} (\lambda + z_V)' (\lambda + z_V) \frown W(K_2, I_L, \lambda'\lambda)$.

(c) For $\frac{1}{2} < \delta < \infty$, $K_2 G_{Tn} \xrightarrow{d} z'_V z_V \frown W(K_2, I_L, 0)$.

(5) Bekker (1994) considers the many instruments model in Eqs. (4.1) and (4.2), where y_i and Y_i are 1×1 scalars, Z_i is an $l \times 1$ vector of exogenous instruments with $l \to \infty$. For simplicity, we assume conditional homoskedasticity and normalize the variances to unity:

$$\text{var}\left(\begin{pmatrix} u_i \\ V_i \end{pmatrix} \middle| Z_i \right) = \begin{pmatrix} 1 & \rho \\ \rho & 1 \end{pmatrix}.$$

Assume that the number of instruments l is increasing proportionately with the sample size $l/n \to \alpha$, where α is a nonnegative constant. Further assume

$$\frac{1}{n} \sum_{i=1}^{n} \gamma' Z_i Z'_i \gamma \xrightarrow{p} c.$$

Show that

$$\hat{\beta}_{\text{OLS}} \xrightarrow{p} \beta + \frac{\rho}{c+1}$$

and

$$\widehat{\beta}_{2SLS} \xrightarrow{p} \beta + \frac{\alpha\rho}{c + \alpha}.$$

Spell out the conditions you need.

(6) Hahn and Hausman (2005) consider the model in Eqs. (4.1) and (4.2), where $\dim(\Pi) = K$ and

$$u = Z\left(\frac{\gamma}{\sqrt{n}}\right) + e$$

with

$$\begin{pmatrix} e_i \\ V_i \end{pmatrix} \sim N\left(0, \begin{bmatrix} \sigma_{11} & \sigma_{12} \\ \sigma_{12} & \sigma_{22} \end{bmatrix}\right).$$

We also assume $\frac{K}{\sqrt{n}} = \mu + o(1)$ and

$$\frac{1}{n}\Pi'Z'Z\Pi = \Theta + o_p(1),$$

$$\frac{1}{n}\Pi'Z'Z\gamma = \Xi + o_p(1).$$

Show that

$$\sqrt{n}(\widehat{\beta}_{2SLS} - \beta) \xrightarrow{d} N\left(\frac{\Xi + \mu\sigma_{12}}{\Theta}, \frac{\sigma_{11}}{\Theta}\right).$$

(7) Chao and Swanson (2005) consider the model in Eqs. (4.1) and (4.2), where y and Y are, respectively, an $n \times 1$ vector and an $n \times G$ matrix on $G + 1$ endogenous variables, Z is an $n \times K$ matrix on the K IVs, and u and V are, respectively, an $n \times 1$ vector and an $n \times G$ matrix error terms. Assume

$$\frac{K}{n} \to \tau \in [0, 1),$$

$$\frac{1}{r_n}\Pi'Z'Z\Pi \to \Psi,$$

and

$$\frac{r_n}{n} \to k \in [0, \infty).$$

Note that r_n can be interpreted as the rate of which the concentration parameter

$$\Sigma_{VV}^{-1/2}\Pi'Z'Z\Pi\Sigma_{VV}^{-1/2}$$

grows as n increases. Given that the concentration parameter is a natural measure of instrument strength, the quality of instruments is characterized by the order of magnitude of r_n, so that the slower is the divergence of r_n, the weaker are the instruments. Assume

$$\begin{pmatrix} u_i \\ V_i \end{pmatrix} \sim N \left(0, \begin{bmatrix} \sigma_{uv} & \sigma'_{Vu} \\ \sigma_{Vu} & \Sigma_{VV} \end{bmatrix} \right).$$

Let

$$\widehat{\beta} = (Y'P_Z Y - \widehat{\alpha}Y'Y)^{-1}(Y'P_Z y - \widehat{\alpha}Y'y)$$

for some choice of $\widehat{\alpha}$, where

$$P_Z = Z(Z'Z)^{-1}Z'.$$

$\widehat{\beta}$ includes all of the familiar k-class estimator except the OLS. Suppose

$$\frac{n}{K}\widehat{\alpha} = 1 + o_p\left(\frac{r_n}{K}\right)$$

and $r_n \to \infty$ as $n \to \infty$ such that $\frac{\sqrt{K}}{r_n} \to 0$. Show that $\widehat{\beta} \xrightarrow{p} \beta$ as $n \to \infty$.

(8) Chao (2014) considers the following panel model in Eqs. (4.5) and (4.6), where y_{it} and Y_{it} are 1×1 and $G \times 1$ endogenous variables, respectively. Z_{it} is a $K \times 1$ vector of IVs, and μ_i and α_i represent 1×1 individual effects. For simplicity, let us ignore the term X_t. Assume

$$\Pi = \Pi_{nT} = n^{-\delta_1}T^{-\delta_2}D^0$$

for $\delta_1 \geq 0$ and $\delta_2 \geq 0$, where D^0 is a $K \times G$ nonrandom matrix of full column rank $G \leq K$. Define

$$\widehat{\beta}_{2SLS} = (Y'P_Z Y)^{-1}Y'P_Z y,$$

where

$$P_Z = Z(Z'Z)^{-1}Z'.$$

Show that as $(n, T) \to \infty$,

$$T^{\frac{1}{2}-\delta_1-\delta_2}(\widehat{\beta}_{2SLS} - \beta^0) = O_p(1)$$

if $0 \leq \delta_1 + \delta_2 < \frac{1}{2}$. What happens when $\delta_1 + \delta_2 > \frac{1}{2}$ and $\delta_1 + \delta_2 = \frac{1}{2}$, respectively?

Chapter 5

Incidental Parameters Problem in Panel Data Models

One great opportunity that panel data offers us is the ability to control for unobserved heterogeneity through including individual effects and time effects. In this chapter, we consider the fixed effects approach to treat the unobserved heterogeneity as parameters to be estimated, therefore allows arbitrary correlation between the unobserved heterogeneity and the regressors. However, estimation of the unobserved heterogeneity also brings in the incidental parameters problem. This chapter discusses the incidental parameters problem in the context of a dynamic panel model under different setups. In Sec. 5.1, we use Neyman and Scott (1948) to illustrate the incidental parameters problem. In Sec. 5.2, we first explain the Nickell bias and then explore different asymptotic results under stationary and nonstationary panels. In Sec. 5.3, we further introduce time effects and consider different cases where individual effects and time effects are additive. Section 5.4 concludes. For nonlinear panels with incidental parameters, see Arellano and Bonhomme (2011), Fernández-Val and Weidner (2018), and Kao and Wang (2019) for reviews.

One thing we would like to point out is that this chapter is closely related to the previous chapters. They all utilize the basic idea of using one more dimension of the data to recover the identification of the model. As we will see in this chapter, our model is inconsistent under fixed time dimension, T, framework, but once we move from fixed T to large T we are able to recover the consistency and model is therefore identified.

5.1.   Incidental Parameters Problem

5.1.1.   *An example of MLE with large n and finite T*

Consider the following example from Neyman and Scott (1948). Suppose that the measurements are independent and y_{it} is normally distributed with unknown mean μ_{0i} and variance σ_0^2, i.e., $y_{it} \sim N(\mu_{0i}, \sigma_0^2)$ for $i = 1, \ldots, n$; $t = 1, \ldots, T$. Note that it is equivalent to rewrite

$$y_{it} = \mu_{0i} + u_{it},$$

where $u_{it} \overset{i.i.d.}{\sim} N(0, \sigma_0^2)$. It is easy to see that the log-likelihood is

$$\log L_{nT} = -\frac{nT}{2} \log(2\pi\sigma^2) - \frac{1}{2\sigma^2} \sum_{i=1}^{n} \sum_{t=1}^{T} (y_{it} - \mu_i)^2.$$

The MLE of μ_i and σ^2 are

$$\widehat{\mu}_i = \frac{1}{T} \sum_{t=1}^{T} y_{it} = \mu_{0i} + \overline{u}_i$$

and

$$\hat{\sigma}^2 = \frac{1}{nT} \sum_{i=1}^{n} \sum_{t=1}^{T} (y_{it} - \overline{y}_i)^2 = \frac{1}{nT} \sum_{i=1}^{n} \sum_{t=1}^{T} (u_{it} - \overline{u}_i)^2,$$

respectively, where

$$\overline{u}_i = \frac{1}{T} \sum_{t=1}^{T} u_{it}.$$

As shown in Neyman and Scott (1948), we have the following result for the MLE.

Theorem 5.1. *If T is finite, as $n \to \infty$, $\widehat{\mu}_i$ and $\hat{\sigma}^2$ are inconsistent. In particular, we have*

$$\hat{\sigma}^2 \overset{p}{\to} \sigma_0^2 - \frac{\sigma_0^2}{T} = \sigma_0^2 \left(1 - \frac{1}{T}\right)$$

as $n \to \infty$.

Proof.   For $\widehat{\mu}_i$, we have

$$E(\widehat{\mu}_i) = \mu_{0i} + E(\overline{u}_i) = \mu_{0i}$$

and

$$\mathrm{Var}(\widehat{\mu}_i) = E[\widehat{\mu}_i - E(\widehat{\mu}_i)]^2 = E(\overline{u}_i^2) = \frac{\sigma_0^2}{T}.$$

When T is finite, $\mathrm{Var}(\widehat{\mu}_i)$ does not shrink to zero. It follows that $\widehat{\mu}_i$ is inconsistent though it is unbiased.

For $\hat{\sigma}^2$, by an LLN, we have

$$\hat{\sigma}^2 = \frac{1}{nT} \sum_{i=1}^{n} \sum_{t=1}^{T} (u_{it} - \bar{u}_i)^2$$

$$= \frac{1}{nT} \sum_{i=1}^{n} \sum_{t=1}^{T} u_{it}^2 - \frac{1}{n} \sum_{i=1}^{n} \bar{u}_i^2$$

$$\xrightarrow{p} \sigma_0^2 - \frac{\sigma_0^2}{T}$$

as $n \to \infty$ since

$$E\left(\frac{1}{T} \sum_{t=1}^{T} u_{it}^2 \right) = \frac{1}{T} \sum_{t=1}^{T} E(u_{it}^2) = \sigma_0^2$$

and $E(\bar{u}_i^2) = \sigma_0^2/T$. □

As we can see that the inconsistency of $\hat{\sigma}^2$ is coming from the inconsistency of $\widehat{\mu}_i$. Because only a finite number of T of observations are available to estimate each μ_i, the estimation error of $\widehat{\mu}_i$ does not vanish as the sample size n grows, and this error contaminates the estimates of parameters of interest.

Theorem 5.1 can be explained as follows: Substituting $\widehat{\mu}_i = \bar{y}_i$ into the likelihood, we obtain the concentrated log-likelihood, which is

$$\log L_{nT}^c = -\frac{nT}{2} \log(2\pi\sigma^2) - \frac{1}{2\sigma^2} \sum_{i=1}^{n} \sum_{t=1}^{T} (y_{it} - \bar{y}_i)^2.$$

Since

$$\frac{1}{nT} \sum_{i=1}^{n} \sum_{t=1}^{T} (y_{it} - \bar{y}_i)^2 = \frac{1}{nT} \sum_{i=1}^{n} \sum_{t=1}^{T} (u_{it} - \bar{u}_i)^2 \xrightarrow{p} \sigma_0^2 \left(1 - \frac{1}{T} \right)$$

as $n \to \infty$, we have

$$-\frac{1}{nT} \log L_{nT}^c \xrightarrow{p} \frac{1}{2} \log(2\pi\sigma^2) + \frac{\sigma_0^2}{2\sigma^2} \left(1 - \frac{1}{T} \right) \equiv L(\sigma^2)$$

uniformly in σ^2. It follows from the usual extremum estimator properties that as $n \to \infty$ with T fixed, $\hat{\sigma}^2 = \sigma_T^2 + o_p(1)$, where $\sigma_T^2 = \arg\max L(\sigma^2)$.

Now

$$\frac{\partial L(\sigma^2)}{\partial \sigma^2} = \frac{1}{2\sigma^2} - \frac{\sigma_0^2}{2\sigma^4}\left(1 - \frac{1}{T}\right).$$

Set $\frac{\partial L(\sigma^2)}{\partial \sigma^2} = 0$, we have

$$\sigma_T^2 = \sigma_0^2 \left(1 - \frac{1}{T}\right).$$

Clearly $\lim_{T\to\infty} \sigma_T^2 = \sigma_0^2$. Let us illustrate the incidental parameters problem using the following example in R.

Example 5.1.

```
> # small T=5
> set.seed(1234)
> T.obs <- 5
> n.obs <- 50
> nT.obs <- n.obs * T.obs
> mu.i <- rnorm(n.obs)
> sigma <- 1
> y <- matrix(rnorm(nT.obs, mu.i, sigma), n.obs, T.obs)
> sigmasq.hat <- mean((y-rowMeans(y))^2)
> sigmasq.hat
```

[1] 0.8014673

In the example above, the variables are created as $n = 50$ and $T = 5$. The true value of σ^2 is 1. The estimated value is 0.8015, which is less than the true value of 1. The bias is 0.1985, which is close to the theoretical bias $-\sigma^2/T = -1/5 = -0.2$.

5.1.2. *An example of MLE with both large n and T*

Let us go back to the above example but for $(n, T) \to \infty$. We have the following result, e.g., Hahn and Newey (2004, p. 1297).

Theorem 5.2. $\widehat{\mu}_i$ *and* $\hat{\sigma}^2$ *are consistent as* $(n, T) \to \infty$. *If* $\dfrac{n}{T} \to \kappa^2$, *we have*

$$\sqrt{nT}(\hat{\sigma}^2 - \sigma_0^2) \xrightarrow{d} N(-\kappa\sigma_0^2, 2\sigma_0^4)$$

as $(n, T) \to \infty$.

Proof. For $\widehat{\mu}_i$, mirroring the earlier result for the fixed T case, we have

$$\text{Var}(\widehat{\mu}_i) = \sigma_0^2/T \to 0$$

as $(n, T) \to \infty$. Together with the unbiased property of $\widehat{\mu}_i$, we know that $\widehat{\mu}_i$ is consistent.

For $\hat{\sigma}^2$, it is easy to see that $\hat{\sigma}^2 \xrightarrow{p} \sigma_0^2$ as $(n, T) \to \infty$. To derive the limiting distribution, we have

$$\hat{\sigma}^2 - \sigma_0^2 = \frac{1}{nT} \sum_{i=1}^{n} \sum_{t=1}^{T} (u_{it} - \overline{u}_i)^2 - \sigma_0^2$$

$$= \frac{1}{nT} \sum_{i=1}^{n} \sum_{t=1}^{T} (u_{it}^2 - \sigma_0^2) - \frac{1}{n} \sum_{i=1}^{n} \overline{u}_i^2.$$

Since $u_{it} \sim N(0, \sigma_0^2)$, we know that u_{it}^2/σ_0^2 follows a χ_1^2 distribution with mean 1 and variance 2. From this, we know $E(u_{it}^2) = \sigma_0^2$ and $\text{Var}(u_{it}^2) = 2\sigma_0^4$. By a CLT, we have

$$\frac{1}{\sqrt{nT}} \sum_{i=1}^{n} \sum_{t=1}^{T} (u_{it}^2 - \sigma_0^2) \xrightarrow{d} N(0, 2\sigma_0^4)$$

as $(n, T) \to \infty$. Furthermore, as we show for the finite T case, $E(\overline{u}_i^2) = \sigma_0^2/T$. By an LLN, we have

$$\frac{T}{n} \sum_{i=1}^{n} \overline{u}_i^2 = \frac{1}{n} \sum_{i=1}^{n} (T\overline{u}_i^2) \xrightarrow{p} \sigma_0^2$$

as $(n, T) \to \infty$. Therefore, if $\frac{n}{T} \to \kappa^2$, we will have

$$\sqrt{nT}(\hat{\sigma}^2 - \sigma_0^2) = \sqrt{nT} \left[\frac{1}{nT} \sum_{i=1}^{n} \sum_{t=1}^{T} (u_{it}^2 - \sigma_0^2) - \frac{1}{n} \sum_{i=1}^{n} \overline{u}_i^2 \right]$$

$$= \frac{1}{\sqrt{nT}} \sum_{i=1}^{n} \sum_{t=1}^{T} (u_{it}^2 - \sigma_0^2) - \sqrt{\frac{n}{T}} \frac{T}{n} \sum_{i=1}^{n} \overline{u}_i^2$$

$$\xrightarrow{d} N(0, 2\sigma_0^4) - \kappa\sigma_0^2$$

$$= N(-\kappa\sigma_0^2, 2\sigma_0^4). \qquad \square$$

Theorem 5.2 can be rewritten into

$$\sqrt{nT} \left[\hat{\sigma}^2 - \sigma_0^2 \left(1 - \frac{1}{T} \right) \right] \xrightarrow{d} N(0, 2\sigma_0^4).$$

As $(n, T) \to \infty$, the estimator $\hat{\sigma}^2$ is asymptotically normal, although it will be centered at $\sigma_0^2(1 - \frac{1}{T})$. This asymptotic bias is easy to fix by equating the denominator with the correct degrees of freedom $n(T - 1)$. Note that the theorem implies

$$\sqrt{nT}(\hat{\sigma}^2 - \sigma_0^2) = O_p\left(\sqrt{\frac{n}{T}}\right).$$

Equivalently, it could be rewritten as $\hat{\sigma}^2 - \sigma_0^2 = O_p(\frac{1}{T})$. In other words, $\hat{\sigma}^2 - \sigma_0^2 \xrightarrow{p} 0$ as $(n, T) \to \infty$, i.e., $\hat{\sigma}^2$ will be consistent when both n and T are large. Let us illustrate the incidental parameters problem for large T using the following example in R.

Example 5.2.

```
> # large T=50
> set.seed(1234)
> T.obs <- 50
> n.obs <- 50
> nT.obs <- n.obs * T.obs
> mu.i <- rnorm(n.obs)
> sigma <- 1
> y <- matrix(rnorm(nT.obs, mu.i, sigma), n.obs, T.obs)
> sigmasq.hat <- mean((y-rowMeans(y))^2)
> sigmasq.hat

[1] 0.9834838
```

The second example is the same as the first one except that the sample size of T increases to 50. The estimated value is 0.9834, which is still less than the true value of 1. The bias reduces to 0.0165, which is again close to the theoretical bias $-\sigma^2/T = -1/50 = -0.02$. The fixed effects approach treats the unobserved effects as parameters to be estimated, therefore allows arbitrary correlation between the unobserved effects and the regressors. However, estimation of the unobserved effects also brings in the incidental parameter problem and hence the estimator is biased when T is finite. Fortunately, the bias shrinks to 0 as $T \to \infty$.

Our main focus of this chapter is on the dynamic linear model with various forms of unobserved individual specific effects and time effects. We consider

$$y_{it} = \rho y_{i,t-1} + \alpha_i + f_t + u_{it}.$$

In this model, α_i and f_t represent individual effects and time effect, respectively. The time effects f_t represent some unobserved common shocks that account for the cross-sectional dependence in the panel. We will start by discussing the most common case with just the individual fixed effects, i.e., $f_t = \bar{f}$ is a constant.

5.2. Individual Effects

In this section, we discuss the stationary and nonstationary panels when $n \to \infty$ with fixed T, and when $(n, T) \to \infty$, respectively. We consider the following dynamic linear panel model

$$y_{it} = \alpha_i + y_{it}^0, \tag{5.1}$$

$$y_{it}^0 = \rho y_{i,t-1}^0 + u_{it}, \tag{5.2}$$

where α_i are unobservable individual effects and $u_{it} \overset{i.i.d.}{\sim} (0, \sigma^2)$. The panel autoregressive coefficient is $\rho \in (-1, 1]$. This model could be rewritten as

$$y_{it} = \rho y_{i,t-1} + \lambda_i + u_{it}, \tag{5.3}$$

where

$$\lambda_i = (1 - \rho)\alpha_i.$$

This implies $\lambda_i = 0$ when $\rho = 1$. Otherwise, the data generating process will have a discontinuity at $\rho = 1$, at which point the individual effects become individual trends. The error term u_{it} is uncorrelated with $y_{i,t-s}^0$ for $s \geq 1$. The parameter of interest is the panel autoregressive coefficient ρ. The quasi-MLE (QMLE) of ρ has the form

$$\widehat{\rho} = \frac{\sum_{i=1}^n \sum_{t=1}^T (y_{i,t-1} - \overline{y}_{i,-1})(y_{it} - \overline{y}_i)}{\sum_{i=1}^n \sum_{t=1}^T (y_{i,t-1} - \overline{y}_{i,-1})^2}$$

and hence

$$\widehat{\rho} - \rho = \frac{\sum_{i=1}^n \sum_{t=1}^T (y_{i,t-1} - \overline{y}_{i,-1})u_{it}}{\sum_{i=1}^n \sum_{t=1}^T (y_{i,t-1} - \overline{y}_{i,-1})^2},$$

where

$$\overline{y}_i = \frac{1}{T} \sum_{t=1}^T y_{it}$$

and

$$\bar{y}_{i,-1} = \frac{1}{T} \sum_{t=1}^{T} y_{i,t-1}.$$

From Eq. (5.1), it is easy to see that

$$y_{it} - \bar{y}_i = y_{it}^0 - \bar{y}_i^0 \quad \text{and} \quad y_{i,t-1} - \bar{y}_{i,-1} = y_{i,t-1}^0 - \bar{y}_{i,-1}^0,$$

where

$$\bar{y}_i^0 = \frac{1}{T} \sum_{t=1}^{T} y_{it}^0$$

and

$$\bar{y}_{i,-1}^0 = \frac{1}{T} \sum_{t=1}^{T} y_{i,t-1}^0.$$

Then we have

$$\hat{\rho} - \rho = \frac{\sum_{i=1}^{n} \sum_{t=1}^{T} (y_{i,t-1}^0 - \bar{y}_{i,-1}^0) u_{it}}{\sum_{i=1}^{n} \sum_{t=1}^{T} (y_{i,t-1}^0 - \bar{y}_{i,-1}^0)^2}. \tag{5.4}$$

5.2.1. *Fixed T*

We first discuss the case where $n \to \infty$ with a fixed T. When $|\rho| < 1$, Nickell (1981) first shows that $\hat{\rho}$ is inconsistent due to the incidental parameters problem. This bias is known as Nickell Bias. As shown in Harris and Tzavalis (1999), the asymptotic bias is even magnified when $\rho = 1$. The asymptotic results for $\hat{\rho}$ are given in the following theorem.

Theorem 5.3. *As $n \to \infty$, we have the following theorem.*

(1) *If $|\rho| < 1$,*

$$\hat{\rho} - \rho \xrightarrow{p} -\frac{1+\rho}{T} + o\left(\frac{1}{T}\right).$$

(2) *If $\rho = 1$,*

$$\hat{\rho} - 1 \xrightarrow{p} -\frac{3}{T+1} + o\left(\frac{1}{T}\right).$$

In Theorem 5.3, the asymptotic distribution of $\hat{\rho}$ when $\rho = 1$ is based on Theorems 2 in Harris and Tzavalis (1999).

5.2.1.1. When $|\rho| < 1$

When $|\rho| < 1$, from Eq. (5.2), we know

$$y_{it}^0 = \sum_{j=0}^{\infty} \rho^j u_{i,t-j}.$$

For the denominator in Eq. (5.4), we have

$$\frac{1}{n} \sum_{i=1}^{n} \sum_{t=1}^{T} (y_{i,t-1}^0 - \overline{y}_{i,-1}^0)^2 \xrightarrow{p} E\left[\sum_{t=1}^{T} (y_{i,t-1}^0 - \overline{y}_{i,-1}^0)^2\right]$$

$$= E\left[\sum_{t=1}^{T} (y_{i,t-1}^0)^2 - T(\overline{y}_{i,-1}^0)^2\right]$$

$$= TE[(y_{i,t-1}^0)^2] - TE[(\overline{y}_{i,-1}^0)^2]$$

$$= T\frac{\sigma^2}{1 - \rho^2} + O(1) \tag{5.5}$$

as $n \to \infty$ since

$$TE[(y_{i,t-1}^0)^2] = TE\left[\left(\sum_{j=0}^{\infty} \rho^j u_{i,t-j-1}\right)^2\right]$$

$$= TE\left[\sum_{j=0}^{\infty}\sum_{k=0}^{\infty} (\rho^j u_{i,t-j-1})(\rho^k u_{i,t-k-1})\right]$$

$$= T\sigma^2 \sum_{j=0}^{\infty} \rho^{2j} = T\frac{\sigma^2}{1 - \rho^2}$$

and

$$TE[(\overline{y}_{i,-1}^0)^2] = \frac{1}{T}E\left[\left(\sum_{t=1}^{T} y_{i,t-1}^0\right)^2\right]$$

$$= \frac{1}{T}E\left[\left(\sum_{t=1}^{T} y_{i,t-1}^0\right)\left(\sum_{s=1}^{T} y_{i,s-1}^0\right)\right]$$

$$= \frac{1}{T} \left[\sum_{t=1}^{T} \sum_{s=1}^{T} E(y_{i,t-1}^0 y_{i,s-1}^0) \right]$$

$$= \frac{1}{T} \sum_{t=1}^{T} \sum_{s=1}^{T} \rho^{|t-s|} \frac{\sigma^2}{1-\rho^2}$$

$$= \frac{\sigma^2}{1-\rho^2} \frac{1}{T} \sum_{t=1}^{T} \sum_{s=1}^{T} \rho^{|t-s|}$$

$$= \frac{\sigma^2}{1-\rho^2} \frac{1}{T} \sum_{j=-(T-1)}^{T-1} \rho^{|j|} \left[\sum_{t,s=1}^{T} 1\{t-s=j\} \right]$$

$$= \frac{\sigma^2}{1-\rho^2} \frac{1}{T} \sum_{j=-(T-1)}^{T-1} \rho^{|j|} [T - |j|]$$

$$= O(1).$$

For the numerator, we have

$$\frac{1}{n} \sum_{i=1}^{n} \sum_{t=1}^{T} (y_{i,t-1}^0 - \bar{y}_{i,-1}^0) u_{it} = \frac{1}{n} \sum_{i=1}^{n} \sum_{t=1}^{T} y_{i,t-1}^0 u_{it} - \frac{1}{n} \sum_{i=1}^{n} \sum_{t=1}^{T} \bar{y}_{i,-1}^0 u_{it}$$

$$\overset{p}{\to} -\frac{\sigma^2}{1-\rho} + O\left(\frac{1}{T}\right)$$

as $n \to \infty$ since

$$\frac{1}{n} \sum_{i=1}^{n} \sum_{t=1}^{T} y_{i,t-1}^0 u_{it} \overset{p}{\to} \sum_{t=1}^{T} E(y_{i,t-1}^0 u_{it}) = 0$$

and

$$-\frac{1}{n} \sum_{i=1}^{n} \sum_{t=1}^{T} \bar{y}_{i,-1}^0 u_{it}$$

$$\overset{p}{\to} -\sum_{t=1}^{T} E(\bar{y}_{i,-1}^0 u_{it})$$

$$= -\frac{1}{T} \sum_{t=1}^{T} E\left(\sum_{s=t+1}^{T} \sum_{j=0}^{\infty} \rho^j u_{i,s-1-j} u_{it} \right)$$

$$= -\sigma^2 \frac{1}{T} \sum_{t=1}^{T} \left(\sum_{j=0}^{T-t-1} \rho^j \right) \quad \text{since } E(u_{i,s-1-j}u_{it}) = \sigma^2 1\{s = t + 1 + j\}$$

$$= -\sigma^2 \frac{1}{T} \sum_{t=1}^{T} \frac{1 - \rho^{T-t}}{1 - \rho}$$

$$= -\frac{\sigma^2}{1 - \rho} + O\left(\frac{1}{T}\right). \tag{5.6}$$

Therefore, as $n \to \infty$, we have

$$\widehat{\rho} - \rho \xrightarrow{p} -\frac{1 + \rho}{T} + o\left(\frac{1}{T}\right). \tag{5.7}$$

As we can see, the QMLE $\widehat{\rho}$ is inconsistent and asymptotically biased downward. As we can see from the proof of Eq. (5.6), the inconsistency arises from the correlation between $\overline{y}_{i,-1}^0$ and u_{it}. By doing within transformation of demeaning to remove the individual fixed effects, we actually induce the correlation between those two terms. The asymptotic bias is $-\frac{(1+\rho)}{T}$, which is nontrivial when T is small. For example, when $T = 5$, the asymptotic bias is -0.2 if $\rho = 0$; the asymptotic bias is -0.3 if $\rho = 0.5$; the asymptotic bias is -0.38 if $\rho = 0.9$.

5.2.1.2.   When $\rho = 1$

Now, we turn to $\rho = 1$. From Eq. (5.2), we have

$$y_{it}^0 = y_{i,t-1}^0 + u_{it} = y_{i,t-2}^0 + u_{i,t-1} + u_{it} = \cdots = \sum_{j=1}^{t} u_{ij}$$

assuming $y_{i0}^0 = 0$ for simplicity. Now we let $\alpha_i = 0$. For the denominator in Eq. (5.4), because

$$\sum_{t=1}^{T} (y_{i,t-1}^0 - \overline{y}_{i,-1}^0)^2$$

$$= \sum_{t=1}^{T} (y_{i,t-1}^0)^2 - \frac{1}{T} \left(\sum_{t=1}^{T} y_{i,t-1}^0 \right)^2$$

$$= \sum_{t=1}^{T} \left(\sum_{j=1}^{t-1} u_{ij} \right)^2 - \frac{1}{T} \left(\sum_{t=1}^{T} (T-t)u_{it} \right) \left(\sum_{s=1}^{T} (T-s)u_{is} \right)$$

$$= \left[\sum_{t=1}^{T}(T-t)u_{it}^2 + 2\sum_{t=1}^{T-1}\sum_{s=t+1}^{T}(T-s)u_{it}u_{is} \right]$$

$$- \frac{1}{T}\left[\sum_{t=1}^{T}(T-t)^2 u_{it}^2 + \sum_{t=1}^{T-1}\sum_{s=t+1}^{T} 2(T-t)(T-s)u_{it}u_{is} \right]$$

$$= \sum_{t=1}^{T}\frac{1}{T}t(T-t)u_{it}^2 + \sum_{t=1}^{T-1}\sum_{s=t+1}^{T}\frac{2}{T}t(T-s)u_{it}u_{is}.$$

we have

$$\frac{1}{n}\sum_{i=1}^{n}\sum_{t=1}^{T}(y_{i,t-1}^0 - \overline{y}_{i,-1}^0)^2$$

$$= \frac{1}{n}\sum_{i=1}^{n}\left[\sum_{t=1}^{T}\frac{1}{T}t(T-t)u_{it}^2 + \sum_{t=1}^{T-1}\sum_{s=t+1}^{T}\frac{2}{T}t(T-s)u_{it}u_{is} \right]$$

$$\xrightarrow{p} \sum_{t=1}^{T}\frac{1}{T}t(T-t)E(u_{it}^2) + \sum_{t=1}^{T-1}\sum_{s=t+1}^{T}\frac{2}{T}t(T-s)E(u_{it}u_{is})$$

$$= \sigma^2\sum_{t=1}^{T}\frac{1}{T}t(T-t) = \frac{(T^2-1)\sigma^2}{6} + O(T) \tag{5.8}$$

as $n \to \infty$.

For the numerator, we have

$$\frac{1}{n}\sum_{i=1}^{n}\sum_{t=1}^{T}(y_{i,t-1}^0 - \overline{y}_{i,-1}^0)u_{it}$$

$$= \frac{1}{n}\sum_{i=1}^{n}\sum_{t=1}^{T}y_{i,t-1}^0 u_{it} - \frac{1}{n}\sum_{i=1}^{n}\sum_{t=1}^{T}\overline{y}_{i,-1}^0 u_{it}$$

$$\xrightarrow{p} -\frac{\sigma^2}{2}(T-1) + o(T)$$

as $n \to \infty$ since

$$\frac{1}{n}\sum_{i=1}^{n}\sum_{t=1}^{T}y_{i,t-1}^0 u_{it} \xrightarrow{p} E(y_{i,t-1}^0 u_{it}) = 0$$

and

$$-\frac{1}{n}\sum_{i=1}^{n}\sum_{t=1}^{T}\overline{y}_{i,-1}^{0}u_{it}$$

$$\overset{p}{\to} -E\left[\sum_{t=1}^{T}(\overline{y}_{i,-1}^{0}u_{it})\right]$$

$$= -E\left[\frac{1}{T}\left(\sum_{t=1}^{T}y_{i,t-1}^{0}\right)\left(\sum_{t=1}^{T}u_{it}\right)\right]$$

$$= -E\left[\frac{1}{T}\sum_{t=1}^{T}(T-t)u_{it}^{2} + \frac{1}{T}\sum_{t=1}^{T-1}\sum_{s=t+1}^{T}(2T-s-t)u_{it}u_{is}\right]$$

$$= -\frac{1}{T}\sum_{t=1}^{T}(T-t)\sigma^{2}$$

$$= -\frac{(T-1)\sigma^{2}}{2} + O(1). \tag{5.9}$$

Therefore, as $n \to \infty$, we have

$$\widehat{\rho} - \rho \overset{p}{\to} -\frac{3}{T+1} + o\left(\frac{1}{T}\right). \tag{5.10}$$

When $\rho = 1$, the bias term in Eq. (5.10) could be very large when T is small. For example, when $T = 5$, the bias is -0.5; when $T = 3$, the bias is -0.75.

5.2.2.   *Large T*

When the time-series dimension of the panel is large, Hahn and Kuersteiner (2002a) propose to use $(n, T) \to \infty$ asymptotics to characterize the asymptotic bias of the fixed effect estimator that arises from the incidental parameters λ_i. Hahn and Kuersteiner derive the limit distribution of $\hat{\rho}$ by allowing $(n, T) \to \infty$ with $\frac{n}{T} \to \kappa^2$, where $0 < \kappa < \infty$.

Theorem 5.4. *Assume* $(n, T) \to \infty$.

(1) *If* $|\rho| < 1$,

$$\sqrt{nT}\left(\hat{\rho} - \rho + \frac{1+\rho}{T}\right) \overset{d}{\to} N(0, 1 - \rho^2).$$

(2) *If $\rho = 1$,*

$$\sqrt{n}T\left(\hat{\rho} - 1 + \frac{3}{T+1}\right) \xrightarrow{d} N\left(0, \frac{51}{5}\right).$$

Note that the asymptotic distribution of $\hat{\rho}$ in this theorem is the same as Theorems 2.9 in Chapter 2.

5.2.2.1. When $|\rho| < 1$

When $|\rho| < 1$, mirroring the earlier result in Eqs. (5.5) and (5.6) for fixed T case, we have

$$\frac{1}{nT} \sum_{i=1}^{n} \sum_{t=1}^{T} (y_{i,t-1}^0 - \overline{y}_{i,-1}^0)^2 \xrightarrow{p} \frac{\sigma^2}{1 - \rho^2} \tag{5.11}$$

and

$$-\frac{1}{n} \sum_{i=1}^{n} \sum_{t=1}^{T} \overline{y}_{i,-1}^0 u_{it} \xrightarrow{p} -\frac{\sigma^2}{1 - \rho} \tag{5.12}$$

as $(n, T) \to \infty$. Furthermore, from a CLT

$$\frac{\frac{1}{\sqrt{nT}} \sum_{i=1}^{n} \sum_{t=1}^{T} y_{i,t-1}^0 u_{it}}{\sqrt{\frac{1}{nT} \text{Var} \left(\sum_{i=1}^{n} \sum_{t=1}^{T} y_{i,t-1}^0 u_{it}\right)}} \xrightarrow{d} N(0,1).$$

It can be shown that

$$\frac{1}{\sqrt{nT}} \sum_{i=1}^{n} \sum_{t=1}^{T} y_{i,t-1}^0 u_{it} \xrightarrow{d} N\left(0, \frac{\sigma^4}{1 - \rho^2}\right). \tag{5.13}$$

Together with Eq. (5.12), we have

$$\frac{1}{\sqrt{nT}} \sum_{i=1}^{n} \sum_{t=1}^{T} (y_{i,t-1}^0 - \overline{y}_{i,-1}^0) u_{it}$$

$$= \frac{1}{\sqrt{nT}} \sum_{i=1}^{n} \sum_{t=1}^{T} y_{i,t-1}^0 u_{it} - \sqrt{\frac{n}{T}} \frac{1}{n} \sum_{i=1}^{n} \sum_{t=1}^{T} \overline{y}_{i,-1}^0 u_{it}$$

$$\xrightarrow{d} N\left(-\kappa \frac{\sigma^2}{1 - \rho}, \frac{\sigma^4}{1 - \rho^2}\right).$$

with $\frac{n}{T} \to \kappa^2$. Using Eq. (5.11), we have the following result:

$$\sqrt{nT}(\hat{\rho} - \rho)$$

$$= \left[\frac{1}{nT} \sum_{i=1}^{n} \sum_{t=1}^{T} (y_{i,t-1} - \overline{y}_{i,-1})^2 \right]^{-1} \left[\frac{1}{\sqrt{nT}} \sum_{i=1}^{n} \sum_{t=1}^{T} (y_{i,t-1} - \overline{y}_{i,-1})u_{it} \right]$$

$$\xrightarrow{d} \left(\frac{\sigma^2}{1 - \rho^2} \right)^{-1} N\left(-\kappa \frac{\sigma^2}{1 - \rho}, \frac{\sigma^4}{1 - \rho^2} \right)$$

$$= N(-\kappa(1 + \rho), 1 - \rho^2) \tag{5.14}$$

or equivalently

$$\sqrt{nT} \left(\hat{\rho} - \rho + \frac{1 + \rho}{T} \right) \xrightarrow{d} N(0, 1 - \rho^2).$$

That is, QMLE of ρ is consistent but asymptotically biased with $\frac{n}{T} \to \kappa^2$. The bias is involved in a normal limiting distribution which is not centered at 0. This bias, like that for the fixed T case, is due to the presence of the incidental parameters λ_i. A finite sample implication of (5.14) is that the bias of $\hat{\rho}$ can be approximated by $-\frac{1+\rho}{T}$. Hahn and Kuersteiner (2002a) suggest the following bias-corrected estimator:

$$\check{\rho} = \hat{\rho} + \frac{1}{T}(1 + \hat{\rho}) = \frac{T + 1}{T}\hat{\rho} + \frac{1}{T}$$

which has the following correctly centered limiting distribution:

$$\sqrt{nT}(\check{\rho} - \rho) \xrightarrow{d} N(0, 1 - \rho^2).$$

5.2.2.2. When $\rho = 1$

When $\rho = 1$, we have

$$\frac{1}{nT} \sum_{i=1}^{n} \sum_{t=1}^{T} (y_{i,t-1}^0 - \overline{y}_{i,-1}^0)^2 \xrightarrow{p} \frac{\sigma^2}{6} \tag{5.15}$$

as $(n, T) \to \infty$. Furthermore, note that

$$\frac{\frac{1}{\sqrt{nT}} \sum_{i=1}^{n} \sum_{t=1}^{T} \left[(y_{i,t-1}^0 - \overline{y}_{i,-1}^0)u_{it} + \frac{3}{T+1}(y_{i,t-1}^0 - \overline{y}_{i,-1}^0)^2 \right]}{\sqrt{\text{Var}\left\{ \frac{1}{\sqrt{nT}} \sum_{i=1}^{n} \sum_{t=1}^{T} \left[(y_{i,t-1}^0 - \overline{y}_{i,-1}^0)u_{it} + \frac{3}{T+1}(y_{i,t-1}^0 - \overline{y}_{i,-1}^0)^2 \right] \right\}}}$$

$$\xrightarrow{d} N(0, 1).$$

It can be shown that

$$\text{Var}\left\{\frac{1}{\sqrt{nT}}\sum_{i=1}^{n}\sum_{t=1}^{T}\left[(y_{i,t-1}^0 - \overline{y}_{i,-1}^0)u_{it} + \frac{3}{T+1}(y_{i,t-1}^0 - \overline{y}_{i,-1}^0)^2\right]\right\} = \frac{17\sigma^4}{60}.$$

$$(5.16)$$

Then

$$\frac{1}{\sqrt{nT}}\sum_{i=1}^{n}\sum_{t=1}^{T}\left[(y_{i,t-1}^0 - \overline{y}_{i,-1}^0)u_{it} + \frac{3}{T+1}(y_{i,t-1}^0 - \overline{y}_{i,-1}^0)^2\right]$$

$$\xrightarrow{d} N\left(0, \frac{17\sigma^4}{60}\right).$$

Finally we obtain

$$\frac{1}{\sqrt{nT}}\left(\widehat{\rho} - \rho + \frac{3}{T+1}\right)$$

$$= \frac{\frac{1}{\sqrt{nT}}\sum_{i=1}^{n}\sum_{t=1}^{T}\left[(y_{i,t-1}^0 - \overline{y}_{i,-1}^0)u_{it} + \frac{3}{T+1}(y_{i,t-1}^0 - \overline{y}_{i,-1}^0)^2\right]}{\frac{1}{nT^2}\sum_{i=1}^{n}\sum_{t=1}^{T}(y_{it-1}^0 - \overline{y}_{i,-1}^0)^2}$$

$$\xrightarrow{d} \frac{N\left(0, \frac{17\sigma^4}{60}\right)}{\frac{\sigma^2}{6}} = N\left(0, \frac{51}{5}\right).$$

5.3.   Additive Fixed Effects

In this section, we consider time effects as additional incidental parameters in the model

$$y_{it} = \rho y_{i,t-1} + \lambda_i + f_t + u_{it}. \qquad (5.17)$$

In model (5.17), incidental parameters exist in both individual and time dimensions. After eliminating the individual effect λ_i and time effect f_t we have

$$y_{it} - \overline{y}_i - (\overline{y}_t - \overline{y}) = \rho[(y_{i,t-1} - \overline{y}_{i,-1}) - (\overline{y}_{t-1} - \overline{y}_{-1})]$$

$$+[u_{it} - \overline{u}_i - (\overline{u}_t - \overline{u})],$$

where

$$\bar{f} = \frac{1}{T} \sum_{t=1}^{T} f_t,$$

$$\bar{u}_i = \frac{1}{T} \sum_{t=1}^{T} u_{it},$$

$$\bar{y}_t = \frac{1}{n} \sum_{i=1}^{n} y_{it},$$

$$\bar{y} = \frac{1}{nT} \sum_{i=1}^{n} \sum_{t=1}^{T} y_{it},$$

$$\bar{y}_{t-1} = \frac{1}{n} \sum_{i=1}^{n} y_{i,t-1},$$

$$\bar{y}_{-1} = \frac{1}{nT} \sum_{i=1}^{n} \sum_{t=1}^{T} y_{i,t-1},$$

$$\bar{u}_t = \frac{1}{n} \sum_{i=1}^{n} u_{it}$$

and

$$\bar{u} = \frac{1}{nT} \sum_{i=1}^{n} \sum_{t=1}^{T} u_{it}.$$

Hence

$$\tilde{\rho} = \left(\sum_{i=1}^{n} \sum_{t=1}^{T} \tilde{y}_{i,t-1}^2 \right)^{-1} \sum_{i=1}^{n} \sum_{t=1}^{T} \tilde{y}_{i,t-1} \tilde{y}_{it}, \qquad (5.18)$$

where

$$\tilde{y}_{it} = y_{it} - \bar{y}_i - \bar{y}_t + \bar{y}$$

and

$$\tilde{y}_{i,t-1} = y_{i,t-1} - \bar{y}_{i,-1} - \bar{y}_{t-1} + \bar{y}_{-1}.$$

When $|\rho| < 1$, Hahn and Moon (2006) show that

$$\sqrt{nT}(\tilde{\rho} - \rho) \xrightarrow{d} N(-\kappa(1+\rho), 1 - \rho^2). \qquad (5.19)$$

Note that the limit distribution of $\tilde{\rho}$ in Eq. (5.19) is identical to Theorem 5.4.

5.4. Conclusion

The main thrust of the results of Chapters 1–4 has been that identification and consistency can be achieved with high-dimensional data. In this chapter, we focus on incidental parameters problem in the dynamic panel model under different asymptotics and setups. Again the identification and consistency can be recovered using high-dimensional data which is the theme of this book.

5.5. Technical Proofs

Proofs of Theorems 5.3 and 5.4 can be found in Harris and Tzavalis (1999) and Hahn and Kuersteiner (2002a), respectively.

5.6. Exercises

(1) Prove Eq. (5.18).
(2) Prove Eq. (5.13).
(3) Revisit Hahn and Moon (2006) when $\rho = 1$.
(4) Explain why the limit distribution of $\tilde{\rho}$ in Eq. (5.19) is identical to Theorem 5.4.
(5) Revisit Theorem 5.4 when the error follows an AR(1)

$$u_{it} = \delta u_{i,t-1} + v_{it}$$

with $|\delta| \leq 1$, where v_{it} is a white noise with variance σ_v^2.
(6) Prove Eq. (5.16).
(7) Chamberlain (1980) considers the following binary choice model:

$$P(y_{it} = 1 | x_{it}, \alpha_i) = F(x_{it}\beta_0 + \alpha_i),$$

where y_{it} is a sequence of independent binary random variables taking the value 1 or 0, β_0 is a scalar, α_i are the nuisance parameters, and F is given as

$$F(z) = \frac{e^z}{1 + e^z}.$$

For simplicity, we assume $T = 2$ with $x_{i1} = 0$ and $x_{i2} = 1$. Let $\widehat{\beta}$ be the MLE of β. Show that $\widehat{\beta} \xrightarrow{p} 2\beta_0$.
(8) Chamberlain (2010) considers a binary panel model

$$P(y_{it} = 1 | x_i, \alpha_i) = F(x_{it}'\beta + \alpha_i)$$

$t = 1, 2$, where $y_{it} = 0$ or 1 and $x'_i = (x'_{i1}, x'_{i2})$. Show that if x_i has bounded support, then β is not point-identified unless F is the logistic distribution. Spell out the conditions you need.

(9) Evdokimov (2010) considers the following panel data model:

$$y_{it} = m(x_{it}, \alpha_i) + u_{it}, \qquad (5.20)$$

where x_{it} is a vector of the explanatory variable, y_{it} is a scalar outcome variable, scalar α_i represents persistent heterogeneity (possible correlated with x_{it}), and u_{it} is a scalar error term. We assume $T = 2$. $m(x_{it}, \alpha_i)$ is an unknown structure function. Let $x_i = (x_{i1}, x_{i2})$. Suppose α_i and x_i are independent and α_i has a uniform distribution on $[0, 1]$. Then (5.20) is identified, i.e., $m(x, \alpha)$ and $f_{u_{it}|x_{it}}$ are identified for all x, $\alpha \in (0, 1)$ and $t \in \{1, 2\}$. Spell out the conditions you need.

(10) Honore and Kyriazidou (2000) consider a panel dynamic binary choice model

$$y_{it} = 1\{x_{it}\beta + \gamma y_{i,t-1} + \alpha_i + u_{it} > 0\}.$$

As usual x_{it} are (strictly) exogenous explanatory variables, u_{it} is the transitory shock, and α_i is the individual fixed effect which could be arbitrarily correlated with the covariates. Now assume $T = 3$, and u_{it} has a logistic distribution. Show that β is identified if one would concentrate on observations for which $x_{i2} = x_{i3}$ (i.e., covariates for individual i remain the same in periods 2 and 3). Spell out the conditions you need.

(11) Graham, Hahn, and Powell (2009) consider a linear panel model with fixed effect

$$y_{it} = \alpha_i + x'_{it}\beta + \varepsilon_{it}$$

with $T = 2$, where ε_{it} is i.i.d. with density equal to

$$f(e) = \begin{cases} \left(\frac{1}{\tau} + \frac{1}{1-\tau}\right)^{-1} \exp(-\tau|e|) & \text{if } e > 0, \\ \left(\frac{1}{\tau} + \frac{1}{1-\tau}\right)^{-1} \exp(-(1-\tau)|e|) & \text{if } e < 0. \end{cases}$$

Assume (x_{i1}, x_{i2}) is independent of $(\varepsilon_{1i}, \varepsilon_{2i})$. The MLE solves

$$\min_{\alpha_1, \dots, \alpha_n, \beta} \sum_{i=1}^{n} \sum_{t=1}^{2} \left[\tau(y_{it} - \alpha_i - x'_{it}\beta)^+ + (1-\tau)(y_{it} - \alpha_i - x'_{it}\beta)^-\right].$$

Verify that the log-likelihood is numerically equivalent to the objective function of a quantile regression model. Show that regardless of τ, the concentrated likelihood function is numerically equivalent to the least absolute deviations model of $y_{i2} - y_{i1}$ on $x_{i2} - x_{i1}$:

$$\min_{\alpha_1,\ldots,\alpha_n} \sum_{i=1}^{n} \sum_{t=1}^{2} \left[\tau(y_{it} - \alpha_i - x'_{it}\beta)^+ + (1-\tau)(y_{it} - \alpha_i - x'_{it}\beta)^- \right]$$

$$= \sum_{i=1}^{n} |(y_{i2} - y_{i1}) - (x_{i2} - x_{i1})'\beta|.$$

(12) Lee (2012) considers a homogeneous pth-order univariate autoregressive model with exogenous regressors x_{it}, i.e., an ARX(p) model given by

$$y_{it} = \mu_i + \sum_{j=1}^{p} \alpha_{pj} y_{i,t-j} + \beta' x_{it} + u_{it},$$

where the lag order p is assumed to be finite. Assume $u_{it} \overset{i.i.d.}{\sim} (0, \sigma^2)$. Suppose the true lag order p is unknown and we choose q instead, where $1 \leq q \leq p$. Denote $\widehat{\alpha}(p,q) = (\widehat{\alpha}_{p,q1}, \widehat{\alpha}_{p,q2}, \ldots, \widehat{\alpha}_{p,qq})$, where $\widehat{\alpha}_{p,qr}$ for $r = 1, 2, \ldots, q$ is the within-group estimator of the coefficient of $y_{i,t-r}$ when ARX(p) process is fitted to ARX(q). Similarly, denote $\alpha(p,q) = (\alpha_{p,q1}, \alpha_{p,q2}, \ldots, \alpha_{p,qq})$ as the theoretical parameter value from the ARX(q) fitting. For example, $\alpha(p,1) = \alpha_{p,11}$ is the first-order autocorrelation coefficient of y_{it} for the pure autoregressive case. When $p = 2$, $q = 1$ and there are no exogenous regressors x_{it}, $\alpha(2,1) = \alpha_{2,11} = \alpha_{21}/(1 - \alpha_{22})$. When n tends to infinity but T is fixed, show that

$$p \lim_{n \to \infty} (\widehat{\alpha}(2,1) - \alpha(2,1)) = -\frac{1}{T-2}(1 + \alpha_{22})(1 + \rho_1)$$

$$- \frac{1}{T-2}\alpha_{22}\left(\frac{1+\alpha_{22}}{1-\alpha_{22}}\right)(1 + \rho_1) + O\left(\frac{1}{T^2}\right),$$

where $\rho_1 = \alpha_{21}/(1 - \alpha_{22}) = \alpha(2,1)$. Verify that when $p = q = 1$, the above is equivalent to Nickell bias.

(13) Phillips (2018) considers the model in Eq. (5.3), where α_i are fixed effects for which $\sigma_\alpha^2 = \lim_{n \to \infty} \sum_{i=1}^{n} \alpha_i^2 < \infty$, the error terms $u_{it} \overset{i.i.d.}{\sim}$ $(0, \sigma^2)$, the initial conditions $y_{i0} = O_p(1)$ for all i and are independent of u_{it} for all i and t. Define

$$\widehat{\rho}_{IV} = \frac{\sum_{i=1}^{n} \sum_{t=2}^{T} y_{i,t-2} \triangle y_{it}}{\sum_{i=1}^{n} \sum_{t=2}^{T} y_{i,t-2} \triangle y_{i,t-1}}$$

with $c < 0$. Show that if $\rho = 1$,

$$\sqrt{T}(\widehat{\rho}_{IV} - 1) \xrightarrow{d} 2C$$

as $(n, T) \to \infty$, where C is a Cauchy random variable. If $\rho_T = 1 + \frac{c}{\sqrt{T}}$,

$$\sqrt{nT}(\widehat{\rho}_{IV} - \rho_T) \xrightarrow{d} N(0, 4).$$

(14) Han, Phillips, and Sul (2014) consider the model in Eq. (5.3) and define an X-difference estimator as

$$\widehat{\rho} = \frac{\sum_{i=1}^{n} \sum_{t=4}^{T} \sum_{s=1}^{t-3}(y_{i,t-1} - y_{i,s+1})(y_{it} - y_{is})}{\sum_{i=1}^{n} \sum_{t=4}^{T} \sum_{s=1}^{t-3}(y_{i,t-1} - y_{i,s+1})^2}.$$

Show that as $(n, T) \to \infty$,

$$\sqrt{nT}(\widehat{\rho} - \rho) \xrightarrow{d} N(0, 1 - \rho^2) \quad \text{if } |\rho| < 1$$

and

$$\sqrt{nT}(\widehat{\rho} - 1) \xrightarrow{d} N(0, 9) \quad \text{if } \rho = 1.$$

(15) Hahn, Kuersteiner, and Cho (2004) consider a panel AR(1) model

$$y_{it} = \rho y_{i,t-1} + \alpha_i + u_{it}. \tag{5.21}$$

Assume $u_{it} \overset{i.i.d.}{\sim} N(0, \sigma^2)$ and $\frac{n}{T} \to c$, where $0 < c < \infty$, $|\rho| < 1$,

$$\frac{1}{n} \sum_{i=1}^{n} y_{i0}^2 = O(1)$$

and

$$\frac{1}{n} \sum_{i=1}^{n} \alpha_i^2 = O(1).$$

We now consider the MLE computed under the possibly incorrect assumption that α_i is a normally distributed random variable independent of y_{i0}:

$$\alpha_i | y_{i0} \sim N(\mu, \omega^2). \tag{5.22}$$

The nature of misspecification is that α_i is assumed to be independent of y_{i0} when in fact they may have an arbitrary correlation. Show that the log-likelihood under (5.22) is

$$L(\sigma^2, \rho, \lambda, \mu) = -nT \log \sigma^2 + n \log \lambda - n \log(T + \lambda) - \frac{n\mu^2}{\sigma^2}\lambda$$

$$- \frac{1}{\sigma^2} \sum_{i=1}^{n} \sum_{t=1}^{T}(y_{it} - \rho y_{i,t-1})^2 + \frac{1}{\sigma^2}\frac{1}{T + \lambda}\sum_{i=1}^{n}[T(\bar{y}_i - \rho \bar{y}_{i,-1}) + \lambda\mu]^2$$

where $\lambda = \frac{\sigma^2}{\omega^2}$. Let $\widehat{\rho}_{\mathrm{RE}} = \arg\max_{\sigma,\rho,\lambda,\mu} L(\sigma^2, \rho, \lambda, \mu)$. Show that $\sqrt{nT}(\widehat{\rho}_{\mathrm{RE}} - \rho) \overset{d}{\to} N(0, 1 - \rho^2)$. Note that the asymptotic distribution of $\widehat{\rho}_{\mathrm{RE}}$ is the same as the bias-corrected MLE developed in Hahn and Kuersteiner (2002a), and the result holds regardless of the correctness of the random effects assumption.

(16) Hsiao and Zhou (2019) consider the model in Eq. (5.21) with $|\rho| < 1$. We assume the errors are independent of α_i and *i.i.d.* over i and t with mean zero and constant variance $\sigma_u^2 = 1$. We also assume $\alpha_i \overset{i.i.d.}{\sim} (0, \sigma_\alpha^2)$. Let $y_i = (y_{i1}, \ldots, y_{iT})'$, $y_{i,-1} = (y_{i0}, \ldots, y_{i,T-1})'$, $u_i = (u_{i1}, \ldots, u_{iT})'$ and 1_T be a $T \times 1$ vector of ones. Then we write

$$y_i = y_{i,-1}\rho + 1_T\alpha_i + u_i.$$

Under the assumption y_{i0} are constants. Show that the quasi-likelihood function has the form

$$L = \prod_{i=1}^{n} (2\pi)^{-\frac{T}{2}} |V|^{-\frac{1}{2}} \exp\left\{ -\frac{1}{2}(y_i - \rho y_{i,-1})'V^{-1}(y_i - \rho y_{i,-1}) \right\},$$

where

$$V = I_T + \sigma_\alpha^2 1_T 1_T'$$

and hence

$$V^{-1} = I_T - \frac{\sigma_\alpha^2}{1 + T\sigma_\alpha^2} 1_T 1_T'.$$

The QMLE of ρ, $\widehat{\rho}$ is obtained by maximizing $\log L$. When σ_u^2 and σ_α^2 are known, show that QMLE is the native GLS

$$\widehat{\rho} = \left(\sum_{i=1}^{n} y_{i,-1}'V^{-1}y_{i,-1} \right)^{-1} \left(\sum_{i=1}^{n} y_{i,-1}'V^{-1}y_i \right).$$

When $y_{i0} = 0$, show that

$$\sqrt{nT}(\widehat{\rho} - \rho) \overset{d}{\to} N(0, 1 - \rho^2)$$

as $(n, T) \to \infty$.

(17) Hsiao and Zhou (2016) consider the model in Eq. (5.21) with $|\rho| < 1$, $u_{it} \overset{i.i.d.}{\sim} (0, \sigma_u^2)$ has finite fourth moment. Let $y_i = (y_{i1}, \ldots, y_{iT})'$,

$y_{i,-1} = (y_{i0}, \ldots, y_{i,T-1})'$, $u_i = (u_{i1}, \ldots, u_{iT})'$ and 1_T be a $T \times 1$ vector of ones. Then we write

$$y_i = y_{i,-1}\rho + 1_T \alpha_i + u_i.$$

Let

$$\widetilde{y}_{it} = y_{it} - y_{i0}.$$

Note

$$\widetilde{y}_{it} = \rho \widetilde{y}_{i,t-1} - \xi_i + u_{it}$$

with

$$\xi_i = (1 - \rho)(1 - \rho L)^{-1} u_{i0}.$$

In vector form

$$\widetilde{y}_i = \widetilde{y}_{i,-1}\rho - \xi_i 1_T + u_i, \qquad (5.23)$$

where

$$E(-\xi_i 1_T + u_i) = 0$$

and

$$\Omega = \operatorname{Var}(-\xi_i 1_T + u_i) = \sigma_\xi^2 1_T 1_T' + \sigma_u^2 1_T.$$

The inverse of Ω takes the form

$$\Omega^{-1} = \frac{1}{\sigma_u^2}\left[Q + \psi \frac{1}{T} 1_T 1_T'\right],$$

where

$$Q = I_T - \frac{1}{T} 1_T 1_T'$$

and

$$\psi = \frac{\sigma_u^2}{\sigma_u^2 + T\sigma_\xi^2}.$$

The log-likelihood function of Eq. (5.23) is

$$\log L = -\frac{nT}{2}\log|\Omega| - \frac{1}{2}\sum_{i=1}^{n}(\widetilde{y}_i - \rho\widetilde{y}_{i,-1})'\Omega^{-1}(\widetilde{y}_i - \rho\widetilde{y}_{i,-1}).$$

Conditional on Ω, the QMLE of ρ is

$$\widehat{\rho} = \left(\sum_{i=1}^{n}\widetilde{y}_{i,-1}'\Omega^{-1}\widetilde{y}_{i,-1}\right)^{-1}\left(\sum_{i=1}^{n}\widetilde{y}_{i,-1}'\Omega^{-1}\widetilde{y}_i\right).$$

Show that as $(n, T) \to \infty$,

$$\sqrt{nT}(\widehat{\rho} - \rho) \xrightarrow{d} N(0, 1 - \rho^2).$$

(18) Phillips and Han (2015) consider the model in Eq. (5.21) with $|\rho| < 1$, $u_{it} \overset{i.i.d.}{\sim} (0, \sigma^2)$,

$$y_{i0} = \frac{\alpha_i}{1 - \rho} + \sum_{j=0}^{\infty} \rho^j u_{i,-j}$$

and $\alpha_i \overset{i.i.d.}{\sim} (0, \sigma_\alpha^2)$. Define levels and difference IV estimators to be

$$\widehat{\rho}_l = \frac{\sum_{i=1}^{n} \sum_{t=2}^{T} y_{it-2} \triangle y_{it}}{\sum_{i=1}^{n} \sum_{t=2}^{T} y_{it-2} \triangle y_{it-1}}$$

and

$$\widehat{\rho}_d = \frac{\sum_{i=1}^{n} \sum_{t=3}^{T} y_{it-2} \triangle y_{it}}{\sum_{i=1}^{n} \sum_{t=3}^{T} \triangle y_{it-2} \triangle y_{it-1}},$$

where

$$\triangle y_{it} = y_{it} - y_{it-1}.$$

Show that as $(n, T) \to \infty$,

$$\sqrt{nT}(\widehat{\rho}_l - \rho) \overset{d}{\to} N(0, 2(1 + \rho))$$

and

$$\sqrt{nT}(\widehat{\rho}_d - \rho) \overset{d}{\to} N\left(0, \frac{2(1 + \rho)(3 - \rho)}{(1 - \rho)^2}\right).$$

(19) Hsiao, Pesaran, and Tahmiscioglu (2002) consider the model in Eq. (5.21) with $u_{it} \overset{i.i.d.}{\sim} (0, \sigma_u^2)$. In FD form

$$\triangle y_{it} = \rho \triangle y_{i,t-1} + \triangle u_{it}.$$

Assume $|\rho| < 1$, $E(\triangle y_{i1}) = 0$,

$$\text{Var}(\triangle y_{i1}) = \frac{2\sigma_u^2}{1 + \rho}.$$

Let

$$\Omega = \sigma_u^2 \begin{bmatrix} \omega & -1 & 0 & \cdots & 0 & 0 \\ -1 & 2 & -1 & \cdots & 0 & 0 \\ 0 & -1 & 2 & \cdots & 0 & 0 \\ \vdots & \vdots & \vdots & \ddots & \vdots & \vdots \\ 0 & 0 & 0 & \cdots & 2 & -1 \\ 0 & 0 & 0 & \cdots & -1 & 2 \end{bmatrix}$$

with

$$\omega = \frac{2}{(1+\rho)\sigma_u^2}.$$

The QMLE $\widehat{\rho}$ maximizes

$$\log L = \frac{-nT}{2}\log(2\pi) - \frac{n}{2}\log|\Omega| - \frac{1}{2}\sum_{i=1}^{n} \triangle u_i' \Omega^{-1} \triangle u_i$$

with

$$\triangle u_i = (\triangle y_{i1}, \triangle y_{i2} - \rho \triangle y_{i1}, \ldots, \triangle y_{iT} - \rho \triangle y_{i,T-1})'.$$

Show that the QMLE is consistent and asymptotically normal for a fixed T.

Bibliography

Anderson, T. W., and Rubin, H. (1949). Estimators of the Parameters of a Single Equation in a Complete Set of Stochastic Equations. *Annals of Mathematical Statistics*, 21, 570–582.

Arellano, M., and Bonhomme, S. (2011). Nonlinear Panel Data Analysis. *Annual Review of Economics*, 3, 395–424.

Aue, A., and Horváth, L. (2013). Structural Breaks in Time Series. *Journal of Time Series Analysis*, 34, 1–16.

Bai, J. (1994). Least Squares Estimation of a Shift in Linear Processes. *Journal of Time Series Analysis*, 15, 453–472.

Bai, J. (1996). A Note on Spurious Break and Regime Shift in Cointegrating Relationship. *Working Paper 96-13*, Department of Economics, MIT.

Bai, J. (1997). Estimation of a Change Point in Multiple Regression Models. *Review of Economics and Statistics*, 79, 551–563.

Bai, J. (1998). A Note on Spurious Break. *Econometric Theory*, 14, 663–669.

Bai, J. (2010). Common Breaks in Means and Variances for Panel Data. *Journal of Econometrics*, 157, 78–92.

Bai, J., Lumsdaine, R. L., and Stock, J. H. (1998). Testing for and Dating Common Breaks in Multivariate Time Series. *Review of Economic Studies*, 65, 395–432.

Baltagi, B. H. (2013). *Econometric Analysis of Panel Data* (5th ed.) New York: Wiley.

Baltagi, B. H., Feng, Q., and Kao, C. (2016). Estimation of Heterogeneous Panels with Structural Breaks. *Journal of Econometrics*, 191, 176–195.

Baltagi, B. H., and Kao, C. (2000). Nonstationary Panels, Cointegration in Panels and Dynamic Panels: A Survey. *Advances in Econometrics*, 15, 7–51.

Baltagi, B. H., Kao, C., and Liu, L. (2008). Asymptotic Properties of Estimators for the Linear Panel Regression Model with Random Individual Effects and Serially Correlated Errors: The Case of Stationary and Non-stationary Regressors and Residuals. *Econometrics Journal*, 11, 554–572.

Baltagi, B. H., Kao, C., and Liu, L. (2012). On the Estimation and Testing of Fixed Effects Panel Data Models with Weak Instruments. *Advances in Econometrics*, 30, 199–235.

Baltagi, B. H., Kao, C., and Liu, L. (2014). Test of Hypotheses in a Time Trend Panel Data Model with Serially Correlated Error Component Disturbances. *Advances in Econometrics*, 33, 347–394.

Baltagi, B. H., Kao, C., and Liu, L. (2017). Estimation and Identification of Change Points in Panel Models with Nonstationary or Stationary Regressors and Error Term. *Econometric Reviews*, 36, 85–102.

Baltagi, B. H., Kao, C., and Liu, L. (2019). Testing for Shifts in a Time Trend Panel Data Model with Serially Correlated Error Component Disturbances. *Econometric Reviews*, forthcoming.

Baltagi, B. H., Kao, C., and Na, S. (2011). Test of Hypotheses in Panel Data Models When the Regressor and Disturbances are Possibly Nonstationary. *Advances in Statistical Analysis*, 95, 329–350.

Baltagi, B. H., Kao, C., and Wang, F. (2017). Identification and Estimation of a Large Factor Model with Structural Instability. *Journal of Econometrics*, 197, 87–100.

Baltagi, B. H., and Krämer, W. (1997). A Simple Linear Trend Model with Error Components. *Econometric Theory*, 13, 463–463.

Baltagi, B. H., and Li, Q. (1991). A Transformation That Will Circumvent the Problem of Autocorrelation in an Error Component Model. *Journal of Econometrics*, 52, 371–380.

Bekker, P. A. (1994). Alternative Approximations to the Distributions of Instrumental Variable Estimators. *Econometrica*, 62, 657–681.

Bunzel, H., and Vogelsang, T. J. (2005). Powerful Trend Function Tests That are Robust to Strong Serial Correlation, with an Application to the Prebisch-Singer Hypothesis. *Journal of Business and Economic Statistics*, 23, 381–394.

Cai, Z., Fang, Y., and Li, H. (2012). Weak Instrumental Variables Models for Longitudinal Data. *Econometric Reviews*, 31, 361–389.

Canay, I. A., and Shaikh, A. M. (2017). Practical and Theoretical Advances in Inference for Partially Identified Models. In B. Honor, A. Pakes, M. Piazzesi, and L. Samuelson, eds., *Advances in Economics and Econometrics: 11th World Congress (Econometric Society Monographs)*, 2, 271–306.

Canjels, E., and Watson, M. W. (1997). Estimating Deterministic Trends in the Presence of Serially Correlated Errors. *Review of Economics and Statistics*, 79, 184–200.

Chamberlain, G. (1980). Analysis of Covariance with Qualitative Data. *Review of Economics Studies*, 47, 225–238.

Chamberlain, G. (2010). Binary Response Models for Panel Data: Identification and Information. *Econometrica*, 78, 159–168.

Chan, J., Horváth, L., and Husková, M. (2013). Darling-Eros Limit Results for Change-point Detection in Panel Data. *Journal of Statistical Planning and Inference*, 143, 955–970.

Chao, J. (2014). Panel Structural Modeling with Weak Instrumentation and Covariance Restrictions. *Econometric Theory*, 30, 839–881.

Chao, J. C., and Swanson, N. R. (2005). Consistent Estimation with a Large Number of Weak Instruments. *Econometrica*, 73, 1673–1692.

Choi, I. (1999). Testing the Random Walk Hypothesis for Real Exchange Rates. *Journal of Applied Econometrics*, 14, 293–308.

Chu, C. S. J., and White, H. (1992). A Direct Test for Changing Trend. *Journal of Business and Economic Statistics*, 10, 289–299.

Cragg, J. G., and Donald, S. G. (1993). Testing Identifiability and Specification in Instrumental Variable Models. *Econometric Theory*, 9, 222–240.

Donald, S. G., and Newey, W. K. (2001). Choosing the Number of Instruments. *Econometrica*, 69, 1161–1191.

Emerson, J., and Kao, C. (2001). Testing for Structural Change of a Time Trend Regression in Panel Data: Part I. *Journal of Propagations in Probability and Statistics*, 2, 57–75.

Emerson, J., and Kao, C. (2002). Testing for Structural Change of a Time Trend Regression in Panel Data: Part II. *Journal of Propagations in Probability and Statistics*, 2, 207–250.

Evdokimov, K. (2010). Identification and Estimation of a Nonparametric Panel Data Model with Unobserved Heterogeneity. Working Paper, *Department of Economics*, Princeton University.

Feng, Q., Kao, C., and Lazarová, S. (2009). Estimation and Identification of Change Points in Panel Models. *Syracuse University Working Paper*.

Fernández-Val, I., and Weidner, M. (2018). Fixed Effect Estimation of Large-T Panel Data Models. *Annual Review of Economics*, 10, 109–138.

Gengenbach, C., Palm, F. C., and Urbain, J. P. (2006). Cointegration Testing in Panels with Common Factors. *Oxford Bulletin of Economics and Statistics*, 68, 683–719.

Graham, B. S., Hahn, J., and Powell, J. (2009). The Incidental Parameter Problem in a Non-Differentiable Panel Data Model. *Economics Letters*, 105, 181–182.

Hahn, J., and Hausman, J. (2005). Estimation with Valid and Invalid Instruments. *Annales d'Economie et Statistique*, 79/80, 25–57.

Hahn, J., and Kuersteiner, G. (2002a). Asymptotically Unbiased Inference for a Dynamic Panel Model with Fixed Effects When Both n and T are Large. *Econometrica*, 70, 1639–1657.

Hahn, J., and Kuersteiner, G. (2002b). Discontinuities of Weak Instrument Limiting Distributions. *Economics Letters*, 75, 325–331.

Hanh, J., Kuersteiner, G., and Cho, M H. (2004). Asymptotic Distribution of Misspecified Random Effects Estimator for a Dynamic Panel Model with Fixed Effects When Both n and T are Large. *Economics Letters*, 84, 117–125.

Hahn, J., and Moon, H. R. (2006). Reducing Bias of MLE in a Dynamic Panel Model. *Econometric Theory*, 22, 499–512.

Hahn, J., and Newey, W. (2004). Jackknife and Analytical Bias Reduction for Nonlinear Panel Models. *Econometrica*, 72, 1295–1319.

Hall, P., and Heyde, C. C. (1980). *Martingale Limit Theory and Its Application*. Academic Press, New York.

Han, C., Phillips, P. C. B., and Sul. D. (2014). X-Differencing and Dynamic Panel Model Estimation. *Econometric Theory*, 30, 201–251.

Harris, R. D., and Tzavalis, E. (1999). Inference for Unit Roots in Dynamic Panels Where the Time Dimension is Fixed. *Journal of Econometrics*, 91, 201–226.

Hong, H., and Tamer, E. (2003). Endogenous Binary Choice Model with Median Restrictions. *Economics Letters*, 80, 219–225.

Honoré, B. E., and Kyriazidou, E. (2000). Panel Data Discrete Choice Models with Lagged Dependent Variables. *Econometrica*, 68, 839–874.

Honoré, B. E., and Tamer, E. (2006). Bounds on Parameters in Panel Dynamic Discrete Choice Models. *Econometrica*, 74, 611–629.

Horváth, L., and Husková, M. (2012). Change-Point Detection in Panel Data. *Journal of Time Series Analysis*, 33, 631–648.

Horváth, L., Husková, M., Rice, G., and Wang, J. (2017). Asymptotic Properties of the Cusum Estimator for the Time of Change in Linear Panel Data Models. *Econometric Theory*, 33, 366–412.

Hsiao, C. (2014). *Analysis of Panel Data* (3ed ed.). Cambridge University Press, Cambridge.

Hsiao, C., Pesaran, M. H., and Tahmiscioglu, A. K. (2002). Maximum Likelihood Estimation of Fixed Effects Dynamic Panel Data Models Covering Short Time Periods. *Journal of Econometrics*, 109, 107–150.

Hsiao, C., and Zhou, Q. (2016). Asymptotic Distribution of Quasi-maximum Likelihood Estimation of Dynamic Panels Using Long Difference Transformation when both N and T are Large. *Statistical Methods and Applications*, 25, 675–683.

Hsiao, C., and Zhou, Q. (2019). Incidental Parameters, Initial Conditions and Sample Size in Statistical Inference for Dynamic Panel Data Models. *Journal of Econometrics*, forthcoming.

Hsu, C., and Lin, C. (2011). Change-Point Estimation for Nonstationary Panel Data. *Working Paper,* Department of Economics, National Central University, Taiwan.

Joseph, L., and Wolfson, D. B. (1993). Maximum Likelihood Estimation in the Multi-path Change-Point Problem. *Annals of the Institute of Statistical Mathematics*, 45, 511–530.

Kao, C. (1999). Spurious Regression and Residual-Based Tests for Cointegration in Panel Data. *Journal of Econometrics*, 90, 1–44.

Kao, C., and Chiang, M-H. (2000). On the Estimation and Inference of a Cointegrated Regression in Panel Data. *Advances in Econometrics*, 15, 179–222.

Kao, C., and Emerson, J. (2004). On the Estimation of a Linear Time Trend Regression with a One-Way Error Component Model in the Presence of Serially Correlated Errors: Part I. *Journal of Probability and Statistical Science*, 2, 213–243.

Kao, C., and Emerson, J. (2005). On the Estimation of a Linear Time Trend Regression with a One-Way Error Component Model in the Presence of Serially Correlated Errors: Part II. *Journal of Probability and Statistical Science*, 3, 59–96.

Kao, C., and Wang, F. (2019). Fixed Effects Likelihood Approach for Large Panels. *Panel Data Econometrics*, forthcoming.

Kim, D. (2011). Estimating a Common Deterministic Time Trend Break in Large Panels with Cross Sectional Dependence. *Journal of Econometrics*, 164, 310–330.

Kim, D. (2014). Common Breaks in Time Trends for Large Panel Data with a Factor Structure. *Econometrics Journal*, 17, 301–337.

Kim, D., Oka, T., Estrada, F., and Perron, P. (2019). Inference Related to Common Breaks in a Multivariate System with Joined Segmented Trends with Applications to Global and Hemispheric Temperatures. *Journal of Econometrics*, forthcoming.

Kleibergen, F. (2002). Pivotal Statistics for Testing Structural Parameters in Instrumental Variable Regression. *Econometrica*, 70, 1781–1803.

Kruskal, W. (1968). When are Gauss–Markov and Least Squares Estimators Identical? A Coordinate Free Approach. *Annals of Mathematical Statistics*, 39, 70–75.

Lee, Y. (2012). Bias in Dynamic Panel Models Under Time Series Misspecification. *Journal of Econometrics*, 169, 54–60.

Moon, H. R., Perron, B., and Phillips, P. C. B. (2007). Incidental Trends and the Power of Panel Unit Root Tests. *Journal of Econometrics*, 141, 416–459.

Moreira, M. J. (2003). A Conditional Likelihood Ratio Test for Structural Models. *Econometrica*, 71, 1027–1048.

Moreira, M. J. (2009). Tests with Correct Size when Instruments Can be Arbitrarily Weak. *Journal of Econometrics*, 152, 131–140.

Mundlak, Y. (1978). On the Pooling of Time Series and Cross-Section Data. *Econometrica*, 46, 69–85.

Neyman, J., and Scott, E. L. (1948). Consistent Estimates Based on Partially Consistent Observations. *Econometrica*, 1, 1–32.

Nickell, S. (1981). Biases in Dynamic Models with Fixed Effects. *Econometrica*, 49, 1417–1426.

Nunes, L. C., Kuan, C. M., and Newbold, P. (1995). Spurious Breaks. *Econometrics Theory*, 11, 736–749.

Perron, P., and Yabu, T. (2009a). Estimating Deterministic Trends with an Integrated or Stationary Noise Component. *Journal of Econometrics*, 151, 56–69.

Perron, P., and Yabu, T. (2009b). Testing for Shifts in Trend with an Integrated or Stationary Noise Component. *Journal of Business and Economic Statistics*, 27, 369–396.

Perron, P., and Zhu, X. (2005). Structural Breaks with Deterministic and Stochastic Trends. *Journal of Econometrics*, 129, 65–119.

Pesaran, M. H. (2006). Estimation and Inference in Large Heterogeneous Panels with a Multifactor Error Structure. *Econometrica*, 74, 967–1012.

Pesaran, M. H. (2015). *Time-series and Panel Data Econometrics for Macro-Economics and Finance*. Oxford University Press.

Phillips, P. C. B. (1986). Understanding Spurious Regressions in Econometrics. *Journal of Econometrics*, 33, 311–340.

Phillips, P. C. B. (2018). Dynamic Panel Auderson–Hsiao Estimation with Root Near Unity. *Econometric Theory*, 34, 253–276.

Phillips, P. C. B., and Han, C. (2015). The True Limit Distributions of the Anderson–Hsiao IV Estimators in Panel Autoregression. *Economics Letters*, 127, 89–92.

Picard, D. (1985). Testing and Estimating Change-Points in Time Series. *Advances in Applied Probability*, 17, 841–867.

Ploberger, W., Krämer, W., and Kontrus, K. (1989). A New Test for Structural Stability in the Linear Regression Model. *Journal of Econometrics*, 40, 307–318.

Roy, A., Falk, B., and Fuller, W. A. (2004). Testing for Trend in the Presence of Autoregressive Error. *Journal of the American Statistical Association*, 99, 1082–1091.

Seo, M. H., and Shin, Y. (2016). Dynamic Panels with Threshold Effect and Endogeneity. *Journal of Econometrics*, 195, 169–186.

Shaikh, A., and Vytlacil, E. (2008). Endogenous Binary Choice Models with Median Restrictions: A Comment. *Economics Letters*, 98, 23–28.

Song, M. (2013). Asymptotic Theory for Dynamic Heterogeneous Panels with Cross-Sectional Dependence and Its Applications. *Columbia University Working Paper*.

Staiger, D., and Stock, J. H. (1997). Instrumental Variables Regression with Weak Instruments. *Econometrica*, 65, 557–587.

Stock, J. H., Wright, H. J. and Yogo, M. (2002). A Survey of Weak Instruments and Weak Identification in Generalized Method of Moments. *Journal of Business and Economic Statistics*, 20, 518–529.

Stock, J. H., and Yogo, M. (2005). Testing for Weak Instruments. In Linear IV regression. In D. W. K. Andrews and J. H. Stock (Eds.). *Identification and Inference for Econometric Models: Essays in Honor of Thomas Rothenberg*, Chapter 5, 80–108. Cambridge University Press, Cambridge, UK.

Van de Geer, S., and Wegkamp, M. (1996). Consistency for the Least Squares Estimator in Nonparametric Regression. *Annals of Statistics*, 24, 2513–2523.

Vogelsang, T. J., and Fomby, T. B. (2002). The Application of Size Robust Trend Analysis to Global Warming Temperature Series. *Journal of Climate*, 15, 117–123.

Vogelsang, T. J., and Franses, P. H. (2005). Testing for Common Deterministic Trend Slopes. *Journal of Econometrics*, 126, 1–24.

Vogelsang, T. J., and Nawaz, N. (2017). Estimation and Inference of Linear Trend Slope Ratios With an Application to Global Temperature Data. *Journal of Time Series Analysis*, 38, 640–667.

Wansbeek, T., and Kapteyn, A. (1983). A Note on Spectral Decomposition and Maximum Likelihood Estimation in ANOVA Models with Balanced Data. *Statistics and Probability Letters*, 1, 213–215.

Wooldridge, J. (2002). *Econometric Analysis of Cross Section and Panel Data* (2nd ed.). MIT Press, Cambridge.

Wu, C. F. (1981). Asymptotic Theory of Nonlinear Least Squares Estimation. *Annals of Statistics*, 9, 501–513.

Xu, K. L. (2015). Testing for Structural Change Under Non-stationary Variances. *Econometrics Journal*, 18, 274–305.

Xu, K. L., and Yang, J. C. (2015). Towards Uniformly Efficient Trend Estimation Under Weak/Strong Correlation and Non-stationary Volatility. *Scandinavian Journal of Statistics*, 42, 63–86.

Index